Foundations of Spiritual Formation

Foundations of Spiritual Formation

A Community Approach to Becoming Like Christ

Paul Pettit

EDITOR

Foundations of Spiritual Formation: A Community Approach to Becoming Like Christ

Published by Kregel Publications, a division of Kregel, Inc., P.O. Box 2607, Grand Rapids, MI 49501.

Library of Congress Cataloging-in-Publication Data
Foundations of spiritual formation: a community approach to becoming like Christ / edited by Paul Pettit.
p. cm.
Includes indexes.
1. Spiritual formation. 2. Church group work. 3. Small groups. I. Pettit, Paul
BV4511.F68 2008
248—dc22
2008017157

ISBN: 978-0-8254-3469-3

Printed in the United States of America
08 09 10 11 12 / 5 4 3 2 1

To Dr. Howard and Jeanne Hendricks

May their tribe increase

Contents

Foreword

Howard Hendricks

It's not an accident that when Jesus Christ practiced discipleship he took a group of twelve men, forsook the large crowds, and took so much time to build into the lives of those men. Ultimately, he is the model for ministry. He is the one who set the pattern, and that is why my passion for students participating in character formation groups is so strong. Every student headed toward vocational Christian service needs a small group experience. Below, I've described characteristics of the special kinds of group interaction students need. The contributors to this volume provide insights for making these characteristics a reality.

Honest Accountability

First, students need a group with accountability in order to develop their credibility. In Hebrews 13:7 we read: "Remember your leaders, who spoke the word of God to you. Consider the outcome of their way of life and imitate their faith." And later, verse 17 says, "Obey your leaders and submit to their authority. They keep watch over you as men who must give an account. Obey them so that their work will be a joy, not a burden, for that would be of no advantage to you."

It is my thoughtful conclusion that any man or woman in college or graduate school without an accountability group is an accident waiting to happen. It is just a matter of time. Character failure is seldom a blowout; it is usually the result of a long, slow leak. We all need someone who loves us but is not impressed with us, someone who will ask us the hard questions.

You need a group who loves you, but loves you so much that they will not allow you to remain the way you are. They should accept you as you are, but not allow you to remain that way. We all need someone who will help us become responsible Christians.

We are all well aware of the statue in New York Harbor called the Statue of *Liberty*, but what is really lacking—and I am recommending that it be put in San Francisco Bay—is a statue of *responsibility*. The two concepts, liberty and responsibility, are intimately related; you cannot have one without the other. And these two components can be honestly discussed and practiced in an accountability group.

I've never forgotten the time my wife, Jeanne, and I were invited to Thanksgiving dinner with a group of third-year seminary students. Every Thanksgiving seven couples would get together, and they would have a blast! One year they invited Jeanne and me to be their guests. We had a time like I do not think I have ever had in fifty-six years as a seminary professor.

We ate together, we played games, we laughed, we cried, we prayed together, and finally we left to go home. The moment I got into the car I leaned over and announced, "Sweetheart, if every student training for vocational Christian service were involved in a small group like that, we would reduce the attrition rate to zero."

From what I understand, that special group continues to meet together as a team on an annual basis. They pray together, they study and think together, they evaluate and hold each other accountable. I could not name seven more significant and influential couples. Are you involved in an accountability group like that?

Those students didn't have a formal small group program when they were in school, but they formed one on their own. They certainly sealed in my mind the notion that experiencing authentic community is essential for ministry preparation.

Strong Support

Second, you need a group that knows and cares for you, people who are willing to take a personal interest in you to help, pray for, and encourage you. You need a support group.

In 1 Corinthians 12:12–13 we read, "The body is a unit, though it is made up of many parts, and though all its parts are many, they form one body. So it is with Christ. For we were all baptized by one Spirit into one body—whether Jews or Greeks, slave or free—and we were all given the one Spirit to drink." You cannot make it alone in the ministry. We are a desperate people. I desperately need you, and you desperately need me, and we desperately need each other. There is no room for an independent in the body of Christ because we are all interdependent upon each other—we are one body.

When you get to be my age, you begin to look back over your life and ask, Who were the people who made the greatest impact on me? My most influential friends were the product of four years of college and four years of seminary. I was a student leader at Wheaton College and it was a wonderful experience, but it couldn't begin to compare with the privilege I had as a senior to have as my "little brother" Jim Elliot, the missionary martyr who died in Ecuador. I have heard a lot of people speak, and I have gotten to know a lot of people, but I have never known a human being quite in his league.

When we met, Jim was eighteen years old, and I was supposed to be developing him. But the truth of the matter is that he changed the whole course of my life and ministry. I enrolled at Dallas Seminary, and there were several fellow students from Wheaton in my class, but they were not the ones who necessarily made the greatest impact on me.

I met, for the first time in my life, a man by the name of Ray Stedman. Ray and I used to stay up till one and two o'clock in the morning reviewing our theology, testing each other, dreaming about what God wanted to do with us in the ministry upon graduation. We formed a philosophy of ministry. We dreamed and prayed about it; we discussed it. He would take one side of a theological argument and lay out all the potential options, and I would take the other side. Then the following evening we would switch sides and argue from the opposing positions. We sharpened each other.

Ray graduated and went off to Palo Alto, California, and I stayed on to teach at Dallas Seminary. As he faithfully served Peninsula Bible Church, he implemented the *body life* concept we had dreamed about, and I had the privilege of teaching it to seminary students.

I came from a broken home. I never had a natural brother relationship, but Ray Stedman was like a brother to me. My last memories of Ray are of laughing and reminiscing with him at his bedside as he said, "Howie, it won't be long before I will be in heaven, and I'm so glad we got to spend my last hours together."

You see, it's life-changing experiences like the ones I had with Jim Elliot and Ray Stedman that so mark you, even twenty, thirty, or forty years later, that you realize you will never be the same again. And by the way, this is particularly true for those of us who are married. Graduate schools are famous for ruining marriages. This is true in medicine, in law, and it is true in Christian higher education as well. You need somebody who will hold you and your partner together and aid you in the whole process of growing up in your marriage and being the kind of people that God can use. So whether you are married or single, you need a group that supports you as you build authentic community. Are you involved in a support group like this?

Godly Desires

Third, you need to spend time with a group of men or women for whom the number one passion in their lives is becoming more like Jesus Christ. You need to be involved in a godly group, not a perfect group—there aren't any—but a group passionate about God, so that when you arrive at graduation you have something significant to offer to a lost society.

The type of group I'm describing will stretch you, challenge you, and provide a model for you. I believe the best part of participating in a spiritual formation group is that it helps you design and construct a similar experience for the people to whom God is calling you to minister.

If you can't take it any other way, take it by faith: the process of spiritual formation does not end when you graduate. That is just the beginning. You will spend many hours equipping yourself through this type of group, and God will be working in and through the group members to mold and shape you and to give you a vision that will never depart. In fact, it will only grow stronger as you move out into the world and into the particular area in which God wants you to minister. As you pursue godliness together, you will be equipped and changed like never before.

The Incredible Value of Participation in Small Groups

I have already written about my experiences with Jim Elliot in college and Ray Stedman in seminary. Because of these unique friendships, I'll never be the same. The only explanation I have is that God supernaturally brought significant people into my life who so shaped and molded me that they made me distinctive as a result of what they built into my life. Involvement in a small group is an effective way of building significant personal relationships.

Being involved in a small group during ministry training also prepares you to lead a small group in your future ministry. It's very hard to lead such a group when you have not been in one.

People often say, "Well, we don't have small groups in our church." I say, "You're wrong. You have a lot of small groups in your church. We call them cliques, and you ought to have open season on them because they will tear your church to shreds!"

On the other hand, when you have groups of people who are falling in love with Jesus Christ and welding themselves together in godly relationships, watch how significant they will be in your church and what a vital part of your ministry they will become.

Small groups help believers appreciate the body of Christ in its very giftedness. Students often say to me, "Well, you know, he's not like me." To which I say, "Thank God for that—we don't need more of you!" We need distinctively different people, and this generation includes some of the most distinctively different people I have met in a long time. And God has called today's students into ministry service because they have a contribution to make that nobody else will make. There is nobody like you—never has been, never will be—and God wants to use you to influence this world and make a unique contribution.

Spiritual growth is best nurtured and promoted in small groups. In fact, I believe this is the missing ingredient in the evangelical church. I'm privileged to see a lot of students going out to do ministry, and I often ask them, "What are you going to *do*?" And they reply, "Well, Prof, I'm committed to what the Scriptures say. I'm going to equip the saints for their work in the ministry." And I say, "Wonderful! *How* are you going to do that?" And the answer they often come up with is, "by teaching and preaching."

My friend, I have news for you. You are not going to change very many people that way. Preaching is one means of bringing to the surface the truths of the Word of God that people need to apply in their own lives. But watch what happens when you get a group of disciples around you!

Walt, a Sunday school teacher of mine years ago, went out into the community and picked up eleven of us kids approximately nine years of age. Nine of those eleven eventually went into full-time vocational ministry. Walt, who built into our lives, who shaped and molded us, never went beyond the sixth grade! He loved me for Christ's sake, and I saw Walt develop what I often look long and hard to find—a pastor, a professional minister, who has produced nine leaders for the body of Christ. Walt developed us by loving us, praying with us, and playing with us. And the results remain today while he has long since gone on to heaven. May his tribe increase!

I urge students to get involved in an authentic spiritual formation small group because loners are not biblical. It is not even an option for the Christ follower. Student leaders generally follow the same pattern: They have learned to keep their ego in check. They are individuals who come to realize that "it's not all about me; it's about the people God allows me to influence. I am just his instrument, that's all, and he wants to use me to help bring about change in the lives of others." And he wants you to do the same.

Some of us older members of the faculties of Christian higher education institutions are not going to be teaching that much longer. I don't mean you need to begin preparing our funerals; I'm just being realistic. And what I really care about is that students will spend the rest of their lives building into the lives of other people who will never be the same again. God wants to reproduce in today's generation like he did in ours. I pray for that every single day.

I have come to the conclusion that independence is not what Jesus Christ is seeking to develop. I undertook a study of men who failed in ministry for moral reasons. I became so passionate and burdened about this problem because it is one of my responsibilities to help develop students for vocational Christian ministry.

I told the subjects of my study that I would never use their names in any form and that all I was asking of them was the privilege of using their experience for teaching purposes. Every single one of the study's participants agreed. As I closely examined the results, one of the most fascinating items I discovered was the reasons why they failed morally in ministry. The thing that literally leaped off the research pages was the answer that every one of the participants gave when I pointedly asked, "Did you ever expect that this would happen to you?" Every single one said, "I never expected it. In fact, had you told me that I would fall in this manner, I certainly would have said that you don't have prophetic gifts."

When I asked them to tell me about their accountability group, every one of the participants except one responded, "I have no accountability group and never have had one." The only one who said that he did was searched out by a close friend in ministry who informed me, "I found him in a bar with a collection of women, and he was trying to convince me these were the people with whom he was accountable." What a fake. What a fraud. He was a loner in ministry.

This study on moral failure and its results is one of the reasons I place accountability right at the outset of those requirements that constitute a great group.

I want you to graduate highly qualified. Not highly qualified to be utterly useless, but highly qualified to distinguish your generation so that it ends up producing proportionately more people with spiritual impact. It is my prayer that you reproduce in kind, that you flourish in your authentic community groups, and that you end up producing individuals who remind us of Jesus Christ.

What a privilege you have of representing Christ in your generation. May you do it, with thanksgiving, in Christ's wonderful name. Go for it!

Contributors

Richard Averbeck serves as professor of Old Testament and Semitic languages at Trinity Evangelical Divinity School. He has been published in several journals and has contributed numerous articles to the *Evangelical Dictionary of Biblical Theology*; *Faith, Tradition, and History*; *Cracking Old Testament Codes: Guide to Interpreting Old Testament Literary Forms*; and the *New International Dictionary of Old Testament Theology and Exegesis*. He is cofounder of the Spiritual Formation Forum.

Darrell L. Bock is research professor of New Testament studies and professor of spiritual development and culture at Dallas Theological Seminary. He has written numerous books and journal articles, including *Jesus According to Scripture*, *Purpose-Directed Theology*, and several commentaries on Luke. He is cofounder of the Spiritual Formation Forum.

George Hillman received his Ph.D. from Southwestern Baptist Theological Seminary. He serves at Dallas Theological Seminary as associate professor of spiritual formation and leadership. He was formerly a staff pastor in Texas and Georgia.

Klaus Issler is professor of Christian education and theology at Talbot School of Theology, Biola University. He also serves as adjunct faculty for the Institute for Spiritual Formation, and he is the author of numerous journal articles and several books, including *Wasting Time with God*.

Gordon Johnston is associate professor of Old Testament studies at Dallas Theological Seminary, where he also received his Th.D. He has served on several archaeological digs, has been published in numerous scholastic journals, and is a contributor to the NET Bible.

Reid Kisling serves as registrar at George Fox University in Newberg, Oregon. Reid led several spiritual formation groups and theological reflection groups all at Dallas Theological Seminary, where he earned the Master of Theology degree. He recently completed a Ph.D. in organizational leadership at Regent University.

Bill Miller earned a Ph.D. at the University of Dallas. He currently teaches at a university in Prague, Czech Republic. Previously he served on staff at the Center for Christian Leadership, Dallas Theological Seminary, where he was extensively involved in the spiritual formation program, leading groups, training leaders, and writing curriculum. He also served on staff with Campus Crusade for Christ at Stanford University.

Jonathan Morrow has a Master of Divinity and a Master of Arts in Philosophy of Religion and Ethics from Talbot School of Theology. He served for two years as a Spiritual Formation Fellow at the Howard G. Hendricks Center for Christian Leadership of Dallas Theological Seminary before becoming the discipleship coordinator for Student Ministries at Biola University. He is the founder of Think Christianly (www.thinkchristianly.org) and the author of *Welcome to College: A Christ-Follower's Guide for the Journey*. Currently, Jonathan is the equipping pastor at Fellowship Bible Church in Murfreesboro, Tennessee.

Paul Pettit has received degrees from the University of Kansas, Moody Bible Institute, and Dallas Theological Seminary. He serves as director of spiritual formation at Dallas Theological Seminary, where he completed the Doctor of Ministry degree. He and his wife, Pamela, have five children.

Andrew Seidel serves as executive director of the Center for Christian Leadership at Dallas Theological Seminary. He is the former senior pastor of Grace Bible Church, College Station, Texas, and served for several years as a missionary in Eastern Europe. He is the author of *Charting a Bold Course.*

Gail Seidel serves on the spiritual formation team at Dallas Theological Seminary, where she received the Master of Arts in Christian Education degree. She has served as a missionary in Eastern Europe and coordinates a ministry training program for women in Russia. Gail is currently completing a Doctor of Ministry degree at Gordon-Conwell Seminary.

Harry Shields serves as senior pastor of Calvary Bible Church in Neenah, Wisconsin. He came to Calvary from Moody Bible Institute where he served as chairman of the department of pastoral studies since 1994 and now teaches in the graduate school. In addition to holding other faculty positions, Harry served as senior pastor of churches in Denver and Elmwood Park, Illinois. He has also served as a conference speaker and radio guest host and has authored books and articles. Dr. Shields received a Master of Theology degree from Dallas Theological Seminary and a Doctor of Ministry degree from Trinity Evangelical Divinity School.

Introduction

Paul Pettit

Christie enjoys hanging out at her neighborhood coffee shop, "Hot Java Lava." She enjoys the music, the atmosphere, and the international blend of customers who drop in to sit, sip, and chat. "I love the *spiritual* atmosphere they've created here," Christie says.

Through the years, Barry has taken several martial arts and Eastern exercise classes at his local community recreation center. His current favorite is labeled "meditative yoga." At first he admitted feeling a little weird following his instructor's advice to spend the first half hour of class completely *freeing his mind*. But now Barry says, "I had no idea how peaceful . . . how *spiritual* . . . these relaxation techniques could be."

Dr. Evans has made it a requirement that his *Spiritual Life 101* students spend considerable time in service projects to help the underprivileged in his college's blighted inner-city area. At the outset of his course, Dr. Evans announced, "I can assure you the work you do helping the poor will be more *spiritually forming* than any activity you'll encounter at your church!"

What is spiritual formation? Certainly both the term itself and the topic as a field of study have become popular discussion fodder in recent years. While many are actively involved in this "process" of study and discussion, others aren't even sure what the term means—and for good reason! When beginning an investigation into the field of spiritual formation, it's important to note that its most basic, historic tenets are as old as the early Christian church, while other aspects of its development are as current as the latest three-day conference with "noted experts in the field."

This volume explores the foundational underpinnings of spiritual formation and how spiritual formation as an academic discipline functions in several key arenas. Each of the contributors to this text teaches on the topic and/or labors in the field of vocational Christian ministry, with an emphasis on spiritual formation.

The Change Process: Physical and Spiritual

At the most basic, foundational level of any discussion on spiritual formation is the topic of change, and it is there we must start.

The ideas and patterns involved in the process of spiritual formation involve a Christian changing or maturing from one form to another. The idea of *spiritual* change can be illustrated by comparing it to another way in which humans desire change. Scores of us long to change our *physical* appearance. And change in the physical arena is similar to change in the spiritual realm.[1]

Many North Americans are interested in changing the "form" of their bodies. People spend millions of dollars annually on exercise programs, diet pills, and health club memberships. Weight-loss books continually top the best-seller lists. And now, liposuction, plastic surgery, and a drastic technique called "stomach banding" are becoming routine for many. The fact that so many overweight people want to change their appearance or physical form has made the weight-loss industry an economic force all its own. People are desperate for physical change!

In a similar way, God desires that his children see change in their physical *and* spiritual lives. God desires nothing less than to transform or reformat our lives.[2] Change in one's physical appearance is fairly easy to detect. When a person loses weight, clothes hang a little more loosely, muscles begin to appear where flab once reigned, and others take notice of the new slimmed-down appearance. However, changes in our inner condition—our character and our spiritual life—are not so easy to see. Change on the inside is often hard to detect and measure.

How do believers know whether they are becoming more and more like Jesus Christ? How do we measure or benchmark a maturing Christ follower? What are the telltale signs we could or should chart? Which "dashboard lights" should flash when authentic, Christlike change is occurring? And for those of us who plow in fields of vocational Christian ministry,

---

1. This is not to imply that the spiritual realm does not closely integrate with the physical also. A healthy, balanced approach to spiritual formation involves a focus on both our material *and* immaterial aspects.

2. Whether we like it or not, we've already been formed by our family of origin, lifestyle choices, habits and patterns of thinking, and influences from outside sources. What God longs to do is *transform* (Rom. 12:2) us into his habits and patterns of thinking and relating. Our minds need to be reformed by Scripture and the godly influence of fellow believers.

how do we know if and when those we are working with are learning and growing in the faith we are proclaiming?

Spiritual Formation Communities

Again, the most basic parameters of any discussion on spiritual formation must include the idea of life change. Inherent in the idea of spiritual formation is the notion that a particular person is being changed (formed) at the core of the person's being (spirit). Some of these changes can be seen immediately—like when a friend begins to practice kindness instead of anger. Other transformations take longer to notice—like when a person begins to understand the importance of practicing concepts such as stillness or gratitude before God in order to improve his or her patience or gratefulness.

The second most basic, foundational underpinning of the spiritual formation process is the idea of *other persons*, or those in one's particular *community*. That is, change for the Christian does not normally involve change that occurs in isolation from others. The change we seek is not change for change's sake. And the change we seek is not solely for self-improvement. Christians are to be *in process* and undergoing renovation so that the individual believer is able to influence and interact with *others* in a more Christlike manner. Christians are *in process* for *influence*.

Purpose of This Book

A primary purpose of this volume is to introduce and explore the subject of spiritual formation for those who have not read widely in the field or studied the topic in depth. In the first section, we begin by exploring the *foundational* aspects of spiritual formation. What is the philosophy and theory informing the discipline? What does the Bible have to say about this discipline? The second section is devoted to several key *functional* aspects of this field of study. How is spiritual formation practiced? How does it work in our congregations, ministries, and schools and in our daily lives?

It is helpful to understand at the outset that spiritual formation is not defined by one particular approach. It is not a specific twelve-step program, an ongoing accountability group, or a specific study of a biblical passage or a theological doctrine (although all of these disciplines and more may be involved at times). It is not closely tied with one particular denomination or a specific group of Christians. While spiritual formation means different things to different groups and definitions are agreeably difficult to arrive at, at the very least we can state the following two principles with conviction. First, *spiritual formation is the holistic work of God in a believer's life whereby systematic change renders the individual continually closer to the image and actions of Jesus Christ.* And second, *the change or transformation that occurs in the believer's life happens best in the context of authentic, Christian community and is oriented as service toward God and others.*

Formation as Change

Change is not optional for the believer in Jesus Christ. It's tragic when a small child does not grow and mature into adolescence and adulthood. Everyone knows something is not right when a child does not learn to walk, talk, or function on his own. Similarly, developmental change is certainly expected for the growing Christ follower. To encourage the early followers of Christ in Corinth toward the process of life change, the apostle Paul wrote,

> But we all, with unveiled face, beholding as in a mirror the glory of the Lord, are *being transformed* into the same image from glory to glory, just as from the Lord, the Spirit. (2 Cor. 3:18 NASB, emphasis mine)

One glorious day all those who have placed their trust in Christ (justification) will enter into God's presence (glorification) and enjoy a long-awaited pilgrim's rest. But until that day, each of us who places faith in Jesus Christ and is living out the life of faith here on earth is being (present tense) transformed (sanctification) into the image and likeness of our Savior. The term for this change process is *spiritual formation*, and a description and discussion of the activities and habits that inform the change are the topic of this book.[3]

The Terms Spiritual and Formation

One way to arrive at what we mean by spiritual formation is to define the terms and provide understandable "flesh" to the sometimes overly academic "bones." By using the term *spiritual*, we are referring to the dynamic, holistic, maturing relationship between the individual believer and God, and between the individual believer and others (both believers and unbelievers). It is a dynamic interaction in that there is movement. The relationships involved are not static. Since God is spirit, the inherent nature of the relationship is primarily immaterial, yet carried out in our bodies.[4]

Another reason why the relationship is described as dynamic or interactive is because the relationship should be continually growing, improving, and maturing. All Christian believers should be growing while learning what it means to live by faith and follow Jesus Christ on a daily basis.

---

3. We have chosen to use the popular term *spiritual formation* because of its wide use. However, one could also accurately label this process Christian formation, spiritual transformation, or Christian transformation. Theologians use the Latin word *sanctus* (holy, set apart for service) and label the process of growth toward Christlikeness *sanctification*.

4. Jesus' original disciples physically walked and talked with him as they carried out their religious apprenticeship. While today's Christians do not physically interact with Jesus of Nazareth, we follow the scriptural mandate to closely interact with the corporate body of Christ; that is, we should live in authentic Christian community with our believing brothers and sisters. The Christian is not to live in isolation.

When we use the term *formation*, we mean the ongoing process of the believer's actions and habits being continually transformed (morphed) into the image of Jesus Christ. Make no mistake: maturing as a Christian is a process. It is not a second step, a higher plane, a sacred blessing, or a lightning bolt moment when God invades and brings the Christian to a perfected place. A lifelong transformation is set into motion when one places his or her faith in Jesus Christ and seeks to follow him (discipleship, apprenticeship). Notice how the apostle Paul uses the idea of lifestyle transformation (process) when he writes:

> Those whom he foreknew he also predestined to be *conformed* to the image of his Son, that his Son would be the firstborn among many brothers and sisters. (Rom. 8:29 NET, emphasis mine)
>
> And we all, with unveiled faces reflecting the glory of the Lord, are being *transformed* into the same image from one degree of glory to another, which is from the Lord, who is the Spirit. (2 Cor. 3:18 NET, emphasis mine)
>
> Do not be conformed to this present world, but be *transformed* by the renewing of your mind, so that you may test and approve what is the will of God—what is good and well-pleasing and perfect. (Rom. 12:2 NET, emphasis mine)
>
> My dear children, for whom I am again in the pains of childbirth until Christ is *formed* in you . . . (Gal. 4:19, emphasis mine)

Individual and Corporate Aspects of Growth

In the current renewal of spiritual formation programs, classes, and small groups, one of the key elements making this fresh movement attractive is the intentional attempt to include both the individual and the corporate aspects of maturity in Christ. Evangelical leaders believe in the importance of the Christian becoming individually conformed more and more into the image of Jesus Christ. And they take seriously those admonishments that call the believer to mature and grow in Jesus Christ. But problems arise when an overemphasis is placed on the individual believer—apart from his or her Christian community.[5]

In addition to individual growth, we also must seriously consider the many scriptural admonishments calling for growth *in* and *within* the body

---

5. Much of the current evangelical discussion surrounding Christian growth emanates from an individualistic and privatized viewpoint. How many times have we seen books or seminars titled: *You and Jesus*, *You and Your Bible*, or *You and Your Growth*? However, the New Testament exclusively speaks of growth in community, so that the "you" is in a second-person plural form. The New Testament approach would have these same topics read: *You All and Jesus*, *You All and Your Bible*, or even the southern colloquial form, *Y'all and Your Growth*.

of Christ as well. The Christian life is not to be lived in isolation but in interaction with other believers, as well as nonbelievers. Christian growth and maturity is best measured by those who know us well.

In other words, all believers should be growing as individual believers *in community*. This means Christians should find their place of service and participation within the larger, corporate body, the church. This is why a helpful spiritual formation program or study requires one to carve out an intentional time or space to be spent with other people in an attempt to provide a context for real life change. While spending time in solitude is necessary, even vital, life change happens best in the context of authentic, biblical community.

Many of the New Testament writers, picking up where Jesus left off, use the metaphor of the body to describe the church. The church is a living organism made up of mutually supporting members who interact with each other in highly interdependent, not independent, ways. Real Christian growth is always growth "in the body." There are no healthy "lone rangers," or isolated Christians, in the church. The goal is to know and to be known by other believers.

A Sports Metaphor

I enjoy golf. I have played for many years. No one ever masters golf, yet one can improve and grow as a golfer. What would it take for me to grow and learn as a golfer? Well, for one I need to be actively involved in the game. I may decide to take lessons from a professional or someone who is developmentally further along in the game. Second, I need to practice. I can't transform my golf game by wishful thinking or by hoping I can score better. I need to pick up my clubs, get out on the golf course, and practice.

No one would think it odd if I even set aside a specific time each week to practice, say, every Wednesday afternoon. Finally, I need to check in with others to see how my game is progressing. I need to play a round of golf with friends or possibly enter a tournament to see if I am maturing as a golfer.

And so it is with the Christian life. Spiritual formation involves the believer's intentional attempt at setting aside sacred spaces (intentional times) for God to bring about life change. It is healthy to regularly meet with other believers for prayer, confession, or accountability. Using *lectio divina*[6] or practicing spiritual disciplines[7] is not a quick fix or a shortcut to Christian

---

6. *Lectio divina* (lit. "words from God" or "sacred readings") is a historic spiritual discipline that invites the reader or hearer of a particular Scripture passage to contemplate or even meditate on a specific word or phrase from the passage in an attempt at carrying the thought throughout the day and seeking to implement the idea into one's life (see Ps. 1:2). It is critical that meditation be done with Scripture. Nowhere does the Bible advocate "clearing" or "emptying" one's mind. These are pagan notions.

7. For a helpful overview of spiritual disciplines, see Dallas Willard, *The Spirit of the Disciplines: Understanding How God Changes Lives*, 2nd ed. (San Francisco: Harper & Row, 1999).

growth. In the same way no one would question my motives in practicing for golf or taking lessons from a professional, Christians need feel no shame in admitting we need help from others in implementing the life change we seek.

Growth Comes from God

God is the one who enables and brings about the change. However, all believers are called to seek to implement life change *with others*. This is why the relationship between the believer and the Holy Spirit is dynamic, interactive, and purposeful. Salvation is more than justification alone or escaping the penalty of sin. For too long, salvation has been defined only as going to heaven, not hell, after death. Salvation also includes the process of sanctification and yielding to God in order to avoid the power, not only the penalty, of sin. You were not saved to escape from this world and dwell in a cave or sit on a pole somewhere. When God is ready to bring you into his presence (glorification) to escape the very presence of sin, he will do it in his good time. But until then, Christians are to be about the business of growth and mission in the world. Christ followers are called to become salt and light in the world.

God's Work, Man's Cooperation

Theologians often wrestle with using the right language to describe how a person comes to faith in Christ. Obviously, God calls, or woos, the lost person. And yet, in a mysterious way, the individual is also responsible to respond to the call, to respond in faith. This call and response is as valid in the process of sanctification (the resultant life of salvation) as it is in the process of justification (the moment of salvation).

God continually calls the individual believer into a deeper, more mature walk of faith. God uses his Word, his church, other believers, circumstances, prayer, and a host of other vehicles to bring individuals and communities of believers into close, intimate relationship. The Scriptures warn that an individual believer can "grieve" the Holy Spirit because of wrong choices or sin (Eph. 4:30).

In addition, believers are continually admonished to grow, to walk worthy, to not stumble, to press on, and to run the race. We are told to work out our salvation, and to strive, to yield, to obey, and even to be holy.

So then, the process of spiritual formation (the believer becoming more like Christ) is a mysterious outworking of *both* God's initiative and involvement over time *and* a concerted response or action plan by the individual believer who fully understands that growth graciously proceeds from God. And again, the process of spiritual formation certainly involves the individual, yet it takes place in community and with others. The "bride" of Christ is not an individual believer but instead is the collection of believers called "the church."

Spiritual Formation and Marriage

Another metaphor that illustrates this dynamic relationship between God and the believer is seen in the picture of marriage, the relationship the apostle Paul called a mystery or illustration of Christ and the church (Eph. 5:23–33). In a marriage relationship, each partner must work at growing closer to the other. Each partner should learn what the other loves and appreciates. Any marriage relationship that is not growing and maturing quickly becomes routine and stagnant.

In my marriage I can choose to work at serving well or at being served. Over time I may begin to view my spouse as one who has been put on the planet to meet my needs and bring me happiness. Or, hopefully, I begin to see myself as one uniquely called upon and graciously gifted to joyfully serve my spouse regardless of the response or outcome—my own happiness being a potential by-product.

Jesus Christ calls all who would follow him to *take up their cross.* That is, Jesus Christ asks each of us to die to our own individualistic and privatized dreams, desires, and life plans and humbly and sensitively follow him into new avenues of relationship and service in the Christian kingdom. He asks us to allow him to form us and shape us into his own desired ends. Since God is Creator, he has at his disposal any means necessary to eventually bring about this type of close conformity. Are you up for the spiritual formation challenge?

Toward a Definition

Since this is an introduction to spiritual formation, we must begin with a working definition that will hold us in good stead as we explore the many subtopics related to our larger topic. Spiritual formation, then, is *the ongoing process of the triune God transforming the believer's life and character toward the life and character of Jesus Christ—accomplished by the ministry of the Spirit in the context of biblical community.*

This process should not be divided into the spiritual and physical, or private and public, or secular and sacred. It involves the integrated, whole person—one's manner of thinking, habits and behaviors, and manner of relating with God and others—and it should result in a life of loving God and loving others well.

Introducing the Contributors

The unique contribution this interdisciplinary book makes is twofold. First, it is penned from a thoroughly evangelical stance. Since the contributors hold to the inerrant, authoritative, revealed Word of God and are convinced of its primacy in relation to truth and its standard of authority as a rule for living, they believe spiritual formation should never be practiced in isolation from Holy Scripture. Second, this book emphasizes the individual believer being rooted in and surrounded by an authentic, biblical Christian community (God's people), and this community involvement is held to be of utmost importance.

We may be so bold as to assert that the New Testament writers do not encourage the believer to seek growth in isolation or to see formation occur only individually. Jesus always called individuals to join with others who had taken up his kingdom cause as a "way of life." Can you imagine your thumb growing individually, apart from the rest of your hand?

As a believer in Jesus Christ, you are a part of the body of Christ and are connected to the other members of the body. We are to grow in relation to, not apart from, the other members. The body metaphor is not simply a catchy way of describing Christianity—it is Christianity! It is the manner in which God designed his kingdom program to operate. We are not called to carry our cross in isolation. We are not called to growth in isolation. We are not called to maturity in isolation. We are called to growth *in the body*. We are called to become spiritually formed *as a body*.

Chapter Previews

In the opening chapter of the foundational section, Jonathan Morrow develops an evangelical theology of spiritual formation, which underpins the process as a whole. He then examines how God spiritually forms believers into the image of Christ with the essential resources of God's Word, God's Spirit, and God's people (the church).

Next, Richard Averbeck, a leading figure in the evangelical spiritual formation movement, shows us how to "look life squarely in the face" by living a life of worship. He writes about worship and spiritual formation because "life looks different when we look at it with God at the center of our vision."

Then two skilled biblical exegetes lead us into the text of Scripture to ensure we remain grounded in revealed truth. Old Testament scholar Gordon Johnston writes on how the Hebrew word *edah* (community) functioned before the appearance of the Messiah and the giving of the Spirit at Pentecost. And rounding out our foundational section, prolific New Testament scholar Darrell Bock shows the key role the Spirit of God plays in forming and transforming the people of God. He focuses his attention on Paul's letter to the Ephesians.

With a strong foundational emphasis as backdrop, we develop the functional aspects of spiritual formation in part 2. Christian educator Klaus Issler writes on the importance of internal obedience. These "matters of the heart" are often ignored in evangelical circles or dismissed as being "too mystical." Following in a similar vein, Reid Kisling demonstrates the vital connection between character development and spiritual formation. He focuses his research and writing on the most significant aspects of character and character development, which are self-transcendence, self-directedness, and cooperativeness.

Next, Bill Miller explores the proper motivation for all true spiritual formation work: love. He shows how much of what passes for Christian maturity is in reality nothing more than "sin management." Leadership development expert Andy Seidel writes on the importance of an individual knowing fully his or her own identity in Christ—even before any leading of others is undertaken in the name of "ministry."

Field educator George Hillman provides a vocational emphasis with an intriguing chapter on calling and service in the body of Christ. Certainly every member of the body is a minister, but how does one know whether to enter into ministry as a vocation? The chapter by Hillman and the creative writing of Gail Seidel help answer that pressing question by calling the reader to examine his or her own "life story." One can often see where God is leading an individual believer over time, by sensitively listening and looking at where God has already led in the past.

Finally, pastor Harry Shields takes us inside the walls of the local congregation to show how public preaching impacts spiritual formation. He argues that the Word of God proclaimed can be one of the primary means God uses to bring about significant life change.

Abbreviations

Bibles

ASV	American Standard Version
CEV	Contemporary English Version
ESV	English Standard Version
HCSB	Holman Christian Standard Bible
KJV	King James Version
LXX	Septuagint
MT	Masoretic Text
NASB	New American Standard Bible
NET	NET Bible
NIV	New International Version
NKJV	New King James Version
NRSV	New Revised Standard Version
RSV	Revised Standard Version
TEV	Today's English Version
TNIV	Today's New International Version

Qumran Scrolls

1QM	1Q*Milḥamah* or *War Scroll*
1QS	1Q*Serek Hayaḥad* or *Rule of the Community*
CD	Cairo Genizah copy of the *Damascus Document*

Reference Works

BDAG	Bauer, Walter, and Frederick W. Danker. *A Greek-English Lexicon of the New Testament and Other Early Christian Literature*. 3rd ed. Chicago: University of Chicago Press, 2000.
BDB	Brown, F., S. R. Driver, and C. A. Briggs. *A Hebrew and English Lexicon of the Old Testament*. Oxford: Oxford University Press, 1907.

HALOT Koehler, L., W. Baumgartner, and J. J. Stamm. *The Hebrew and Aramaic Lexicon of the Old Testament.* Translated and edited under the supervision of M. E. J. Richardson. Study ed. 2 vols. Leiden: E. J. Brill, 2001.

NIDOTTE VanGemeren, W. A., ed. *New International Dictionary of Old Testament Theology and Exegesis.* 5 vols. Grand Rapids: Zondervan, 1997.

THAT Jenni, E., ed. *Theologisches Handwörterbuch zum Alten Testament.* With assistance from C. Westermann. 2 vols. Stuggart, 1971–1976.

TWOT Harris, R. L., G. L. Archer Jr., and B. K. Waltke, eds. *Theological Wordbook of the Old Testament.* 2 vols. Chicago: Moody, 1980.

Part 1

Laying the Foundations of Spiritual Formation

CHAPTER 1

INTRODUCING SPIRITUAL FORMATION

Jonathan Morrow

> Beloved, now we are children of God, and it has not appeared as yet what we will be. We know that when He appears, we will be like Him, because we will see Him just as He is.
>
> —1 John 3:2 NASB

> The Bible alone, and the Bible in its entirety, is the Word of God written and is therefore inerrant in the autographs. God is a Trinity, Father, Son, and Holy Spirit, each an uncreated person, one in essence, equal in power and glory.
>
> —Doctrinal Statement, Evangelical Theological Society

Spiritual formation[1] has had many traditional and denominational expressions throughout church history.[2] In recent years resurgence in thinking about spiritual formation has swept over the evangelical landscape. Our purpose here is to set forth a distinctively evangelical view of spiritual formation. Our journey will begin as we (1) examine the necessary

---

1. For the sake of simplicity, I will use *spiritual formation* synonymously with terms like *sanctification* and *the spiritual life*. Also, you will notice that I include ample footnotes. This is so that you, as a student, will be able to track down the information I am drawing from and you will have fruitful avenues for further study and exploration.

2. Evangelical spiritual formation differs significantly from the traditional Roman Catholic emphasis upon the sacraments as the means of grace for the Christian life. See *Catechism of the Catholic Church: With Modifications from the Edito Typica* (New York: Doubleday, 1995), 341–470. With that said, evangelicals can and should learn much from the lives and practices of holy men and women throughout the history of Christendom, for God has been at work in the lives of his people—conforming them to the image of Christ—for two thousand years. One recent work that highlights the diverse contributions of various Christian traditions to spirituality is Richard J. Foster, *Streams of Living Water: Celebrating the Great Traditions of Christian Faith* (San Francisco: HarperSanFrancisco, 2001).

preconditions for doing distinctively evangelical spiritual formation. We will then (2) examine spiritual formation in light of the gospel and (3) explore in panorama the theological implications for spiritual formation. We will conclude our journey, equipped with theological clarity and content, as we (4) show how God spiritually forms believers into the image of his Son, Jesus Christ.

Preconditions for Doing Evangelical Spiritual Formation

Certain preconditions for doing distinctively evangelical spiritual formation will frame our approach. These are the indispensable rails on which the following discussion runs. One essential distinctive of an evangelical approach to spiritual formation is a high view of Scripture.[3] All else derives from this unique source of God's special revelation to humanity. Before examining God's special revelation in the Bible, it should be noted that evangelicals also affirm God's general revelation through what he has made. God has not left himself without witness since all of creation is stamped with the divine fingerprint.[4]

God has spoken. But what precisely does that mean? Evangelicals confess that God has spoken truly[5] and authoritatively[6] through his Word (spe-

---

3. Evangelicalism is a diverse group that allows for many doctrinal nuances. That being said, Alister McGrath (*Historical Theology: An Introduction to the History of Christian Thought* [Oxford: Blackwell, 1998], 249) observes that the "authority and sufficiency of Scripture" is a core evangelical commitment. Moreover, evangelicals affirm the Trinity, the full deity and humanity of Christ, and the spiritual lostness of humanity. Concerning the work of Christ, it is recognized that the atonement is multifaceted, but the central claim is that Christ died as our substitute and was raised bodily from the dead. Salvation is freely offered to all and is achieved by faith alone in Christ alone. For an excellent survey of these core beliefs recognized throughout church history, see John D. Hannah, *Our Legacy: History of Christian Doctrine* (Colorado Springs: NavPress, 2001).

4. See Psalm 19:1–4; Acts 14:17; and Romans 1:19–20. Demarest describes the content of what can be known through general revelation: "While not imparting truths necessary for salvation—such as the Trinity, the incarnation, or the atonement—general revelation conveys the conviction that God exists and that he is transcendent, immanent, self-sufficient, eternal, powerful, good and a hater of evil" (Bruce Demarest, "General Revelation," in *Evangelical Dictionary of Theology*, ed. Walter A. Elwell [Grand Rapids: Baker, 2001], 1019–21).

5. While it must be recognized that an infinite God cannot reveal himself *completely* to finite creatures, he has revealed himself *truly*.

6. There is growing confusion over the nature and source of biblical authority. David K. Clark (*To Know and Love God: Method for Theology*, Foundations of Evangelical Theology [Wheaton, IL: Crossway, 2003], 65) clarifies that

> the functional view of authority makes a grievous error to the degree that it collapses the critical distinction between the *recognition of the Bible's authority* by the church and the *Bible's inherent possession of authority*. For evangelical theology, a community's act of recognizing a document as authoritative for its thought and life is essential, but this is not the reality, the power, or the force that gives a document its divine authority. That is, the church's act of receiving the Bible as divine is not the *ontological ground* of the Bible's being God's Word. Rather, for evangelical theology, it is God's act of inspiration that grounds the Bible's status as God's revelation.

cial revelation). David Clark in his comprehensive work, *To Know and Love God*, offers a crisp summary of the evangelical view of Scripture.

> [The Bible] alone is the unique, written revelation of God, a permanent, meaningful, and authoritative self-expression by God of his nature and will. The Holy Spirit's act of superintendence—inspiration—was decisive in the writing of Scripture and is the reason the Bible possesses unique status as revelation. Through inspiration, the Holy Spirit aided those who wrote the Bible. The Spirit then guided the church in identifying inspired works and collecting them as the canon. This supervision renders Scripture uniquely authoritative for Christian believers. Of course, the Spirit also preserved the Bible and now guides in interpreting the Bible, but these activities are distinct from the Spirit's work in inspiration.[7]

This conviction is evident in the Evangelical Theological Society's doctrinal statement that must be affirmed annually by its members.[8] Prominent evangelical theologian David Dockery offers a helpful definition of inerrancy by stating that "when all the facts are known, the Bible (in its original writings) properly interpreted in light of which culture and communication means had developed by the time of its composition will be shown to be completely true (and therefore not false) in all that it affirms, to the degree of precision intended by the author, in all matters relating to God and his creation."[9] Evangelicals maintain that respect for and submission to

---

So this is the salient distinction: the *ontological ground of the text's authority* is not the same as the *epistemic acceptance of the text's authority*. For evangelical theology, the first idea, the ontological ground of authority, lies rooted in the objective reality of the triune God speaking through the Spirit's inspiration. The second concept, the subjective recognition of the Bible as God's Word by a believing community, is the appropriate human response to the authority of Scripture. These two ideas work together, and both are absolutely necessary. The objective authority of the Bible rooted in God's inspiring action stands against allowing any contemporary agendas to gain control over the theology. The subjective recognition of the Bible as authoritative guards against a dead orthodoxy that pays lip service to divine truth even as it pursues other agendas.

7. Ibid., 61.

8. For the Evangelical Theological Society's (ETS) doctrinal statement, see the epigraph at the beginning of this chapter (http://www.etsjets.org/doctrine.html). The ETS began in 1950. For an excellent treatment of what ETS is and the role it plays within evangelicalism, see Darrell L. Bock, *Purpose-Directed Theology: Getting Our Priorities Right in Evangelical Controversies* (Downers Grove, IL: InterVarsity Press, 2002), 53–71. Bock is a former president of the ETS. The classic evangelical statement on the inspiration and authority of the Scriptures drafted in 1978 by the International Council on Biblical Inerrancy can be found in Norman Geisler, *Systematic Theology, Vol. 1: Introduction and Bible* (Minneapolis: Bethany House, 2002), 418–22.

9. David S. Dockery, *Christian Scripture: An Evangelical Perspective on Inspiration, Authority,*

the Scriptures is a vital presupposition for spiritual formation. David Clark attests, "Those who refuse to acknowledge the Bible's authority will not experience spiritual transformation by the Spirit and through the Word."[10] Paul demonstrated the link between viewing God's Word as authoritative and the work of spiritual formation when he wrote, "For this reason we also constantly thank God that when you received the word of God which you heard from us, you accepted it not as the word of men, but for what it really is, the word of God, which also performs its work in you who believe" (1 Thess. 2:13 NASB; cf. John 17:17; 2 Tim. 3:16–17).

Now that we have established an evangelical foundation for our discussion, let us examine some important philosophical issues that will allow greater precision for our study. Every generation of Christian theologians faces a different set of cultural and philosophical issues. This was the case for Augustine and Aquinas, and it is no different today. In our generation, postmodernism must be critically assessed because it—as a philosophical system—impacts one's view of God's special revelation in the Bible. Postmodernism can also shape our ability to derive a biblical/systematic theology from the Bible, which in turn informs the spiritual formation process. Students forming their views regarding these cultural and philosophical issues, as well as those serving in ministries where people are also forming their convictions on these issues, need to be aware of the contemporary cultural atmosphere so that they can think *Christianly* within it. America at the beginning of the twenty-first century has shifted toward postmodernism, though few would know to label themselves as postmodernists. College graduates from the 1950s up to the present have been shaped by central ideas undergirding postmodern thought.[11] Many from this generation have become disillusioned with the unkept promises of the Enlightenment (i.e., that scientific advancement and knowledge *alone* would solve all of humanity's problems). This disillusionment has led many to deny the classical (and commonsense) notion of the correspondence theory of truth[12] and reject the idea that language has meaning outside of a socially constructed context.[13] Many are unconvinced that there is

---

and Interpretation (Nashville: Broadman & Holman, 1995), 64. This is a clear, thorough, yet accessible discussion of these topics. For two robust arguments for the rationality of inerrancy and biblical authority, see J. P. Moreland, "The Rationality of Belief in Inerrancy," *Trinity Journal* 7, no. 1 (1986): 75–86; and Douglas Blount, "The Authority of Scripture," in *Reason for the Hope Within*, ed. Michael J. Murray (Grand Rapids: Eerdmans, 1999).

10. Clark, *To Know and Love God*, 65.

11. R. Scott Smith, *Truth and the New Kind of Christian: The Emerging Effects of Postmodernism in the Church* (Wheaton, IL: Crossway, 2005), 78–93.

12. This denial leads to the belief that there is no Truth with a capital *T*, only truths with a lowercase *t*, which are relative to individuals and cultures. In other words, something can be "true for you but not true for me." See Douglas R. Groothuis, *Truth Decay: Defending Christianity Against the Challenges of Postmodernism* (Downers Grove, IL: InterVarsity Press, 2000).

13. This stems from "reader response criticism" and the posture of "deconstructionism"

a way the world actually is and that we have access to it and dismiss the whole idea of metanarratives (which is what the Bible claims to provide).[14] Unfortunately, some within the evangelical community are beginning to embrace philosophical postmodernism's presuppositions and absorb them into their views of truth, knowledge, biblical interpretation, and the enterprise of theology as a whole.[15] In the final analysis, evangelicals must affirm that objective truth can be discovered,[16] known, and communicated because *all* truth is ultimately grounded in the person of God and the propositional revelation of that God.[17]

---

toward language taught in many liberal arts departments in American universities. On this view, meaning does not reside in the intention of the author or the text itself but in the reader's response to the text. Consequently, there can be as many possible interpretations as there are interpreters. For more on the ideas that gave rise to postmodernity, see Millard J. Erickson, *Truth or Consequences: The Promise and Perils of Postmodernism* (Downers Grove, IL: InterVarsity Press, 2001), 75–167.

14. The growing sentiment is that language creates reality or at least we have no direct access to reality. Rejecting this view, Bock suggests (and I think correctly) that evangelicals adopt "critical realism," by which he means "there is a reality external to us. . . . We have awareness and knowledge of it, so that our accounts of that reality at least roughly correspond with it, though we're not infallible or exhaustive in our understanding of it" (*Purpose-Directed Theology*, 22). This concept is discussed in more detail in Smith, *Truth and the New Kind of Christian*, 170–90.

15. Paul did write about becoming "all things to all men" so that he might "by all means save some" (1 Cor. 9:22 NASB). And in this sense learning to contextualize the Christian gospel for a postmodern audience should be pursued because we are Christ's ambassadors urging humanity to be reconciled to God (2 Cor. 5:18–21). However, it is unwise and ultimately harmful to the vitality of Christianity to embrace the underpinnings of philosophical postmodernism. Perhaps the most prominent evangelical work in which this is occurring is Stanley J. Grenz and John R. Franke, *Beyond Foundationalism: Shaping Theology in a Postmodern Context* (Louisville: Westminster John Knox Press, 2001). For a clear philosophical explanation of truth and postmodernism, see J. P. Moreland and William Lane Craig, *Philosophical Foundations for a Christian Worldview* (Downers Grove, IL: InterVarsity Press, 2003), 130–53. For a helpful theological critique of these trends, see Millard J. Erickson, Paul Kjoss Helseth, and Justin Taylor, eds., *Reclaiming the Center: Confronting Evangelical Accommodation in Postmodern Times* (Wheaton, IL: Crossway, 2004). And for a timely discussion regarding how postmodernism—as expressed by *some* within the "emerging church"—is affecting the church, see D. A. Carson, *Becoming Conversant with the Emerging Church: Understanding a Movement and Its Implications* (Grand Rapids: Zondervan, 2005).

16. William Dembski helps us see this by advocating an approach he labels "moderate contextualism," which "affirms that all human inquiry occurs within contexts and must therefore acknowledge the role of contexts in shaping how we view the world. Reason functions within contexts and cannot be divorced from contexts. . . . Objectivity is not lost by acknowledging the role that contexts play in shaping how we learn about the world . . . while acknowledging the obvious, does not open the door to unbridled skepticism or relativism" ("The Fallacy of Contextualism," in *Unapologetic Apologetics: Meeting the Challenges of Theological Studies*, ed. William A. Dembski and Jay Wesley Richards [Downers Grove, IL: InterVarsity Press, 2001], 46).

17. Ronald Nash reminds us that "God has endowed humans with a structure of rationality patterned after the ideas of His own mind: we can know truth because God has made us like Himself [i.e., in His image]" and that "language is a divinely given gift to facilitate communion between God and humans that is both personal and cognitive" (*The Word of God*

Understanding Spiritual Formation in Light of the Gospel

With these preliminaries firmly established, let us now focus our attention on understanding spiritual formation in light of the gospel. Through an exploration and explanation of the gospel of the kingdom, we can understand better the context in which spiritual formation occurs. The gospel is "good news."[18] There is only one gospel. But for practical purposes it is helpful to make a distinction between the gospel as an invitation offered to unbelievers[19] and the gospel as God's full kingdom program.[20] The good news that Christians share with unbelievers provides them the opportunity to "enter the eternal kind of life now" through Jesus Christ.[21] But this is only the beginning. The more we explore what God has said, done, and promised, the bigger the good news gets! The kingdom story we find ourselves in (the true metanarrative if you will) encompasses all of reality. This is the gospel in the fullest sense. Darrell Bock captures this sentiment well by stating, "The gospel is about far more than heaven."[22]

An analogy might be helpful. Think of the content of what we share

---

and the Mind of Man: The Crisis of Revealed Truth in Contemporary Theology [Phillipsburg, NJ: Presbyterian and Reformed, 1992], 81, 132). Christianity requires *both* propositional (knowledge that) and personal (knowledge of) knowledge. One without the other can result in a deficient understanding. Yet, our knowledge of whom we are worshiping and what we are experiencing is always guided and informed by the propositional content of the Bible—which is, in fact, true. For more on this, see Gordon R. Lewis, "Is Propositional Revelation Essential to Evangelical Spiritual Formation?" *Journal of the Evangelical Theological Society* 46, no. 2 (2003).

18. In 1999, leaders from many denominations came together to draft an evangelical statement on what the gospel is and is not. This wonderful and historic statement can be found in "The Gospel of Jesus Christ: An Evangelical Celebration," *Christianity Today*, June 14, 1999, 51–56. A follow-up article was written with shorter gospel statements, allowing for more nuanced language. See "What's the Good News? Nine Evangelical Leaders Define the Gospel," *Christianity Today*, February 7, 2000, 46–51.

19. We must be careful, no matter how well intentioned, not to add or frontload *effects* of the gospel (e.g., changed behavior, baptism, lordship, verbal confession, good works, intense emotions, etc.) to the only condition of salvation, which is faith alone (*sola fide*). The only requirement—and it is a serious one—for entering into the eternal relationship God offers (John 17:3) only in Jesus Christ (John 14:6; Acts 4:12; 1 Tim. 2:5) is trusting in what Christ has done for us and in faith resting in that relationship through Christ. Classically faith includes (1) understanding (*notitia*), (2) assent (*assensus*), and (3) trust (*fiducia*). The clearest summary of the core of the gospel message can be found in 1 Corinthians 15:1–4. It is certainly bigger than this, but definitely no less than this.

20. Saucy summarizes this program: "God's kingly rule is brought to the earth through the mediation of the kingdom of the Messiah. According to biblical prophecy, the coming of the kingdom involves the redemption of creation from all the effects of sin through the personal salvation of individuals, the socio-political salvation of the nations, and finally the salvation of the earth and heavens through re-creation. This pervasive mediatorial kingdom program, ultimately fulfilled in the reign of Christ, is the theme of Scripture and the unifying principle of all aspects of God's work in history" (Robert L. Saucy, *The Case for Progressive Dispensationalism: The Interface Between Dispensational and Non-Dispensational Theology* [Grand Rapids: Zondervan, 1993], 28).

21. Dallas Willard, *The Divine Conspiracy: Rediscovering Our Hidden Life in God* (San Francisco: HarperSanFrancisco, 1997), 1–58.

22. "What's the Good News?" 47.

with unbelievers in evangelism as being similar to the preview of a novel printed on the dust jacket. Does that preview fully capture the novel? Of course not! But it does give the person the opportunity to join the never-ending story. And it is within this never-ending, kingdom story that the process of spiritual formation occurs. Just as a precious jewel shines most brilliantly against the background of lavish velvet, so the process of spiritual formation shines brightest in light of the gospel of the kingdom.

Theological Implications for Spiritual Formation in Panoramic View

Viewing the fullness of the gospel ushers our discussion into theological implications for spiritual formation. As we look at the panorama of God's revelation, we must climb four prominent peaks (the Trinity, humanity in the image of God, the God-man Jesus Christ, and salvation) and descend into one murky valley (the fall and sinfulness of humanity). We will describe the theological truths discovered along the way and then show their relationship to spiritual formation.

The Trinity

The most prominent of the four peaks is the Trinity, and it is this doctrine that serves as the ultimate reference point for all of reality. As we stand at the base of this mountain, we gaze in wonder and awe as the majestic disappears into the clouds beyond our sight. And while this doctrine is ultimately *beyond* reason,[23] God has been pleased to reveal the boundaries of orthodoxy in his Word to ensure accurate understanding among his people. Bruce Ware offers a salient summary of the classic biblical teaching on the Trinity:

> The Christian faith affirms that there is one and only one God, eternally existing and fully expressed as three Persons, the Father, the Son, and the Holy Spirit. Each member of the Godhead is equally God, each is eternally God, and each is fully God—not three gods but three Persons of the one Godhead. Each Person is equal in essence as each possesses fully the identically same, eternal divine nature, yet each is also an eternal and distinct personal expression of the one undivided divine nature.[24]

---

23. This is one of those truths that is ultimately beyond reason, not against reason. The early church fathers were careful to formulate a definition/creedal statement of the Trinity that was not *explicitly* contradictory at Nicaea (325), Constantinople (381), and Chalcedon (451), as seen in John H. Leith, *Creeds of the Churches: A Reader in Christian Doctrine, from the Bible to the Present*, 3rd ed. (Atlanta: John Knox Press, 1982), 28–36. For a defense of the coherence of the Trinity without a removal of mystery, see the excellent explanation of Thomas D. Senor, "The Incarnation and the Trinity," in *Reason for the Hope Within*, ed. Michael J. Murray (Grand Rapids: Eerdmans, 1999).

24. Bruce A. Ware, *Father, Son, and Holy Spirit: Relationships, Roles, and Relevance* (Wheaton, IL: Crossway, 2005), 43. I am grateful to Scott Horrell for shaping and informing

So we see that God, from all eternity, exists in a self-giving (often termed *perichoretic*) love relationship as Father, Son, and Holy Spirit. In short, God is essentially relational. For any view of spiritual formation to be adequate, it must be fully Trinitarian. As Klaus Issler puts it, "Christian spirituality involves a deepening trust and friendship with God for those who are in Christ Jesus. More specifically, it is an ever growing, experientially dynamic relationship with our Trinitarian God—Father, Son and Holy Spirit—through the agency of the indwelling Spirit of God."[25]

Perhaps the single most significant philosophical question that all worldviews and religions have to answer is, "Why is there *something* instead of *nothing*?" God in his aseity[26] (lit. "from or by himself") did not *have* to create. He was completely satisfied in himself and did not need creation to express his attributes. Why did he create then? The Scriptures hint at the reason. It seems that God's purpose in creation was so that he could invite a community of his image bearers in Christ to participate in the eternal love relationship that the Trinity enjoys, thus displaying his glory (John 17:20–25; cf. Eph. 3:11). James Beilby puts it this way: "Creation is a gift of God's love—unmerited and unnecessitated . . . [in which] the glory of God finds its fullest expression."[27] Indeed, the doctrine of the Trinity in all its magnificence is foundational for evangelical spiritual formation.

Humanity in the Image of God

The next peak we need to explore on our expedition is that of who we are as humans. What does it mean to be human (both male and female) in the image of the triune God? Where does our innate desire for relationship come from? What is it that is being spiritually formed? Answering these questions will help us better understand the process of spiritual formation.

There has been much discussion regarding what it means to be made in the image or likeness of God.[28] The Hebrew words for "image" and "likeness" "refer to something that is *similar* but not identical to the thing it rep-

---

my view of the importance of the Trinity to all of life. He has been a great encouragement to me.

25. Klaus Issler, *Wasting Time with God: A Christian Spirituality of Friendship with God* (Downers Grove, IL: InterVarsity Press, 2001), 25–26.

26. James Beilby offers a precise explanation of "arguably God's most fundamental divine attribute" by proposing, "First, God is *ontologically a se*. He is uncaused, without beginning, not dependent on an external person, principle, or metaphysical reality for his existence. Second, God is *psychologically a se*. There is no lack or need in God. He is fully satisfied, not needing anything outside of himself to be happy or fulfilled" ("Divine Aseity, Divine Freedom: A Conceptual Problem for Edwardsian-Calvinsim," *Journal of the Evangelical Theological Society* 47, no. 4 [2004]: 648).

27. Ibid., 658.

28. For good evangelical discussions, see Gordon R. Lewis and Bruce A. Demarest, *Integrative Theology* (Grand Rapids: Zondervan, 1996), 123–80; and Millard Erickson, *Christian Theology*, 2nd ed. (Grand Rapids: Baker, 2001), 517–36.

resents or is an 'image' of."[29] There are generally three different views of the image of God (substantive, relational, and functional), but Ware's definition best integrates these aspects together:

> The image of God in man as functional holism means that God made human beings, both male and female, to be created and finite representations (images of God) of God's own nature, that in relationship with Him and each other they might be His representatives (imaging God) in carrying out the responsibilities He has given to them. In this sense, we are images of God in order to image God and His purposes in the ordering of our lives and the carrying out of our God-given responsibilities.[30]

Supplementing this definition, Robert Saucy contributes the following implications of the "endowments of personality" implicit in the image of God: self-conscious rationality (I would include emotional capacities as well), self-determination or freedom, moral nature, and original righteousness (i.e., Adam was created good by God).[31] The obvious inference is that humans are distinct from all of the animal creation in that we alone bear the image of God (Gen. 1:27; James 3:9).

Also, we are inherently relational because we are made in the image of a relational God. Thus the rugged individualism and "lone-ranger Christianity" so prevalent in America is opposed to God's intention. A man, alone with God, would seem to be the pinnacle of spirituality in our culture, but God said, "It is not good for the man to be alone" (Gen. 2:18). Authentic community is God's intention for humanity. In short, as humans we were created in the image of God in order to experience a vibrant relationship with our triune Creator God and to experience authentic relationships in community with one another.[32]

God created humanity as male and female. Discussions of gender often arouse strong emotions. Ware offers a needed word of clarification: "After affirming the complete essential equality of men and women as created in

---

29. Wayne A. Grudem, *Systematic Theology: An Introduction to Biblical Doctrine* (Grand Rapids: Zondervan, 2000), 442.

30. Bruce A. Ware, "Male and Female Complementarity and the Image of God," in *Biblical Foundations for Manhood and Womanhood*, ed. Wayne Grudem (Wheaton, IL: Crossway, 2002), 79.

31. Robert L. Saucy, "Theology of Human Nature," in *Christian Perspectives on Being Human: A Multidisciplinary Approach to Integration*, ed. J. P. Moreland and David M. Ciocchi (Grand Rapids: Baker, 1993), 27–28.

32. "The very fact that God, though singular in nature, is plural and societal in person, indicates that we should not view ourselves as isolated individuals who happen to exist in close proximity to others, but as interconnected, interdependent relational persons in community. . . . God intends that there be a created community of persons in which there is an interconnection and interdependence, so that what one does affects another; what one needs can be supplied by another, and what one seeks to accomplish may be assisted by another" (Ware, *Father, Son, and Holy Spirit*, 134).

the image of God, an obvious observation must be made that has important implications: While male is fully human, male is also male, not female; and while female is fully human, female is also female, not male. That is, while God did intend to create male and female as equal in their essential nature as human, he also intended to make them *different expressions* of that essential nature, as male and female reflect different ways, as it were, of being human."[33] Gender does affect the spiritual formation process. Men and women must discover how they express the image of God as distinctively male and female.[34]

We often overlook the fact that we were created to relate to God as physical beings on a physical earth. The popular notion that the ideal state of relating to God is blissfully floating as an ethereal spirit is simply false. Human beings are composed of both material (body) and immaterial (soul) aspects functioning as unified entities (holistic dualism).[35] Saucy explains that "Although the human person is a basic duality, these two aspects of his nature are joined together in a functional holism of life."[36] Humans are called to love God with all of their heart, soul, mind, and strength (Luke 10:27). In other words, we are to love God with an *integrated devotion*.[37] The term that ap-

---

33. Ware, "Male and Female Complementarity and the Image of God," 81.

34. For more on imaging God as male/female, see John Coe, "Being Faithful to Christ in One's Gender: Theological Reflections on Masculinity and Femininity," in *Women and Men in Ministry: A Complementary Perspective*, ed. Robert L. Saucy and Judith K. TenElshof (Chicago: Moody Press, 2001). On imaging God as husband/wife and within the family, see the excellent work by Andreas J. Köstenberger and David W. Jones, *God, Marriage, and Family: Rebuilding the Biblical Foundation* (Wheaton, IL: Crossway, 2004). For how male and female image God within the church, see Saucy and TenElshof's work above. The aforementioned positions are complementarian, which is the position I take to be biblically accurate.

35. An excellent book that interacts with the relevant biblical, theological, and philosophical data defending this view and critiquing other views is John W. Cooper, *Body, Soul, and Life Everlasting: Biblical Anthropology and the Monism-Dualism Debate*, updated ed. (Grand Rapids: Eerdmans, 2000). When we ask "What is being spiritually formed?" and "How does this occur?" the discipline of philosophical anthropology can help us think more clearly. For example, Dallas Willard has set forth a helpful way of thinking about how the different aspects of the human person interact in spiritual formation in *Renovation of the Heart: Putting on the Character of Christ* (Colorado Springs: NavPress, 2002), 38–42. We must remember that the body (and its members, cf. Rom. 6:12–13) is essential to spiritual formation. The body is where our habits (tendencies to act, think, or feel in certain ways without willing to do so) reside. And our character is the sum total of our habits. As Moreland notes, "To change our habits and to interact differently with the world, we need to retrain our bodies to form new habits that replace the old ones" (J. P. Moreland, *Love Your God with All Your Mind: The Role of Reason in the Life of the Soul* [Colorado Springs: NavPress, 1997], 66; cf. idem, "Spiritual Formation and the Nature of the Soul," *Christian Education Journal*, no. NS 4 [Fall 2000]: 25–43).

36. Saucy, "Theology of Human Nature," 39.

37. My friend Cole Huffman introduced this terminology to me, and I think it captures the thrust of this passage well. For learning how to love God more with your mind, see Moreland, *Love Your God with All Your Mind*. For emphasis on loving God more with your heart, see Willard, *Renovation of the Heart*.

pears more than any other in Scripture is *heart*.[38] "It is important to grasp the biblical truth that in the heart, the operating center from which all behavior flows, thought, feeling, and will all come together in a unified whole."[39]

In sum, humanity in the image of God as male and female is the highest of the created order and was intended to function in vibrant physical relationship with our triune God and in authentic community with one another. They've lived happily ever after, right? Unfortunately they have not.

The Fall and Sinfulness of Humanity

We are now at the low point in our journey, slogging through a murky valley far below the prominent peaks explored thus far. Our survey of the carnage found here reveals what was created good in the beginning has been corrupted and wrecked by sin and death. A great fall has occurred (Gen. 3), and we must honestly deal with this fact if we are to be spiritually transformed. The sin of Adam has stained all of his progeny with sin and death due to his disobedience as humanity's head (Rom. 5:12–21).[40] Everyone born after Adam validates his initial act of disobedience through sins of commission (doing what we should not do) and sins of omission (not doing what we ought to do).

The wreck known as *the fall* defaced the image of God in humanity, but mercifully it did not erase it. The wages of death now spread to all men and women. We all have fallen tragically short of the glory of God (Rom. 3:23). Humanity now finds itself in a sinful state[41] that is agonizingly *not the way it was supposed to be.* In Cornelius Plantinga's words, "Shalom [i.e., peace or wholeness] is God's design for creation and redemption; sin is blamable human vandalism of these great realties and therefore an affront to their architect and builder."[42] Shalom has been vandalized. The consequences are staggering. Humanity has been spiritually separated from God, separated from themselves,[43] separated from their fellow human beings (hostility), and

---

38. *Heart* is used some 726 times in the NASB; *spirit* is used 570 times; *soul* 276 times; and *mind* 144 times.

39. Saucy, "Theology of Human Nature," 42.

40. Helpful discussions of original sin and the effects of sin can be found in Paul Copan, "Original Sin and Christian Philosophy," *Philosophia Christi* 5, no. 2 (2003): 519–34; Henri Blocher, *Original Sin: Illuminating the Riddle* (Grand Rapids: Eerdmans, 1997); and Norman L. Geisler, *Systematic Theology, Vol. 3: Sin and Salvation* (Minneapolis: Bethany House, 2004), 80–178.

41. The terminology of "sin nature" needs to be clearly defined or not used at all because of potential misunderstandings that can occur—especially within the church—if taken in the wrong sense. I prefer "corrupted nature" for the sake of precision. See the discussion in Copan, "Original Sin and Christian Philosophy," 522–27, as well as Walt Russell, "The Apostle Paul's View of the 'Sin Nature'/'New Nature' Struggle," in *Christian Perspectives on Being Human: A Multidisciplinary Approach to Integration*, ed. J. P. Moreland and David M. Ciocchi (Grand Rapids: Baker, 1993).

42. Cornelius Plantinga, *Not the Way It's Supposed to Be: A Breviary of Sin* (Grand Rapids: Eerdmans, 1995), 16.

43. Sin did something that was never intended to occur—namely cause the separation of the body and soul by death. The body goes into the ground and the soul goes to be with

separated from the ruling relationship they were intended to have over nature. Nature itself has been corrupted and subjugated by sin (Rom. 8:20–22). The consequences of the fall are extensive and affect the total person (i.e., total depravity).[44] What has been deformed by the ugliness of sin (the whole person) must now be reformed according to the ideal image of perfect humanity found in Jesus Christ. Dallas Willard observes that "the greatest need you and I have—the greatest need of collective humanity—is renovation of our heart. That spiritual place within us from which outlook, choices and actions come has been formed by a world away from God. Now it must be transformed."[45]

The God-Man, Jesus Christ

The second person of the Godhead became incarnate in the person of Jesus Christ in order to reveal the Father, defeat Satan and his works, seek and save the lost, and become humanity's substitute and Savior by atoning for the sins of the whole world[46] so that whosoever believes in him will not perish but have everlasting life (John 3:16). Jesus is the expression of the triune God in human flesh, in whom God was pleased to allow all the fullness of deity to dwell (Col. 1:19; 2:9). Jesus—the perfect and unique God-man—is fully God and fully human. Being fully God, he can save us; and being fully human, he can identify with us. Both are necessary. He possesses all that it requires to be God and has added to his divine nature a human nature like ours in every respect—except sin (Heb. 4:15). All that was said above about our (pre-fall) human nature is true of the human nature of Christ. He is the perfect image of God.

These are lofty statements that are orthodox, wonderful, and true. And yet, many Christians find it difficult to believe in the full humanity of Jesus. A Jesus who is God is relatively easy to conceive of. But a Jesus who was human in the same way we are and experienced everyday life like we do is sometimes hard to imagine. But the Bible presents Jesus as human as much as it confesses him to be divine. A careful reading of the Gospels reveals the striking humanity of Jesus.[47] He grew in wisdom, stature, and favor with

---

the Lord at death. Humanity must then wait for the day when God reunites body and soul in the resurrection and ultimate glorification.

44. Total depravity does not mean that humans are as bad as they could be at every moment, only that they are in a state of being as "bad off" as they could possibly be. There is no part of our humanness that has not been deeply corrupted by sin.

45. Willard, *Renovation of the Heart*, 14.

46. I find the unlimited atonement view to be the most biblically and theologically compelling (see especially 1 Tim. 2:6; 4:10; 2 Peter 2:1; 1 John 2:2). Demarest's discussion is excellent in Bruce A. Demarest, *The Cross and Salvation: The Doctrine of Salvation*, Foundations of Evangelical Theology (Wheaton, IL: Crossway, 1997), 191–93.

47. This point was brought home to me in a class I took from Darrell Bock using the content found in Bock's *Jesus According to Scripture: Restoring the Portrait from the Gospels* (Grand Rapids: Baker, 2002). The disciples did not understand Jesus to be the second person of the ontological Trinity—they had their brighter moments and not-so-bright moments—during

men and God (Luke 2:52). He hungered (Luke 4:2), wept (John 11:35), was tempted in all ways as we are (Luke 4:2; Heb. 4:15), felt compassion (Matt. 9:36), loved (John 11:5), learned obedience (Luke 22:42; Heb. 5:8), and even got angry (Mark 11:15–17)—but all without sinning. He was prayerfully dependent on the Father (Luke 5:16; John 17), empowered by the Holy Spirit (Luke 4:1), and full of grace and truth (John 1:14). Jesus fulfilled the greatest commandment of loving the Father perfectly and his neighbors as himself. So in the sinful state of deformation that we find ourselves, the Scriptures hold forth Jesus as our ultimate example to follow in spiritual formation.[48] And as we follow him obediently in discipleship (living as he lived), we are increasingly conformed to his image (Luke 6:40; Gal. 4:19; Col. 3:10).

So Great a Salvation

The doctrine of salvation (soteriology) is considered here because we need to see the means by which God can righteously invite us into a love relationship with himself. We will divide our discussion into the truths that are ours already and the ones we have not yet experienced.

When we recognize the depth of our sin and place our trust in the finished work of Christ on our behalf, we become a Christian. At that moment, many truly amazing things happen (and have already been happening to make salvation even possible).[49] What occurs at this beautiful moment is sometimes referred to as positional salvation or justification (Rom. 3:24, 28).[50] We have been freed from the penalty of sin. Some of the benefits acompanying justification include substitution,[51] regeneration (John 3:3; Titus 3:5), redemption (Gal. 3:13), propitiation,[52] reconciliation

---

his earthly ministry. But we must also guard against the heresy of Nestoriansim that sees the divine Jesus calming the storm but the human Jesus weeping over Lazarus. He was fully God and fully human on both occasions.

48. Jesus is certainly more than just our example, but humanly speaking we strive to imitate him. Also, he was without sin and therefore without need of spiritual formation but he is the ideal we strive to emulate.

49. For how the various theological systems within the evangelical spectrum view how the process of salvation is initiated, see these helpful works: Jerry L. Walls and Joseph Dongell, *Why I Am Not a Calvinist* (Downers Grove, IL: InterVarsity Press, 2004); William Lane Craig, "Middle Knowledge: A Calvinist-Arminian Rapprochement," in *The Grace of God and the Will of Man*, ed. Clark H. Pinnock (Minneapolis: Bethany House, 1995); Bruce A. Ware, *God's Greater Glory: The Exalted God of Scripture and the Christian Faith* (Wheaton, IL: Crossway, 2004); and Geisler, *Systematic Theology, Vol. 3: Sin and Salvation*, 181–551.

50. There is variance of opinion within evangelicalism as to how much to separate justification from sanctification. See, for example, Melvin E. Dieter, ed., *Five Views on Sanctification* (Grand Rapids: Zondervan, 1987).

51. Christ died for us in our place (Rom. 5:8; 2 Cor. 5:21; 1 Peter 3:18). While much more was accomplished at the cross, the center of the atonement of Jesus Christ is his substitutionary death. All the other benefits extend like shockwaves from the center stake driven into the ground, demonstrating both the love of God and the justice of God (among other attributes).

52. Christ satisfied God's wrath against sin (Rom. 3:25; 1 John 2:2). See D. A. Carson, "Atonement in Romans 3:21–26: God Presented Him as a Propitiation," in *The Glory of the*

(2 Cor. 5:18–21), adoption (John 1:12; Rom. 8:14–17), baptism by the Holy Spirit,[53] and eternal security/assurance of salvation.[54] These are just some of the blessings that are ours positionally in Christ.

What an astonishing list this is! And yet the process has only begun. It is not complete. Sanctification involves our being progressively freed from the power of sin. As Christians, we live in the now and *not yet*. "Christians are positionally holy by virtue of being in Christ (1 Cor. 1:2; 6:11; Heb. 10:10) although experientially they remain tainted by sin."[55] We are simultaneously "sinning saints" or "saintly sinners." While it is true that we possess everything for life and godliness (2 Peter 1:3), it is also true that we still await our final state of righteousness in glorified bodies. This occurs at glorification when the presence of sin is finally done away with. We see in part now (1 Cor. 13:12), but one day all the blinders of sin will be removed. Sin has initially been dealt with at the cross, but its final (historical) demise is yet future. One day our character will finally be conformed to Christ—positional will become actual. This process is what spiritual formation is all about.

How God Spiritually Forms Believers into the Image of Christ

In this final section, we will seek to unite all of the content above into a cogent theological road map to show how God spiritually forms believers into the image of Christ. Just as salvation occurs by grace alone through faith, so too the spiritual formation process takes place by grace alone through faith empowered by the Holy Spirit, who keeps our eyes steadied on Jesus Christ, the author and perfecter of our faith (Heb. 12:2).

Atonement: Biblical, Historical, and Practical Perspectives, ed. Charles E. Hill and Frank A. James III (Downers Grove, IL: InterVarsity Press, 2004), 119–39.

53. The new believer is baptized (i.e., placed) into the body of Christ (1 Cor. 12:13; cf. Acts 11:15–17) by the Holy Spirit. There are diverse views on this as well, with implications for the process of spiritual formation. Some helpful evangelical treatments are John R. W. Stott, *Baptism and Fullness: The Work of the Holy Spirit Today* (Downers Grove, IL: InterVarsity Press, 1975); J. I. Packer, *Keep in Step with the Spirit* (Grand Rapids: Revell, 2000); Gordon D. Fee, *Paul, the Spirit, and the People of God* (Peabody, MA: Hendrickson, 1996); and Chad Brand, ed., *Perspectives on Spirit Baptism: Five Views* (Nashville: Broadman & Holman, 2004).

54. *Eternal security* is the doctrine that once a person becomes a Christian, that person cannot finally lose his or her salvation. The new believer is sealed by the Holy Spirit, whose presence functions as a guarantee, proof, and divine stamp of authority (Eph. 1:13–14; 4:30; 2 Cor. 1:22). *Assurance of salvation* is the doctrine that concerns a believer's experiential understanding that he or she is saved. A believer can have assurance of his salvation based on the testimony of God's Word (1 John 5:11–12), the inner witness of the Holy Spirit (Rom. 8:16), and the bearing of fruit through obedience in his or her life (Scripture does indicate that at least some fruitfulness will occur in a believer—most notably love for one another (1 John 3:18–19). Bruce Demarest notes, "Unlike justification or adoption, assurance of salvation admits of degrees and thus may fluctuate in strength and intensity. Since much of the evidence (moral, relational, and experiential) is subjective, assurance can be expected to vacillate with our circumstances and feelings. Believers ought not to be shaken by the presence of honest doubts in their lives" (*The Cross and Salvation*, 379).

55. Ibid., 402.

Necessary Resources for Spiritual Formation

Spiritual formation is divinely enabled by God through three essential resources: God's Word, God's Spirit, and God's people (the church).

The first essential resource is exposure to God's Word. By its truth our thinking is renewed and we are able to break free from the anti-Christian mold the world seeks to press us into (Rom. 12:1–2). God's Word is the primary and objective source of truth about Christ and what it means to follow him. It is a lamp to the feet and a light to the path (Ps. 119:105), alive and active (Heb. 4:12), sweeter than honey (Ps. 19:10), more precious than gold (Ps. 19:10), perfect and trustworthy (Ps. 19:7), and true and righteous (Ps. 19:9). Exposure to God's Word provides many benefits to our journey of spiritual formation, such as stability (Eph. 4:12–15), insight/guidance (Ps. 119:9–10; Prov. 3:5–6), and spiritual maturity (1 Peter 2:2–3; cf. 1 Cor. 3:1–3; Heb. 5:14). Walt Russell offers helpful insight concerning hermeneutics, the discipline of Bible reading, and spiritual formation:

> *First*, we must reject the idea that there is a chasm between informational reading and formational reading. No such false dichotomy should exist in our reading of the Bible. Rather, we should first be reading to understand the intention of the biblical author within the biblical book we are reading. This involves *some* "informational" emphasis, but is not an end in and of itself, nor is it as intensive as an academic study of the passage. Rather, it is a means to the end of being spiritually formed according to the meaning of a biblical passage. There can be no true spiritual transforming apart from the true meaning of the biblical text! Although this demands some initial informational emphasis in the reading of the Bible, it should be balanced. It is both author-and text-centered (for the *meaning* of the passage) and reader-responsive (for the *significance* of that meaning to us).[56]

God dynamically uses his Word to form us into the image of Christ.

The third person of the Trinity, the Holy Spirit, is another essential resource for our spiritual formation. When Jesus spoke to his disciples in the Upper Room Discourse, he promised another helper, the Holy Spirit, who not only would be *with* them, but, after Jesus' death, resurrection, and ascension, also would be *in* them (John 14:17). As discussed above, the Holy Spirit indwells us and is at work in our lives. He is a person, not a force. The gifts that the body of Christ enjoys are dispensed by the Holy Spirit for the edification and benefit of the community (1 Cor. 12; Rom.

---

56. Walt Russell, *Playing with Fire: How the Bible Ignites Change in Your Soul* (Colorado Springs: NavPress, 2000), 43.

12; Eph. 4; 1 Peter 4).[57] In short, there is no spiritual formation if there is no activity of the Holy Spirit. As Gordon Fee has aptly said, "The Spirit is . . . the empowering presence of God for living the life of God in the present."[58] Robert Gromacki summarizes some of the Spirit's ministries in the Christian's life: He assists us in prayer, strengthens us, leads and guides us,[59] enables us to resist temptation, aids us in our understanding/ application of the Scriptures, enables us to proclaim the gospel, and empowers us to serve God.[60] The Spirit is both essential and active! But he can be quenched (1 Thess. 5:19) and grieved (Eph. 4:30) by the believer. We desperately need the resources of the Spirit to become more like Jesus (2 Cor. 3:18). It is encouraging to see evangelicals desiring to see more of the Spirit's power emphasized, experienced, and manifested in believers' lives today.[61]

The final essential resource for spiritual formation is the body of Christ (the church). The Christian life is not to be pursued in isolation. It is refreshing to see so many leading evangelical thinkers make this clear in their writings. James White points out that "A . . . myth [about the spiritual life] is that a personal relationship with God through Christ is synonymous with a private relationship with God through Christ. The truth however, is that becoming a truly spiritual person is a team sport."[62] Dallas Willard observes that "Spiritual Formation, good or bad, is always profoundly social. You cannot keep it to yourself. Anyone who thinks of it as a merely private matter has misunderstood it."[63] And Gordon Fee expresses it this way: "God is not just saving individuals and preparing them for heaven; rather, he is creating a people among whom he can live and who in their life together will reproduce God's life and character."[64]

The bottom line is that we need one another in order to be conformed to the image of Christ. The image of Christ has a communal expression (cf. Gal. 4:19—"you" is plural here). Even our knowledge of God is incomplete without one another, as Issler rightly points out: "God is so grand and majestic, and each relationship is so person specific that there will be much

---

57. For the various views on the gifts, see Wayne A. Grudem, *Are Miraculous Gifts for Today? Four Views* (Grand Rapids: Zondervan, 1996).

58. Fee, *Paul, the Spirit, and the People of God*, 183.

59. For insightful discussions on how to develop the discipline of discerning God's leading, see chapter 6 in Issler, *Wasting Time with God*, 151–82; see also Henry Blackaby and Richard Blackaby, *Hearing God's Voice* (Nashville: Broadman & Holman, 2002); and Dallas Willard, *Hearing God: Developing a Conversational Relationship with God* (Downers Grove, IL: InterVarsity Press, 1999).

60. Robert Gromacki, *The Holy Spirit: Who He Is, What He Does*, Swindoll Leadership Library (Nashville: Word, 1999), 197–204.

61. M. James Sawyer and Daniel B. Wallace, *Who's Afraid of the Holy Spirit? An Investigation into the Ministry of the Spirit of God Today* (Dallas: Biblical Studies Press, 2005).

62. James Emery White, *You Can Experience a Spiritual Life* (Nashville: Word, 1999), 30.

63. Willard, *Renovation of the Heart*, 182.

64. Fee, *Paul, the Spirit, and the People of God*, 66.

to learn about God from the stories of other believers' experiences with God. The fullest knowledge of God attainable by human beings will only come about within a growing and God-knowing community of saints. Thus, to know God more fully cannot be accomplished without the larger community of believers."[65] The community of God is not an American phenomenon, and the goal should not be to become a Western evangelical Christian.[66] The wonderful truth is that communities of Christians in every language and from all countries are included in the process of being conformed to the image of Christ. The body of Christ is diverse, and we have much to learn from one another. God is good to give us each other—now if we could only get along as Jesus prayed for us (John 17:20–23)!

So God has given us all we need for the task of spiritual formation through three essential resources that empower us in our journey toward Christlikeness—his Word, his Spirit, and his people.

Spiritual Formation Requires a "Both/And" Approach

Sometimes we make "either/or" decisions when the correct choice is a "both/and." This is especially true in two key spiritual formation areas. The first area requiring a both/and approach concerns the Spirit of God's activity and the believer's activity. An either/or approach here must be rejected. Rather, we should embrace the reality that both the Spirit of God is at work in our lives and we cooperate with that work (Phil. 2:12–13; 1 Thess. 2:13; 2 Peter 1:3–8). Just as the individual must respond in faith in order to be justified, so too must the individual respond in faith during the process of sanctification. As Dallas Willard has put it in *The Great Omission: Reclaiming Jesus's Essential Teachings on Discipleship*, effort does not equal earning. God initiates and enables, and then we respond in faith by cooperating with the work he desires to do in us. It is all motivated by grace.

The second both/and concerns whether spiritual formation is individualized or practiced communally. It is both—we are individuals created to function within a community (Rom. 12:4–5). And that entails that we practice both individual[67] and corporate[68] disciplines. Jesus

---

65. Issler, *Wasting Time with God*, 26.

66. If Philip Jenkins is correct, in fifty years the most populated areas of evangelical Christianity will not be the Western hemisphere, but the Southern. See Philip Jenkins, *The Next Christendom: The Coming of Global Christianity* (Oxford: Oxford University Press, 2002). For more on the diversity that God created and desires (Rev. 5:9), see J. Daniel Hays, *From Every People and Nation: A Biblical Theology of Race*, New Studies in Biblical Theology (Downers Grove, IL: InterVarsity Press, 2003).

67. Helpful lists of the spiritual disciplines can be found in Donald S. Whitney, *Spiritual Disciplines for the Christian Life* (Colorado Springs: NavPress, 1991); Dallas Willard, *The Spirit of the Disciplines: Understanding How God Changes Lives*, 2nd ed. (San Francisco: Harper & Row, 1999); and Richard J. Foster, *Celebration of Discipline: The Path to Spiritual Growth*, 25th anniversary ed. (San Francisco: HarperSanFrancisco, 1998).

68. See Donald S. Whitney, *Spiritual Disciplines Within the Church: Participating Fully in the Body of Christ* (Chicago: Moody Press, 1996).

himself made a point to seek solitude and pray (Matt. 26:36; Luke 5:16). Paul commands us to discipline ourselves "for the purpose of godliness" (1 Tim. 4:7 NASB). Yet, the disciplines are not the end goal but the means.[69] Practicing the disciplines creates a context and opportunity for the Spirit to work in our lives. Some shy away from individual disciplines because they fear they will lead to legalism. And while that can happen, this should not keep Christians from practicing them. Dallas Willard helpfully describes the spiritual disciplines as "the indirect means that allow us to cooperate in reshaping the personality—the feelings, ideas, mental processes and images, and the deep readiness of soul and body—so that our whole being is poised to go with the movements of the regenerate heart that is in us by the impact of the Gospel Word under the direction and energizing of the Holy Spirit."[70] As individuals are conformed to Christ with an integrated devotion and within the community, they do not lose their individuality. They are now functioning in a Trinitarian-informed way in which their individuality is expressed in and for the benefit of the Christian community.

Christians' Spiritual Formation Impacts the Culture

Since salvation is holistic, one possibly obvious implication of the spiritual formation process is that the believer's life should ultimately affect the culture.[71] One of the purposes for which Christ saved us was for us to be a people "eager to do what is good" (Titus 2:14; cf. 1 Peter 2:12).[72] As we seek to be conformed to the image of Christ, we need to be mindful that Jesus' primary role on earth was to glorify the Father. So one way we "image the Son" is by bringing glory to the Father. Jesus said, "In the same way, let your light shine before men, that they may see your good deeds and praise your Father in heaven" (Matt. 5:16). Just prior to this verse we are reminded that we are to be a preserving agent (salt) and a voice of truth (light). This need not result in a "socialized gospel" as long as we continue to offer the gospel of the kingdom to the world (Acts 28:31). Christ followers are to be publicly engaged because transformation occurs as in-

---

69. See the outstanding work by J. P. Moreland and Klaus Issler, *The Lost Virtue of Happiness: Discovering the Disciplines of the Good Life* (Colorado Springs: NavPress, 2006).

70. As quoted in Michael J. Wilkins, *In His Image: Reflecting Christ in Everyday Life* (Colorado Springs: NavPress, 1997), 59.

71. "Because Christ is simultaneously the covenant God who pledged to create a people for Himself and the anointed ruler of that people, the Messiah offers a salvation that cannot be truncated into bare spiritual blessings in one dispensation or mere political authority in another. Therefore, although the church does not yet wield political authority over the nations, it must recognize that the redemption it offers has a social and political element that is intrinsically tied to the gospel itself" (Russell D. Moore, *The Kingdom of Christ: The New Evangelical Perspective* [Wheaton, IL: Crossway, 2004], 129).

72. A thought-provoking work that calls the church to good works is Ronald J. Sider, *Good News and Good Works: A Theology for the Whole Gospel* (Grand Rapids: Baker, 1999).

dividuals within communities live out the good news of the kingdom.[73] Christ was a public figure who impacted the world with the words of life that he spoke, the quality of life that he lived, and the acts of service and compassion that he performed.

Christianity is not just privately true, requiring our attention for only two hours on a Sunday morning; it is public and should affect the totality of life (i.e., a Christian worldview). Unfortunately, evangelicals have withdrawn from ethical, social, political, educational, and cultural issues and institutions.[74] As evangelicals, we need to enter into dialogue in the public square and become part of the solution (not just heralds of the many problems). In previous centuries, Christians understood their responsibility of loving people enough to share the fruit of a "Christian way of life."[75] We would do well to imitate them as they imitated Christ. The sum total of our lives both as individuals and as part of the community of God's people should be no less holistic than that of Christ's. The words of Francis Schaeffer ring as true today as the day they were penned: "True spirituality—the Christian life—flows on into the total culture."[76]

The Finished Product of Spiritual Formation

We live in the *already* and await the *not* yet. The day is still future when spiritual formation will cease. But one day, when Christ appears, we shall be like him (1 John 3:2), and the work God began in us will be complete (Rom. 8:29–30; Phil. 1:6). There will be a final conformity of the believer's life and character to the life and character of Jesus Christ. Along the way we will know we are heading in the right direction as we increasingly display the fruit of the Spirit in our lives (Gal. 5:22–23). We will have a passionate love for God and a visibly compassionate love for people. As we await the finished product, we run hard and seek to finish well—enabled by the Holy Spirit and God's grace.

It will be a journey of heartache and wonder. Mark Buchanan reminds us, "It is the Unseen things that render the things we do see—both the beauty and the ugliness, the grandeur and the bareness, never enough, and yet never too much."[77] Our motivating hope is that one day the unseen will become fully visible. In the new heaven and new earth—throughout eternity—we

---

73. One church's story can be found in Robert Lewis and Rob Wilkins, *The Church of Irresistible Influence* (Grand Rapids: Zondervan, 2001).

74. For a critique and a way to move forward, see J. Daryl Charles, *The Unformed Conscience of Evangelicalism: Recovering the Church's Moral Vision* (Downers Grove, IL: InterVarsity Press, 2002).

75. For the impact of Christianity lived out in culture throughout history, see the excellent book by Alvin J. Schmidt, *How Christianity Changed the World* (Grand Rapids: Zondervan, 2004).

76. Francis A. Schaeffer, *True Spirituality: How to Live for Jesus Moment by Moment*, 30th anniversary ed. (Wheaton, IL: Tyndale House, 2001), 158.

77. Mark Buchanan, *Things Unseen: Living in Light of Forever* (Sisters, OR: Multnomah, 2002), 25.

will fully experience life in the redeemed community, and we will fully enjoy the dynamic love relationship that the Father, Son, and Spirit share. And in that day, we will become *fully human*. I can't wait.[78]

---

78. I want to thank Paul Pettit for offering me the opportunity to be a part of this project. I am also indebted to three friends who read earlier versions of this chapter: Joey Allen, Cole Huffman, and Monty Waldron. Theology is a community exercise and my work was strengthened because of their insights.

Chapter 2

Worship and Spiritual Formation

Richard Averbeck

> Therefore I urge you, brethren, by the mercies of God, to present your bodies a living and holy sacrifice, acceptable to God, which is your spiritual service of worship.
>
> —Romans 12:1 NASB

Worship *is* spirituality. From early Genesis (e.g., Gen. 4:26b, "At that time men began to call on the name of the LORD") to the end of Revelation ("the Lord God Almighty and the Lamb are its temple," Rev. 21:22b), worship is at the core of spiritual life. As individuals and communities of faith, we are temples, and by definition a temple is first of all and above all a place of worship (1 Cor. 3:16–17; 6:19–20; Eph. 2:19–22). Jesus is "the living Stone," in fact, the chosen, precious cornerstone (1 Peter 2:4, 6–7; cf. Eph. 2:20), and we are "like living stones" who "are being built into a spiritual house to be a holy priesthood, offering spiritual sacrifices acceptable to God through Jesus Christ" (1 Peter 2:5).

The term *spiritual formation* is not a biblical term, but then neither is the word *trinity*. Nevertheless, both are expressions we use in referring to important teachings that are most certainly found in the Bible and, in fact, are central to biblical theology and the Christian life. The meaning of the term *spiritual formation* and a biblical understanding of what it is and how it works is best taken from passages in the Bible that refer to the Holy Spirit in the context of *form*ing, trans*form*ing, or con*form*ing a person's life toward Christlikeness ("until Christ is formed in you," Gal. 4:19b).[1] For example, Romans 8:27–29 states, "The Spirit intercedes for

1. For important elements of the biblical theology of the Holy Spirit and the Spirit's importance in spiritual reading of the Bible that underlie the following discussion, see Richard E. Averbeck, "The Holy Spirit in the Hebrew Bible and Its Connections to the New

the saints in accordance with God's will. . . . For those God foreknew he also predestined to be conformed to the likeness of his Son" (cf. Rom. 12:1–2; 2 Cor. 3:17–18).

All three persons of the Trinity come together in this passage. Spiritual formation consists of the Trinitarian work of God in the lives of genuine believers in Christ through the presence and power of the Holy Spirit. The verbal idea in the word *formation* (i.e., to form, transform, conform) emphasizes the active focus of spiritual formation. This includes, first, the *dynamics* of the interaction between the Holy Spirit and our human spirit, and, second, the *activities,* or ways and means, by which we purposefully engage in the dynamics of spiritual formation individually in our private lives, in relationships with others of like purpose in the community of faith, and in our missional engagement with the world.

Worship of the triune God is the most spiritually formative practice available to us as Christians. It is *the* spiritual practice par excellence. Until we get this straight in our minds and allow it to penetrate to the core of our daily lives and communities of faith, we are just going to be working harder at the Christian life and getting nowhere. As Jesus put it to the woman at the well, after all is said and done, what God seeks most of all and above all is worshipers who worship him "in spirit and truth" (John 4:23–24).[2] Whether it is private and personal, or public and communal, it is worship that keeps us most directly engaged with God in life through meditation on his Word (Ps. 1:2), prayer (Ps. 3), penitence (Pss. 32; 51), praise (Pss. 146–150; Heb. 13:15a), thanksgiving (Ps. 100; Heb. 13:15b), lament (Ps. 137), self-sacrifice (Rom. 12:1; 1 Peter 2:5), ministry (Rom. 15:16; Phil. 2:17), doing good works (Heb. 13:16), and more.

The goal of this essay is to develop a biblical theology of worship that shows its primary importance in the spiritual life of individuals and communities of faith and its centrality in spiritual formation. We will treat this in two main sections: worship and the human spirit, and worship and the Holy Spirit. Both of these have roots sunk deep into the soil of the Old Testament and extend into the New Testament for life and worship in the church and the Christian life. We are concerned with a theology of worship built on the whole Bible for the whole person in every part of our lives individually and in community, all directed toward the glory and glorification of God (1 Cor. 10:31).

Worship and the Human Spirit

It all began with creation—"In the beginning God . . ." (Gen. 1:1a)—the

---

Testament" and "God, People, and the Bible: A Spiritually Formative Approach to Biblical Scholarship," in *Who's Afraid of the Holy Spirit? An Investigation into the Ministry of the Spirit of God Today*, ed. Daniel B. Wallace and M. James Sawyer (Dallas: Biblical Studies Press, 2005), 15–36, 137–65.

2. Much of what is written about worship below depends on the exegetical and theological work done in two previously published essays: Richard E. Averbeck, "Worshiping God in Spirit," and "Worshiping God in Truth," in *Authentic Worship: Scripture's Voice, Applying Its Truth*, ed. Herbert W. Bateman IV (Grand Rapids: Kregel, 2002), 79–133.

crowning act of which was the creation of human beings in the "image" and "likeness" of God himself (vv. 26–28). What stands out in the text is the functional nature of this image and likeness. It has to do with how we live and function in the world as the representatives of God's nature and character, his vice-regents, so to speak (cf. also Ps. 8). The passage comes back around to this twice: first, "Then God said, 'Let us make man in our image, in our likeness, *and let them rule over . . .*'" (v. 26, emphasis mine), and, second: "So God created man in his own image, in the image of God he created him; male and female he created them. God blessed them and said to them, 'Be fruitful and increase in number; fill the earth and *subdue it. Rule over* the fish of the sea and the birds of the air and over every living creature that moves on the ground'" (vv. 27–28, emphasis mine).

The point is that the image and likeness terminology leads immediately and directly to the ruling and subduing of the created world, specifically the animal world. As humankind, male and female, God created us to function together as those who represent his authority.

The tragedy comes in Genesis 2–4 with the corruption of this image and likeness. Things go from very good, to bad, to total disaster, so that eventually we read in Genesis 6:5–7, "The LORD saw how great man's wickedness on the earth had become, and that every inclination of the thoughts of his heart was only evil all the time. The LORD was grieved that he had made man on the earth, and his heart was filled with pain. So the LORD said, 'I will wipe mankind, whom I have created, from the face of the earth—men and animals, and creatures that move along the ground, and birds of the air—for I am grieved that I have made them.'"

There are two especially important points in this passage. First, since the Lord is absolutely holy and righteous, he was deeply grieved and pained by the widespread and incessant wickedness of the people he created in his own image and likeness in the first place. In fact, he was grieved (or "sorry," NRSV) that he even created us. This may sound to us like God is unstable and unsure of himself. But in the context of the ancient Israelite and Near Eastern world, it shows how consistent God is in his nature and character. The gods of the other peoples were often unscrupulous and capricious. One could never be certain what they were going to do, whether good or evil, and whether the various gods in the pantheon were going to cooperate or compete. This God, Yahweh of Israel, however, is a God who is consistent within himself as the only God, and he is always good, holy, and righteous. Furthermore, he is committed to manifesting this character through those whom he created to function as his image and likeness in the world. This is what makes our corruption such a disaster in God's view.

This brings us to the second point. The wickedness arose out of a corrupt heart: "every inclination of the thoughts of his heart was only evil all the time" (v. 5). The term for "inclination" is better translated "form" or "shape." It is the noun from the same root as the verb used in Genesis 2:7 for the Lord's shaping of the man's physical body: "The LORD God formed the man from the dust of the ground." In Genesis 6:5 it refers to the "shape" of the "thoughts" that are in the "heart." "Heart" in Hebrew can refer to any element of our inner being, including the way we think and feel, our will and our desires, our memories and our plans, our attitudes, and more. The Hebrew language does not really have another term for "mind" or "brain." Our intellectual capacity is not separate from all the other forms of what takes place in the immaterial part of our being, in our "heart."

The words *heart*, *soul*, and *spirit* do not refer to different segments or parts of our inner person. Instead, they are terms for our whole inner person looked at from different angles and perspectives. They refer to the various kinds of conditions and activities within us. The "heart," for example, refers in general to all that goes on inside us. The Hebrew term for "soul" is notoriously difficult to translate. It can mean simply the "person" as a whole, but it can also refer to the animate life in a human or an animal, among other things. For example, in Genesis 1:24 God created the "living creatures" (lit. "living soul" beings) of the land. Similarly, in Genesis 2:7b the Lord shaped the man from the dust of the ground and breathed into him so that he became "a living being" (lit. "living soul," the same term as for the animals in Gen. 1:24 above).

The Human Spirit in Scripture

This brings us to the term for "spirit," which is our main concern here. On the one hand, in 40 percent of its occurrences the Old Testament Hebrew word "spirit" (*rûaḥ*) means "wind" or "breath," not "spirit" as we use the term in the church today (see, e.g., Ps. 1:4; Ezek. 37:7–9, 14). The New Testament Greek word (*pneuma*) is also sometimes used in this way (cf. John 3:5 with v. 8; 2 Thess. 2:8). On the other hand, these words do often refer to the *human* spirit, and certain passages draw out the correspondence between the Spirit of God and the human spirit, and the importance of God's work through that correspondence in forming us spiritually. We will return to this correspondence later. For now it is important to understand the nature of the human "spirit," a somewhat neglected topic that is especially important for understanding spiritual formation and its connection to worship "in spirit and truth."

Hebrew *rûaḥ* ("spirit") is used about 120 times for all sorts of inner conditions, positions, and dispositions in the Old Testament. For example, it refers to vitality of life (e.g., Gen. 45:27; Josh. 5:1; 1 Kings 10:5; 21:5; Isa. 38:16), moral and spiritual character (e.g., positive: Isa. 26:9; Mal. 2:16; and negative: Isa. 29:24; Ezek. 13:3), capacities of mind and will (e.g., Exod. 28:3; Job 20:3, lit. "the spirit of my understanding"; Pss. 51:10[12], 12[14]; 77:6[7]), and various dispositions or states of the human person and personality (e.g., Num. 5:14, feelings, suspicions; Judg. 8:3, anger, resentment; etc.). According to Ecclesiastes 12:7, "the dust [*'āfār*] returns to the ground it came from, and the spirit [*rûaḥ*] returns to God who gave it" (cf. Job 34:14–15; Ps. 146:4; Isa. 42:5; Zech. 12:1).

The New Testament word *pneuma* ("spirit") occurs in similar usages. For example, Jesus cried out on the cross, "Father, into your hands I commit my spirit" (Luke 23:46). And James wrote, "As the body without the spirit is dead, so faith without deeds is dead" (James 2:26). When the "spirit" of a person departs, the physical body dies. Even in life one can refer to the combination of "body" (*sōma*, or "flesh" [*sarx*]) and "spirit" (*pneuma*) as making up the whole person (e.g., 1 Cor. 7:34; 2 Cor. 7:1; Col. 2:5; and the combination of body, flesh [as embodied sin], and spirit in 1 Cor. 5:3–5), although other combinations also can be used (see, e.g., "soul and body" in Matt. 10:28 and "spirit, soul and body" in 1 Thess. 5:23). The "spirit" is the seat of human character, as well as capacities, dispositions, and attitudes. For example, it is the seat of intuition (Mark 2:8), discouragement or internal despair (Mark 8:12), joy (Luke 1:47, where it is parallel with "soul" in v. 46), intense affection (John 11:33), an internal sense of being (2 Tim. 1:7, a spirit of fear, as opposed to a spirit of power, love, and self-discipline; 1 Cor. 4:21, a spirit of gentleness), and so on.

Thus, "spirit" in Scripture can refer to either the whole immaterial part of a human being or to some element of it, especially the inner conditions and dispositions of the person. It is precisely here that the problem arises. Our "spirit" has become corrupt. We have all been "formed" by our corrupt nature, by the effects of the corrupt nature of others on us, and by the fact that the world around is in a corrupt state and under the influence of the Evil One (Eph. 2:1–2), "that ancient serpent called the devil, or Satan, who leads the whole world astray" (Rev. 12:9).[3] We all "groan" as corrupt people in the midst of a corrupt and groaning world (Rom. 8:22–25). We are in this condition because of the fall into sin in Genesis 3.

This is not the place to delve into all the details of the account of the fall, but there are several points that are pivotal to our concerns here.[4] First, the serpent's temptation was a direct attack on God because it was a direct attack on those created by God in his image and likeness to live and rule as he would, according to his nature and character (see above). This is the exact opposite of worship. It is the shaking of the fist in the face of God, not the bowing of the knee to him and his will. Second, the story of the fall is archetypal. It is not just about what happened in the garden but also what keeps on happening in our lives. We keep on replaying the fall. Third, the narrative theology of Genesis 3 yields a step-by-step description of the processes through which the man and the woman fell into sin

3. For a discussion of the serpent in Genesis 3 in ancient Near Eastern and biblical perspective, see Richard E. Averbeck, "Ancient Near Eastern Mythography as It Relates to Historiography in the Hebrew Bible: Genesis 3 and the Cosmic Battle," in *The Future of Biblical Archaeology: Reassessing Methodologies and Assumptions*, ed. James K. Hoffmeier and Alan R. Millard (Grand Rapids: Eerdmans, 2004), 328–56.

4. For a more detailed description of our fallen condition, see Richard E. Averbeck, "Creation and Corruption, Redemption and Wisdom: A Biblical Theology Foundation for Counseling Psychology," in *Journal of Psychology and Christianity* 25, no. 2 (2006): 111–26.

and experienced the ramifications of it within them, between them, and between them and God.

First came the deception (Gen. 3:1a, 13; cf. 1 Tim. 2:12–14). The serpent was crafty. The deception was meant to raise doubt about the goodness of God (3:1b, 5) and the repercussions of rebellion against God (3:4). The doubt led to illegitimate desire for something forbidden (3:6), and the illegitimate desire led to rebellious disobedience (i.e., the act of sin as a violation of God's command). These dynamics are found not only here in Genesis 3, but also in similar combinations in other passages (see, e.g., James 1:13–16; Rom. 7:9–11). The sin led to shame (contrast Gen. 2:25 with 3:7), and the shame led to fear (3:8–10). Imagine never having felt shame before and then having it strike you full force. Shame is one of those feelings that we take great effort to avoid. Have you noticed that if a person feels shamed, he or she has a hard time looking people in the face? Shame brings with it a visceral desire to avoid being seen, to cover up. The combination of all these dynamics led to what we might call "scrambling." The man and the woman scurried about in the garden trying to hide from God and avoid blame (3:8–13). No one had to teach them to scramble. They did it naturally because they were now corrupt. Thus, the fall had immediate and organic consequences for the man and woman in the garden.

The fall also had divinely imposed consequences. In response to all the above, the Lord cursed the serpent (3:14–15) and the ground (3:17a), which had repercussions for the woman (3:16) and the man (3:17b–19a), respectively. Life would now be hard for both of them, and then they would die (3:19b). Death came as a result of being cast out of the garden so that they no longer had access to the rejuvenating Tree of Life (3:22–24). What a disaster it would be if the man and woman and their offspring (3:20–21) would live forever in this corrupt condition. Lamech gives us a taste of what such a world would look like: "Lamech said to his wives, 'Adah and Zillah, listen to me; wives of Lamech, hear my words. I have killed a man for wounding me, a young man for injuring me. If Cain is avenged seven times, then Lamech seventy-seven times'" (Gen. 4:23–24).

The Human Spirit in Worship

This brief synopsis of the dynamics of the fall and its aftermath applies directly to our ongoing experience. Again, we keep on replaying the fall in our own lives, in our own personal and relational way. Although we have been created in the image and likeness of God, we are now corrupt to the core of our being, down in our human spirit. Our human spirit is now dominated by these dynamics of corruption. A big part of spiritual formation is about transforming our human spirit from corruption to godliness—back to the image of God, having "put on the new self, which is being renewed in knowledge in the image of its Creator" (Col. 3:10). We are all deceived, we doubt, we have sinful desires, and all too often we follow those desires into sinful actions. With this comes shame, fear, and scrambling. In turn, God's curses are his way of "rigging" the world so that it does not work well for us in our fallen condition. They are his way of driving us back to himself. Thus, James writes, "Consider it pure joy, my brothers, whenever you face trials of many kinds, because you know that the testing of your faith develops perseverance. Perseverance must finish its work so that you may be mature and complete, not lacking anything" (James 1:2–4; cf. Rom. 5:3–5).

Now, it is important to observe that the unit of the text extends from Genesis 2:4, "This is the account [lit. 'these are the generations'] of the heavens and the earth," to the next "generations" formula in Genesis 5:1, "This is the written account [lit. 'this is the scroll of the generations'] of Adam's line." We need to read Genesis 2–3 with Genesis 4 in order to get the whole picture. The first part of chapter 4 brings up sacrificial worship in the story of Cain and Abel. At the end of the chapter—in fact, the very last clause of the unit—we find the most important verbal expression of worship in the Bible:

> Adam lay with his wife again, and she gave birth to a son and named him Seth, saying, "God has granted me another child in place of Abel, since Cain killed him." Seth also had a son, and he named him Enosh. At that time men began to call on the name of the LORD. (Gen. 4:25–26)

This is the first occurrence of this well-known clause in the Bible, and its importance in its context cannot be overestimated. It stands in immediate contrastive relationship to the boast of Lamech cited above. Lamech's response (vv. 23–24) was anything but "calling on the name of the LORD" (v. 26). He had no interest in calling on the Lord to handle life. He would handle it himself, and all around him had better look out because he would do it with unmatched vengeance with only his personal welfare in mind.

The expression "call on the name of the Lord" occurs throughout the Old Testament and carries over into the New Testament in Greek translation. In the Old Testament it often refers to the verbal expression that took place specifically in a context of altar worship.[5] For example, in Genesis 12:8 after Abram entered Canaan and received the promise of its inheritance, "he went on toward the hills east of Bethel and pitched his tent, with Bethel on the west and Ai on the east. There he built an altar to the LORD and called on the name of the LORD." The building of the altar probably included making

---

5. See the discussion of this and related passages that contain essentially the same formula in Allen P. Ross, *Recalling the Hope of Glory: Biblical Worship from the Garden to the New Creation* (Grand Rapids: Kregel, 2006), 123, 142–47; and more technical discussion in Allen P. Ross, "Did the Patriarchs Know the Name of the LORD?" in *Giving the Sense: Understanding and Using Old Testament Historical Texts*, ed. David M. Howard Jr. and Michael A. Grisanti (Grand Rapids: Kregel, 2003), 323–39.

offerings, although that is not mentioned explicitly in the text. Abram called on the name of the Lord in order to invoke the divine presence and blessing of God on him in this new land. In part, it would be like the common "invocation" at the beginning of formal church worship services today. Isaac did the same thing in Genesis 26:25.

However, on at least some occasions this may well have included more than just the calling out of the name of the Lord as we would understand it today. In the Israelite world it would likely mean to proclaim and laud the character of the Lord as a means of drawing his attention to the worship. Exodus 34:5–6 suggests this when the same clause introduces the Lord's words on the occasion where he "proclaimed his (own) name" by declaring the qualities of his character, specifically those qualities that enabled his forgiveness of the golden calf debacle and the reestablishment of the covenant: "The LORD, the LORD, the compassionate and gracious God, slow to anger, abounding in love and faithfulness."

When Elijah confronted the prophets of Baal on Mount Carmel, the challenge was that they should "call on the name of" their god, Baal, and Elijah would "call on the name of the LORD." Elijah said, "The god who answers by fire—he is God" (1 Kings 18:24). What they actually did in making the call involved a great deal more than invocation (vv. 25–39). They both built altars and performed extensive activities and prayers in direct relationship to the altar offerings, "calling on the name." Other passages make the same connection between proclamation in worship and the altar actions of worship (e.g., Ps. 116:17; Zeph. 3:9–10). Still others use the same expression for calling on the Lord in the midst of trouble—a simple cry for help, "O LORD, save me!" (Ps. 116:4; cf., e.g., Ps. 50:15). So it seems that this expression can refer to anything from a simple invocation by calling out the name of the Lord, to a pointed cry to God for help, to full-fledged occasions of worship with extensive prayer, praise, or lament, and other worship activities.

The most direct link to the New Testament comes from Joel 2:32a, where "everyone who calls on the name of the LORD will be saved" introduces the call to escape from the coming great and terrible day of the Lord. It is this clause that launches Peter into his sermon on the day of Pentecost. The day of the Lord is coming, so all must "call on the name of the Lord." Since Pentecost, we have been in "the last days," looking for the coming of that great, awesome day when the Lord comes to set all things right. Paul cites the same clause in Romans 10:13 to underline the fact that salvation is based on faith in the Lord. Similarly, in 1 Corinthians 1:2 he addresses the believers at Corinth "together with all those everywhere who call on the name of our Lord Jesus Christ."

The bottom line is this: The only real answer to the dilemma of the fall and our corruption is to "call on the name of the Lord." The last line of the Genesis 2:4–4:26 section is the only resolution to the tragedy that develops within the section. That is why it is the last line, and that is why the line keeps recurring through the rest of Scripture in pivotal places. There are basically only two ways to handle life: the Lamech way or the way of calling on the name of the Lord. They are opposites. When the Lord walked in the garden before the fall, the most natural thing to do would have been to run to him and walk alongside him. After the fall the most natural thing was to run away from him and hide (Gen. 3:8). Lamech's way is to keep on running away. To call on the name of the Lord amounts to turning around and running back to him in order to walk with him right where we are, through all that happens in life. It is the way of worship.

"Calling on the name of the Lord" is at the core of worship. It is the essence of what we do when we go to God in the midst of life's circumstances. Here is where a problem sometimes arises with how we understand what worship is and how it works. Sometimes there is a tendency to think that one needs to leave off their life concerns when they come to worship so they can concentrate on God. This is not what we find in the psalms, which are, above all, words of worship. On the contrary, the Psalter is heavily weighted with the concerns of life and life situations. They are anything but an escape from life. In fact, the main point here is that the heart of true authentic worship is the bringing of one's life and concerns to God so that they might be set before him and worked through in his presence. One "calls on the name of the Lord" in the midst of it all. In a sense, *authentic worship is seeing God while looking life squarely in the face.*

Yes, there are praise songs and hymns, and there is much to praise God for. But worship comes out of a presentation of our life to God all along the way, whether personal or communal. When we present our life to him in worship, we actually have a chance to put it in perspective—divine perspective. The psalms teach us this. Sometimes we give thanks in worship because we are in a thankful place in life. Sometimes we lament in worship because we are lamenting over something in our life. There are other times when we proclaim our confidence in the Lord because that is where our heart is at the time. Sometimes our worship enables us to work our way from lament to praise and confidence in the Lord. Sometimes we just continue in lament. For example, Psalm 88 is the bleakest of the lament psalms. There is hardly anything positive here. How is this worship? The answer is that the writer is presenting his heart and experience to God. It is an authentic call to God. There are times when there is really nothing positive to say. To try to say something positive when one is in such a state of mind is to compromise the authenticity of the worship experience. Worship comes from the "spirit" of the worshiper as it is, if it is indeed worship in spirit and in truth. There is a lot of lament in the psalms because there is a lot of lament in life.

Sometimes we confess our sinful corruption in worship because that is what stands out to us in our life at the time. Sometimes we cry out for help in the midst of trouble. Sometimes we entreat the Lord for answers in the midst of our life circumstances. Sometimes we praise God because we have seen his deliverance, or his goodness, or his justice. The last five psalms in the Psalter constitute an explosion of praise. We have much to praise God about. Psalms 103 and 104 are bound together by their common beginning and ending: "Praise [lit. 'bless'] the LORD, O my soul" with an additional "Praise the LORD" appended to Psalm 104. Psalm 103 contains a beautiful exposition of God's forgiveness and redemptive work. Psalm 104 consists of an equally impressive poem about God's work in creation. These are the two major poles around which all biblical theology revolves. The Bible starts with God as our creator, and it is not long before he also becomes our redeemer. Those of us who know and worship him "in truth," know him as both.

All true worship comes out of the human spirit affected by God, and it is directed to him. Another way of saying this is that worship is about *getting impressed with God* in the depths of our spirit and letting the effects of that work its way into all the nooks and crannies of our lives personally and relationally. Sometimes it takes a while for the effects to become evident, but when one truly sees God with "the eyes" of the "heart," so to speak (see this expression in Eph. 1:18), he or she will undoubtedly be impressed! One of the main reasons people do not worship well is because they are simply more impressed with other things than they are with God. We are impressed with the wrong things. When what we are impressed with changes, our lives change, including our worship, which arises out of the "spirit" of our lives. Real worship arises out of the human spirit that is deeply impacted by God's presence and transforming work through his Holy Spirit in our human spirit right in the middle of real life. This brings us to worship and the Holy Spirit.

Worship and the Holy Spirit

Spiritual formation begins with "calling on the name of the Lord"; that is, it begins with becoming a worshiper of the only true God, bowing the knee and calling upon him. Without this there is no formation into the image of Christ to talk about. From the beginning it all depends on God's revealed grace and, in point of fact, it continues this way through the whole life of the Christian. The Holy Spirit is our companion (our helper, John 14:16–17) in all this. He is the empowering presence of God who works to transform us into the image of Christ according to the will of the Father.

It takes the work of the Holy Spirit in our human spirit to transform us into worshipers who worship "in spirit and truth" (John 4:23–24). Our corruption goes to the core of who we are, so our transformation needs to go there too. If not, it is only superficial, and our God does nothing superficially. First Corinthians 2:10b–12 is especially helpful here: "The *Spirit* searches all things, even the deep things of God. For who among men knows the thoughts of a man except the man's *spirit* [lit. "the spirit of the man"] within him? In the same way no one knows the thoughts of God except *the Spirit* of God. We have not received the spirit of the world but the Spirit who is from God, that we may understand what God has freely given us" (emphasis mine).

Three important points stand out here. First, the Holy Spirit of God knows the depths of God, and the human spirit of a person knows the depths of that person. This is foundational. Second, we have received from God the Holy Spirit, who knows the depths of God. So we have a direct connection with God through the Holy Spirit in our human spirit. This is basic to how the power of the Holy Spirit actually works to transform our human spirit. Third, the power that the Holy Spirit brings to bear in our human spirit is an in-depth, penetrating, and transforming understanding in our spirit of "what God has freely given us."[6]

Thus, the empowerment for our formation into the image of Jesus Christ comes from the gospel ("good news") of God's grace toward us, which is what Paul has been talking about all along in this and the preceding chapter. This is what the Holy Spirit is seeking to impress us with in our human spirit, because when we get impressed with God and what he has freely given us, we become truly spiritual and will worship him in spirit and in truth. Essentially, the Holy Spirit is working the gospel into our human spirit at ever deeper levels to transform us more and more into the image of Jesus. In this way the gospel is always good news for everyone. Even for those of us who already know Jesus, there are always ways the effects of the gospel have not been worked down into the depths of our hearts and from there into the way we live.

In terms of the dynamics of the fall in Genesis 3 (see above), the Holy Spirit works in our human spirit to make the transformation from deception to wisdom (James 3:13–18), from doubt to confident trust (Prov. 3:5–8), from illegitimate desires to good and holy legitimate desires (Gal. 5:16–26), from sinful rebellion against God to obedience (Matt. 28:20), from the depths of shame to the heights of God's love and glory (Eph. 3:14–21), from a spirit of fear to a spirit of adoption (Rom. 8:15–17), from "scrambling" to rest in the soul (Matt. 11:28–30). There is a close correspondence here to the fruit of the Spirit as expressed in Galatians 5:22–23: "love, joy, peace, patience, kindness, goodness, faithfulness, gentleness and self-control."

---

6. Walter C. Kaiser Jr., "A Neglected Text in Bibliology Discussions: 1 Corinthians 2:6–16," *Westminster Theological Journal* 43 (Spring 1981): 310–19, argues that this passage is really about revelation and inspiration through Paul as an apostle rather than about illumination of the believer by the Holy Spirit through the revealed and preached Word. I cannot deal with all the issues here, but in order to take this position, he must take the "we" in verses 6–16 to be the same as the "I" in verses 1–5. This is a serious problem. It seems much more likely that, in the context, the "we" refers to "mature" believers (v. 6) who are "spiritual" (vv. 15–16) as opposed to those who are "fleshly" (3:1ff.). The point is that the Holy Spirit works in us (i.e., in our human spirit) as believers to enable us to truly understand and receive into our lives "what God has freely given us" as believers. See, for example, the discussions in F. W. Grosheide, *Commentary on the First Epistle to the Corinthians*, New International Commentary on the New Testament (Grand Rapids: Eerdmans, 1953), 68–75; and Simon J. Kistemaker, *1 Corinthians*, New Testament Commentary (Grand Rapids: Baker, 1993), 86–95.

Our life in Christ is made up of calling on him as the essence of walking with him in the midst of whatever is going on, day by day, moment by moment—practicing his presence. The fruit of the Spirit emerges in that practicing of the presence.

Worship and the Holy Spirit as "Wind"

Consider what Peter wrote in 2 Peter 1:21 about the prophets who spoke from God "as they were carried along by the Holy Spirit." The term translated "carried along" is the same as that used in Acts 27 (vv. 15 and 17) to describe how Paul's ship was "driven along" by a storm wind on its way to Rome, a wind that eventually wrecked the ship on the island of Malta. The image of wind "driving" a sailboat along is a good one for understanding some of the essential features of spiritual formation. We do not provide the wind. Only the Holy Spirit can do that. If there is no wind blowing, one might as well forget the sails. They will do no good. And it will do no good to have the people on the ship blow into the sails either. We cannot create our own wind. Only God can do that, and he does it through the Holy Spirit of God, the third person of the Trinity. In fact, as noted earlier in this essay, the primary terms for "spirit" are the same as that for wind in both the Hebrew Old Testament (*rûaḥ*) and the Greek New Testament (*pneuma*).

Recall, for example, the valley of dry bones in Ezekiel 37. The bones lie dead and dried out on the valley floor until the "wind" (Hebrew *rûaḥ*, the same word as "spirit" and rendered "breath" in vv. 5–6, 8, 9–10; i.e., "wind" and "breath" are the same word in this chapter) comes and begins bringing them to life. We find out later in the chapter that the "wind" is in fact the "Spirit" of God himself (the same word is used again for [God's] Spirit in v. 14). Jesus used a similar image in John 3:8 in his conversation with Nicodemus. In a play on words, he said: "The wind [the Greek work *pneuma*, from which we get words like *pneumonia*] blows wherever it pleases. You hear its sound, but you cannot tell where it comes from or where it is going. So it is with everyone born of the Spirit [*pneuma*]." The Spirit, the "wind" of God, is essential to the new birth, the birth from above.

The fact of the matter is that in spiritual formation we do not provide the driving force. Only God can provide the wind. And he does it through his Holy Spirit, his own divine wind. That is one of the main biblical reasons for calling it *spiritual* formation. It is first of all, above all, and throughout the work of the Holy Spirit. We are overwhelmingly dependent on God working by his own hand through the Holy Spirit for real formation into the image of Christ to take place in our lives and through us in the lives of others. That is why God has actually given the Holy Spirit to indwell us as individuals and communities of faith in Jesus the Messiah. The wind of God is always in us, working to drive us along, so that we grow closer to him and live more effectively for him in the world.

But this does not mean we have no part in it. We are not passive. If the Holy Spirit is the wind, then we Christians are the boat. The point here is that the wind will not take us very far if our sail is down; that is, if our human spirit is not engaged. Just as the writers of Scripture needed the Holy Spirit to drive them along in writing the Bible, so every Christian needs the same divine wind to drive them along in living the Christian life. The spiritual formation practices that we engage in are like putting up the sail. They are ways of getting our human spirit engaged with the Spirit of God. Again, it will do no good to raise the sails or turn the rudder of the boat without the wind of God blowing. Doing these things does not *cause* spiritual formation to happen, just as putting up the sail on a boat does not make the wind blow.

The various spiritual disciplines are not magic wands we wave in order "get spiritual." But they are part of what is involved in putting up the sail of the Christian life and trimming it well in order to catch the wind of God as he blows into and through our lives. God often works in ways that seem strange to us, and sometimes it may seem that the wind is blowing in the wrong direction or not blowing at all, but that is up to God. Our part in it is getting the sail up and keeping it up by the way we live, privately, in community, and in the world.

Here again is where worship gets at the heart of spiritual formation. The first and foremost way of "putting up our sails" to catch the "wind" of the Holy Spirit in our lives is through genuine worship. Recall the remarks on Genesis 4:26 earlier. Worship is the most important of all the spiritual disciplines because it is the core answer to the dilemma we face as fallen and corrupt people in a fallen and corrupt world. We are called first of all and above all to be worshipers. More than anything else, the main goal of the Christian life is to become better worshipers. God intends that everything else gain its direction and energy from there. As Jesus said to the woman at the well, "A time is coming and has now come when the true worshipers will worship the Father in spirit and truth, for they are the kind of worshipers the Father seeks. God is spirit, and his worshipers must worship in spirit and in truth" (John 4:23–24). What our Father in heaven actually "seeks" is worshipers who truly worship from the depths of their being and according to all that is true about him. Jesus wants to make us into great worshipers, and he has given us the Holy Spirit to empower that transformation in our lives.

The Holy Spirit and Temple Worship

Another part of the Old Testament background for New Testament Christian worship is, of course, the Old Testament tabernacle worship system described in the Hebrew Torah, the first five books of the Bible, otherwise known as the Pentateuch. We talked about the psalms above. They constitute the hymnbook for worship in the tabernacle and, later, the temple. This hymnbook was composed and collected over centuries as the Hebrew Bible as a whole, from Moses to Malachi, was being composed. Music and singing are certainly important in the practice of worship, but they are not the essence of worship. At its base, worship is about the presence of God and our engaging with that presence. Spiritual formation, in turn, is about how to actually go about engaging with the presence of God, walking with him day by day, moment by moment, in worship, prayer, obedience, witness, spiritual disciplines, or whatever.

It seems that Moses met the Lord (Hebrew *Yahweh*), the covenant God of Israel, face-to-face, so to speak, for the first time at the burning bush on Mount Sinai, "the mountain of God" (Exod. 3:1; cf. 4:27; 18:5; 24:13). At that time the Lord promised Moses that he would "be with" him (Exod. 3:12a, "I will be with you"; Hebrew *ʾehyeh ʿimmāk*) in bringing Israel out of Egypt and back to this mountain (v. 12b). From that point forward, the presence of God with Moses and Israel is one of the main features of Old Testament theology. He was with them in his glory cloud (with fire in it by night so that they could see and follow his presence in the dark) from the time they left Egypt all the way to Sinai (Exod. 13:21–22). In this form, God protected them (Exod. 14:19–20) and led them to Sinai, his holy mountain (Exod. 19:1–3; 24:15–18).

This form of his presence continued with them from Sinai in the tabernacle, which was essentially a "movable Sinai"—his tent amid their tents as they traveled through the wilderness to the Promised Land (Exod. 40:34–38; Lev. 9:22–24; 16:1–2; Num. 9:15–23; 10:11–12, 33–36, etc.). In the Lord's introduction to the tabernacle account, he instructed Moses, "Have them [the Israelites] make a sanctuary for me, and I will dwell among them. Make this tabernacle and all its furnishings exactly like the pattern I will show you" (Exod. 25:8–9). The word *tabernacle* itself derives from the verb meaning "to dwell." Near the end of the Sinai revelation, the Lord promised, "I will walk among you and be your God, and you will be my people" (Lev. 26:12). The verb used for God "walking" among his people is the same one used for God walking in the garden "to the wind of the day" (Gen. 3:8, literal translation) and elsewhere for people "walking" with God (Enoch, Gen. 5:22, 24; Noah, Gen. 6:9) or before God (Abraham, Gen. 17:1). The same glory cloud presence of God occupied the later Solomonic temple (1 Kings 8:10–11; 2 Chron. 7:1–3), but Ezekiel recounts the cloud of the Lord's presence abandoning the temple so that it could be destroyed by the Babylonians at the time of the Babylonian exile (ca. 586 B.C.; Ezek. 8:4; 9:3; 10:3–5, 18–19; 11:22–25).

The link to the New Testament, the church, and the Christian life comes through Jesus himself. "The Word became flesh and made his dwelling [i.e., 'tabernacled'] among us. We have seen his glory, the glory of the One and Only, who came from the Father, full of grace and truth" (John 1:14). The connection to the tabernacle dwelling and glory of God is obvious here. In his high priestly prayer, Jesus said to the Father, "I have given them the glory that you gave me, that they may be one as we are one" (John 17:22). So we now get to be the glory of God that shines forth God's presence in the world! Second Corinthians 3:7–18 ties this all to the Holy Spirit's presence, especially in verses 17–18: "Now the Lord is the Spirit, and where the

Spirit of the Lord is, there is freedom. And we, who with unveiled faces all reflect the Lord's glory, are being transformed into his likeness with ever-increasing glory, which comes from the Lord, who is the Spirit" (see also 4:6–7, 16–18; 5:5).

The Holy Spirit is actually "present" in us individually (1 Cor. 6:19–20) and among us corporately, as the body of Christ (1 Cor. 3:16–17; Eph. 2:19–22; 3:14–21; 1 Peter 2:4–12). This makes us the temple of God the Holy Spirit today. Thus, there is a shift between the Testaments from the temple as a holy *place* to the temple as a holy *people*. And since a temple is by nature a place of worship, we return once again to the point that worship must be at the very center of our experience in Christ. People (individuals and communities of faith) who are spiritually well formed are good worshipers. Here we need to return again to John 4 as perhaps the most natural point of departure in the Bible for grasping the intimate connection between the human spirit, the Holy Spirit, and meaningful worship. As Jesus said to the woman at the well when she asked where the appropriate place was to worship—Mount Gerizim or Jerusalem—the Holy Spirit is a "spring of water" (John 4:14; cf. 7:37–39) that gushes up within us to make us people who worship "the Father in spirit and in truth" (John 4:23–24). He turned the worship focus from a place to a people.

In Ephesians the apostle Paul develops this most extensively, especially the community side of it. In the latter part of chapter 2, he is concerned about the unity of the church, the breaking down of the wall between Jew and Gentile: "Now in Christ Jesus you who once were far away have been brought near through the blood of Christ. . . . For through him we both [Jew and Gentile together] have access to the Father by one Spirit" (Eph. 2:13, 18). He goes on to develop the implications of this for us all as the temple of the Holy Spirit:

> Consequently, you are no longer foreigners and aliens, but fellow citizens with God's people and members of God's household, built on the foundation of the apostles and prophets, with Christ Jesus himself as the chief cornerstone. In him the whole building is joined together and rises to become a holy temple in the Lord. And in him you too are being built together to become a dwelling in which God lives by his Spirit. (Eph. 2:19–22)

We are a "household," a "building" built on a "foundation" of stone, Jesus Christ being the "chief cornerstone." From the apostles and prophets down to us, we must all line up with him. And we are not just any old house, but a "holy temple" that has been put together for the actual habitation of God the Holy Spirit. Yes, this is a figure of speech, but that is the point. It carries profound meaning for who we are, and the roots of it are sunk deep into the soil of the Jewish Old Testament world to which even Gentiles who are in Christ have now become joined.

The next chapter begins, "For this reason," introducing an excursus about the mystery of the church that is bound up with this breaking down of the wall of partition (Eph. 3:1a). Verse 14 begins again, "For this reason." In this way Paul returns to the subject he introduced at the end of chapter 2.

> I pray that out of his glorious riches he may strengthen you with power through his Spirit in your inner being, so that Christ may dwell in your hearts through faith. And I pray that you, being rooted and established in love, may have power, together with all the saints, to grasp how wide and long and high and deep is the love of Christ, and to know this love that surpasses knowledge—that you may be filled to the measure of all the fullness of God. Now to him who is able to do immeasurably more than all we ask or imagine, according to his power that is at work within us, to him be glory in the church and in Christ Jesus throughout all generations, for ever and ever! Amen. (Eph. 3:16–21)

It is through the power of the Spirit that works in our inner person that Christ "dwells" in our hearts. The goal, therefore, is to be "rooted" and "established" (better "grounded," NRSV; it is a term for laying the foundation for building something, for example, a house or temple) in the love that is found in Christ and becomes our way of life. This love has dimensions like a temple building does—width, length, height, and depth—and the whole structure is to be filled up with God, like the Old Testament tabernacle and temple were (see above, e.g., Exod. 40:34–Lev. 1:1; 1 Kings 8:10–11). This "power" of the Holy Spirit that works within us is the way the "glory" of God shines forth in and through the church for all time. The whole passage is packed with the importance of our being the temple of the Holy Spirit and, therefore, a place where God's glory shines through worship and service. Ephesians 4:1–7 binds this temple and glory imagery to our unity as one body, with no wall of partition between us. This is very much the same concern Jesus had in his high priestly prayer (John 17:22, cited above), where the glory that he passed on to his followers becomes manifest in the oneness among us, reflecting the oneness between the Father and the Son.

Peter uses the same imagery in 1 Peter 2:4–5: "As you come to him, the living Stone—rejected by men but chosen by God and precious to him—you also, like living stones, are being built into a spiritual house to be a holy priesthood, offering *spiritual sacrifices* acceptable to God through Jesus Christ" (emphasis mine). Again, this is all built on the Old Testament background, but now we have added "sacrifice" to the image. We offer up "spiritual sacrifices" that are "acceptable" to God. There are many other passages in the New Testament that use such terms. For example, in Romans 12:1 we have the metaphorical command, "Offer your bodies as living sacrifices, holy and pleasing to God—this is your spiritual act of worship." In Acts 10:4 the prayers of Cornelius are a "memorial offering" to God. In Romans

15:16 "the Gentiles" are Paul's "offering acceptable to God, sanctified by the Holy Spirit." In Philippians 2:17 Paul considers his life to be a drink offering poured out to God. Hebrews 13:15–16 calls our praise to God, as well as our doing good and sharing with others, sacrifices to God.

Returning now to the book of Ephesians, the "filling" terminology applies to the church as the "fullness" of Christ (Eph. 1:22–23) and the filling of Christians and the church by the Father (3:19), the Son (4:10, 13), and especially the Holy Spirit (Eph. 5:18–21). The latter passage is especially important to us here.

> Do not get drunk on wine, which leads to debauchery. Instead, *be filled* [the only imperative from here on!] with *the Spirit*. Speak [lit. "speaking"] to one another with psalms, hymns and spiritual songs. Sing [lit. "singing"] and make music [lit. "making music," Greek *psallontes*] in your heart to the Lord, always giving thanks to God the Father for everything, in the name of our Lord Jesus Christ. Submit [lit. "submitting"] to one another out of reverence for Christ. (emphasis mine)

The point of the passage is that the main and most immediate effect of the Holy Spirit filling up our human spirit is worship. Again, the first and best thing the Holy Spirit works in us is worship in and from our human spirit. The Holy Spirit's goal is to overwhelm us with God. Maturity yields from this and from this alone. It is the expression of love for God that yields also love for others through submission to one another (vv. 21ff.).

Recall the discussion of 1 Corinthians 2:10–12 above, where the Holy Spirit, who knows the depths of God, comes into our human spirit, which goes to the depths of us. The goal is working down into our lives in ever more transforming ways the things freely given to us so that we become spiritually mature (vv. 12ff.). Another passage where this work of the Spirit in our human spirit comes out clearly is Romans 8:16, "The Spirit himself testifies with our spirit that we are God's children." In that context the issue is our sanctification (Rom. 6–8). In Romans 7:14–24 we hear about the struggle we have between walking in the flesh and walking in the Spirit. Paul ends with a question: "What a wretched man I am! Who will rescue me from this body of death?" The answer is found in Jesus Christ according to the following verses. But what kind of answer is it? How does it actually work?

The key here is the same as in 1 Corinthians 2:12, "what God has freely given us." As Paul puts it in Romans 8:1, "Therefore, there is now no condemnation for those who are in Christ Jesus." Perhaps an illustration will help us here. There is an ancient Greek legend about a special knot that a peasant used to tie a yoke to a chariot. The peasant, Gordius, became king of the region through a special oracle. According to the legend, the person who could untie the knot would become the ruler of all Asia. Eventually,

Alexander the Great came along, took his sword, and cut right through the knot. He did not even try to "untie" it. This is where we get the expression "cutting the Gordian knot," and this is exactly what God did for us through the death of Jesus on the cross. He cut right through the knot of "what I do not want to do, I do; what I want to do, I don't do" (Rom. 7:14–24). We are never going to be able to untie our knotted-up lives. But God did it by his grace in Christ Jesus. He has simply made those who trust in Jesus his children. He has adopted us: "For you did not receive a spirit of slavery to fall back into fear, but you have received a spirit of adoption. When we cry, 'Abba! Father!'" (Rom. 8:15 NRSV). This leads immediately to verse 16: "The Spirit himself testifies with our spirit that we are God's children." The Spirit works deep within us to convince us in our spirit that we are God's adopted children. Being deeply convinced about this is at the core of our spiritual formation.

From this point in the passage, Paul works through our groaning condition in this groaning world (vv. 18–25) to the passage cited in the first few paragraphs of this essay: "The Spirit intercedes for the saints in accordance with God's will. . . . For those God foreknew he also predestined to be conformed to the likeness of his Son" (Rom. 8:27–29). We define the essence of "spiritual formation" from that and related passages. But the textual unit comes to its climax and conclusion in what we could call a "hymn to adoption" in Romans 8:31–39. It is a poetic passage that really does read like a hymn. It gushes forth from the Holy Spirit, the Water of Life that Jesus referred to in John 4, and floods the human spirit with the full force of the truth that nothing can separate us from the love of God.

> If God is for us, who can be against us? He who did not spare his own Son, but gave him up for us all—how will he not also, along with him, graciously give us all things? . . . Who shall separate us from the love of Christ? Shall trouble or hardship or persecution or famine or nakedness or danger or sword? . . . No, in all these things we are more than conquerors through him who loved us. For I am convinced that neither death nor life, neither angels nor demons, neither the present nor the future, nor any powers, neither height nor depth, nor anything else in all creation, will be able to separate us from the love of God that is in Christ Jesus our Lord.

The human spirit that really "gets it" sings this! We live out of this "spirit," and it is first of all and above all a spirit of worship. It is spiritual formation par excellence.

Conclusion

Worship is the core discipline and experience of true spiritual formation. Everything flows from it. The human spirit that turns to God in worship ("to call on the name of the LORD," Gen. 4:26) begins a walk with him.

The believer starts down the road of spiritual formation. The bright center line of the road is worship. It keeps things straight and going in the right direction, under the empowerment and guidance of the Holy Spirit, who works in our human spirit. God wants to be at the center of our vision. And to use another metaphor, we need to keep our eye on the ball. We cannot get distracted from the basic reality of who God is and what he has done, and what all that means about how we can practice his magnificent presence with us.

We are his adopted children, and nothing can separate us from his love. When we grasp how fully we are loved by the God of creation and redemption, there really is nothing else to do with our lives but to love God and people (the two great commandments, Matt. 22:34–40). Nothing else makes sense when we look at the world with God at the center of our vision, which is what worship is all about. There are all sorts of different kinds of worship experiences, and the "worship wars" are not over. That is another subject for another time. For now we can only emphasize the fact that the main issues are not styles of music, whether there is liturgy, or anything else. The real issue in individual or corporate worship is the human spirit overwhelmed by the work of the Holy Spirit enabling a vision of God that is true and transformational.

Chapter 3

Old Testament Community and Spiritual Formation

Gordon Johnston

> He has showed you, O man, what is good. And what does the LORD require of you? To act justly and to love mercy and to walk humbly with your God.
>
> —Micah 6:8

Though it first aired during the 2002 Super Bowl, it remains my all-time favorite commercial. "Terry Tate—Office Linebacker" is a tongue-in-cheek spoof of the art of building community in the corporate business world.[1] Retired NFL linebacker Terry Tate enforces office rules at the headquarters of Felcher & Sons the only way he knows how—with bone-crushing tackles and smashmouth trash talking. Interspersed between scenes of Terry body-slamming lazy employees, sits Ron Felcher, CEO, smiling behind his desk, extolling his innovative strategy for building community.

RON FELCHER: When we asked Reebok to send us Terry Tate, some people thought we were crazy. But I'm a firm believer in paradigm breaking; outside-the-box thinking. . . . Since Terry has been with us, our productivity has gone up 46 percent. . . . We're getting more from our employees than ever before. . . . But what's really impressed me is how Terry has become part of the Felcher "family." . . . He fits right in!

---

1. Reebok's commercial, "Terry Tate, Office Linebacker," originally available for online viewing at www.reebok.com, can now be found at a variety of sites, e.g., http://www.Gofish.vo.llnwd.net (accessed December 6, 2006). The original fifty-eight-second video clip offers a humorous way to introduce the topic of community building to an audience (however, permission for use must be secured).

This ironic monologue plays on the incongruity of contradictory concepts of community: the single-minded corporate pursuit of productivity and the sensitive encouragement of a close-knit family. Felcher's approach raises the question, What is community?

Defining Community

Community is one of the most ubiquitous but ambiguous terms in our culture. The English word is used in three ways, all of which overlap somewhat. Biblical terms for community, as we will see, also reflect a similar threefold range of meanings.

com-mu-ni-ty (noun)

1. designation for society as a whole; public human population
2. group of people who
   a. form a distinct segment of society due to ethnicity, gender, religion, etc.
   b. live in the same location (e.g., nation, region, neighborhood)
   c. have a common background or shared history
   d. identify with one another as members in an organization of choice
   e. share common interests or participate in activities together for common cause
3. sense of interpersonal connectedness; social bonding; sharing; fellowship

As its root indicates, the term refers to people who share something in common. Used objectively, it refers to society as a whole, which shares the same stock of humanity, or to a group that shares some kind of homogeneity. Used subjectively, it connotes a sense of community or experience of community life in a close-knit group. Generally, the larger the objective homogeneous community, the less subjective sense of community there is; the smaller the objective homogeneous community, the more subjective sense of community there is. One's sense of community is greater in a smaller group where individuals share more in common. The chart below depicts the sense of community that an individual may enjoy.

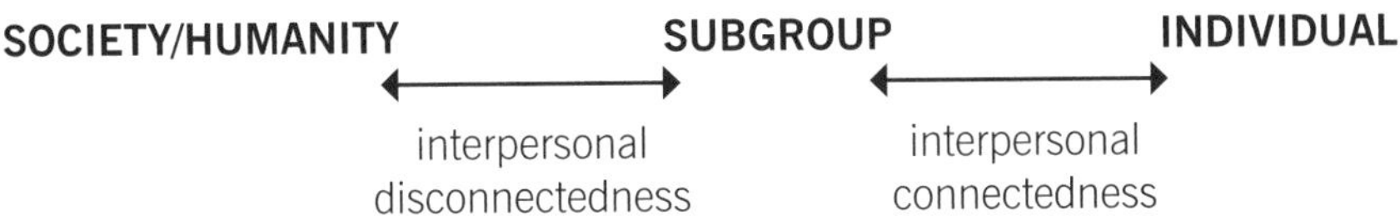

Though the Christian concept of community is unique, community itself is not an exclusively Christian idea. The essence of community is perhaps best expressed by the German sociologist Ferdinand Tönnies. Writing in the mid-nineteenth century, Tönnies voiced concern over the dramatic breakup of traditional community life unfolding before his eyes.[2] From the dawn of civilization, community life had centered around family and clan living together in close proximity over several generations. However, the rise of industrialization and urbanization brought about the demise of this traditional community life.[3] To Tönnies, it was self-evident that small towns fostered more social cohesiveness and community life than burgeoning cities that spawn virtually unbridled individualism. In the village, the individual was connected to community life through deep personal relations with family, neighbors, and traditional institutions, especially the church. These ties were broken when people migrated in anonymous masses to large industrialized cities or immigrated to foreign soil. Tönnies highlighted the dichotomy between the connectedness of community life and disconnectness of society at large by distinguishing *Gemeinschaft* (community) and *Gesellschaft* (society).[4]

Connectedness of Community Life

Gemeinschaft is a community to which individuals are oriented as much if not more than to their own self-interest. Individuals in *Gemeinschaft* are regulated by common moral norms, social mores, and shared beliefs of appropriate behavior and responsibility of every member to each other and to the community as a whole. Such communities feature "unity of will."[5] In such communities, there is seldom need to enforce external social

2. Ferdinand Tönnies, *Community and Civil Society*, ed. Jose Harris (Cambridge, UK: Cambridge University Press, 2001); translation of German original, *Gemeinschaft und Gesellschaft* (1887).

3. T. N. Clark, "Social Contexts of Community," in *International Encylopedia of the Social and Behavioral Sciences*, ed. N. J. Smelser and P. B. Baltes (New York: Elsevier, 2001), 4:2374–78.

4. B. Stråth, "Community/Society: History of the Concept," in *International Encyclopedia of the Social and Behavioral Sciences*, 4:2374–78.

5. Tönnies, *Community and Civil Society*, 22.

control since its members feel strong collective loyalty to its overarching values. *Gemeinschaft* is characterized by strong personal relationships, relatively simple social structure, and moderate division of labor. Tönnies saw the family as the best expression of such community life. He suggested that *Gemeinschaft* was also present in traditional village life, where people were bound together by a shared set of beliefs, norms, traditions, and history. *Gemeinschaften* tend to be racially and ethnically homogeneous and geographically rooted. Tönnies, however, cited the Christian church as the most unique example of an ethnically diverse and globally dispersed *Gemeinschaft*.

Disconnectedness of Society at Large

In contrast, *Gesellschaft* is disconnected, heterogeneous society at large. It lacks the same level of shared moral norms, social mores, historical traditions, and shared beliefs of the *Gemeinschaft*. *Gesellschaften* are characterized by secondary relationships rather than familial or community ties, so there is less individual loyalty to the society. The whole never takes on more importance to the individual than his own self-interest. The society or organization is maintained by individuals acting in their own self-interest. Since it lacks a cohesive fabric, it is more susceptible to class conflict as well as racial and ethnic tensions. Tönnies characterized industrialized urban centers as the prime example of *Gesellschaften*. The business company itself is the extreme example: workers, managers, and owners may share few common beliefs and may not care deeply for the product they make, but it is in their self-interest to come to work to make money so the business continues.[6] Nations once ethnically and racially homogeneous were becoming increasingly more diverse in population under massive influx of foreign immigrants. According to Tönnies, this breakup of traditional community could lead only to social unrest, class conflict, ethnic and racial tension on the broad level, and the despair and alienation of the anonymous soul on the individual level.

Biblical Concept of Community

The concept of community (aka *Gemeinschaft*) permeates the social dimensions of Scripture.[7] Scripture focuses on humans experiencing community with God and with one another. Let us consider a few prominent themes related to biblical community.

---

6. Though Tönnies originally used the term to describe modern industrialized society, in modern twentieth-century business usage, *Gesellschaft* became the technical German term for "company."

7. For insightful discussion of the biblical concept of community, albeit from a historical-critical perspective, see Paul D. Hanson, *The People Called: The Growth of the Community in the Bible* (Louisville: Westminster John Knox, 2001). Also see Niels Peter Lemche, "The Understanding of Community in the Old Testament and in the Dead Sea Scrolls," in *Qumran Between the Old and New Testaments*, ed. Frederick H. Cryer and Thomas L. Thompson (Sheffield: Sheffield Academic Press, 1998), 181–93.

Universal Need for Community

God created humans as community and for community (Gen. 1:26–31).[8] His declaration, "It is not good for man to be alone" (2:18), and Adam's jubilation, "This one at last is bone of my bones and flesh of my flesh" (2:23 NET), are paradigmatic, underscoring our universal need for connectedness.[9] This thirst for a close sense of community is hardwired into our genetic code, so to speak. However, as the garden narrative shows, sin alienates us from God and one another (3:1–24). Cain's punishment for his sin was isolation—loss of community all the days of his life (4:9–16). When the growth in human population was matched only by the depth of its depravity, community life was ruined by violence and society as a whole was placed in jeopardy (6:5–7, 11–13). Thus, the primeval history (Gen. 1–11) is a story about the origin of community as the blessing of God, as well as about the tragic demise of community that comes from sin and wickedness.

Redemptive Restoration of Community

God's program of redemptive covenants restores community between the faithful and God, and with one another.[10] If nothing else, the epic history of salvation unfolds the restoration of community between God and humanity, and between the individual and the rest of human society. Genesis 1–3 and Revelation 21–22 frame this history of redemption, in the contrast between Paradise lost and Paradise restored. Parallels between Genesis 1–3 and Revelation 21–22 reveal that the formation of a redeemed community is at the heart of God's plan: while God created only one couple for the primeval garden, he is re-creating a unified new community for the eschatological city.

Covenant and Community

Community is a crucial aspect of the biblical concept of covenant.[11] Kutsch notes that *bĕrît* (covenant) conveys mutuality in the twin themes of divine commitment and human obligation.[12] Kalluveettil adds that covenant

---

8. Marsha M. Wilfong ("Human Creation in Canonical Context: Genesis 1:26–31 and Beyond," in *God Who Creates* [Grand Rapids: Eerdmans, 2000], 42–52) notes that God created humans to make possible faithful relationship with himself, human community, and the rest of creation.

9. Marsha M. Wilfong ("Genesis 2:18–24," *Interpretation* 42 [1988]: 58–63), suggests that this passage is paradigmatic for human community, which is characterized by diversity and complementarity and interpersonal intimacy and that humans are complete only when they exist in community.

10. Ralph Klein, "Call, Covenant, and Community," *Currents in Theology and Mission* 15 (1988): 120–27.

11. D. J. Elazar, "Covenant and Community," *Judaism* 49 (2000): 387–98; and J. Stephen Harper, "Old Testament Spirituality," *Asbury Theological Journal* 42, no. 2 (1987): 63–77.

12. For example, see Ernst Kutsch, "בְּרִית.," in *Theological Lexicon of the Old Testament*, ed. Ernst Jenni and Claus Westermann (Peabody, MA: Hendrickson, 1997), 1:256–66.

is essentially a relational concept.[13] It forms a new bond between the two contracting parties. While a covenant is typically based on a previously existing relationship, it fundamentally redefines the nature of this relationship by introducing a mutual commitment between the covenanters. Thus, a new dimension of the relationship—a new community—is formed by the inauguration of a covenant. This community is enjoyed by maintenance of the covenant, but breach of the covenant disrupts this communal relationship. Repentance and covenant renewal revitalizes and allows the relationship to continue.

Community and Ethical Morality

Scripture emphasizes the role of the community of faith in cultivating the ethical morality of the individual.[14] While the character of God is the focus of the moral life, the community of faith is its catalyst. At Sinai, God transformed the descendants of Abraham into a covenant community to be characterized, first and foremost, by moral righteousness (Exod. 19:5–6).[15] The primary calling of the covenant community was to pursue moral holiness: "Speak to the whole community of the Israelites and tell them, 'You must be holy because I, Yahweh your God, am holy'" (Lev. 19:2, translation mine).[16] The community was to center around the presence of the holy God, expressing moral holiness in response to the divine presence.[17] The eighth-century B.C. prophets (Amos, Isaiah, Micah) especially emphasized the importance of moral ethics to the community life of Israel.[18] In fact, the preservation of the covenant community was contingent on genuine moral righteousness and ethical justice.[19] The postexilic prophets called for the practice of genuine community, rather than oppressing the poor and excluding outsiders; the people of God must reach out to the excluded and

---

13. Paul Kalluveettil, "Covenant and Community: Insights into the Relational Aspect of Covenant," *Jeevadhara* 11 (1981): 94–104; idem, *Declaration and Covenant: A Comprehensive Review of Covenant Formulae from the Old Testament and the Ancient Near East* (Rome: Biblical Institute Press, 1982), 90–92.

14. Bruce Birch, "Moral Agency, Community, and the Character of God in the Hebrew Bible," *Semeia* 66 (1994): 23–41.

15. Bruce Birch, "Divine Character and the Formation of Moral Community in the Book of Exodus," in *The Bible in Ethics*, ed. J. W. Rogerson, Margaret Davis, M. Daniel Carroll R. (Sheffield: Sheffield Academic Press, 1995), 119–35.

16. Thomas Raitt, "Holiness and Community in Leviticus 19:2ff.," *Proceedings, Eastern Great Lakes and Midwest Biblical Society* 6 (1986): 170–78.

17. Frank Gorman, *Divine Presence and Community: A Commentary on the Book of Leviticus* (Grand Rapids: Eerdmans, 1997).

18. Rick Marrs, "The Prophetic Faith: A Call to Ethics and Community," *Restoration Quarterly* 36 (1994): 304–15; A. Johnston, "A Prophetic Vision of an Alternative Community: A Reading of Isaiah 40–55," in *Uncovering Ancient Stones*, ed. Lewis M. Hopfe (Winona Lake, IN: Eisenbrauns, 1994), 31–40; and Walter Brueggemann, "Prophetic Ministry: A Sustainable Alternative Community," *Horizons in Biblical Theology* 11, no. 1 (1989): 1–33.

19. Dennis J. McCarthy, "Prophets and Covenant Community," *Jeevadhara* 11 (1981): 105–22.

serve the needy.[20] Likewise, the new covenant community is called to moral righteousness and social justice, shown by reaching out to the disenfranchised and meeting the needs of the poor (James 1:22–2:26).

Community and Inclusivity

Though Israel was not to adopt practices of pagan nations (Lev. 18:1–30; Deut. 14:1–21), Yahweh called her to be an obedient "kingdom of priests" (Exod. 19:5–6) and thus draw other nations to worship him (Deut. 4:5–8; Isa. 2:1–5; 42:1–9).[21] Postexilic Judaism developed an "insider" mentality of nationalistic exclusivity that limited membership in the covenant community to ethnic Israel.[22] Isaiah 56:1–8, however, had promised full membership in the new covenant community to Gentile converts who would keep Torah ideals of Sabbath observance and moral ethical behavior.[23] Isaiah's inclusive approach anticipated an even more radical revolution in which full membership in the new covenant community by believing Jews and Gentiles is on the basis of faith in Christ alone, not of ethnic descent from Abraham or the traditional Jewish badges (circumcision, adherence to ceremonial food laws, or observation of Sabbath).

Salvation and Justification by Faith Alone: Individualistic or an Inclusive Community?

Scripture emphasizes that the basis for community is the common salvific work of Christ in the lives of all believers (John 17:11, 21–23; Rom. 12:4–5; 1 Cor. 10:17; 12:11–13, 20; Eph. 2:11–22; 4:1–6; Col. 3:14–15; Titus 1:4; Philem. 6; 2 Peter 1:4; Jude 3). Unfortunately, many popular views of salvation feature a privatized, individualistic approach. However, several evangelicals, such as N. T. Wright, point out that Paul's doctrine of justification by faith is not merely a soteriological formulation but also features a sociological dimension. In opposition to Judaizers, who required that Gentiles not only trust in Christ but also submit to the Jewish "badges" of circumcision, Sabbath, and the ceremonial food laws (cf. Acts 15:1), Paul countered that Jews and Gentiles enter the new covenant community on the basis of faith in Christ alone.[24] Ratzlaff suggests

---

20. M. E. Andrew, "Post-Exilic Prophets and the Ministry of Creating Community," *Expository Times* 93 (1982): 42–46.

21. Eugene H. Merrill, "Royal Priesthood," *Bibliotheca Sacra* 150 (1993): 50–62.

22. Joseph F. Wimmer, "Inside/Outside the Community," *Bible Today* 37 (1999): 217–21; Bob Becking, "Continuity and Community: The Belief System of the Book of Ezra," in *The Crisis of Israelite Religion*, ed. Bob Becking and Marjo C. A. Korpel (Leiden/Boston: Brill, 1999), 256–75; and Pancratius Beentjes, "Identity and Community in the Book of Chronicles," *Zeitschrift für Althebräistik* 12 (1999): 233–37.

23. D. W. Van Winkle, "An Inclusive Authoritative Text in Exclusive Communities," in *Writing and Reading the Scroll of Isaiah*, ed. Craig C. Broyles (Leiden: Brill, 1997), 1:423–40; and Clinton Hammock, "Isaiah 56:1–8 and Redefining the Restoration Judean Community," *Biblical Theology Bulletin* 30 (2000): 46–57.

24. N. T. Wright, *What Saint Paul Really Said* (London: University of Oxford Press, 1997).

that appreciation of this sociological dimension in Paul's doctrine of justification by faith is a critical corrective to contemporary individualism and should redirect our focus onto the importance of the community of the people of God.[25]

Sanctification: A Community Pilgrimage

Fergusson notes that many contemporary models of the Christian life feature an individualistic approach and fail to appreciate the crucial role of community life.[26] As one writer puts it, "The spiritual journey is not to be a solitary walk but a community pilgrimage."[27] The isolated, self-guiding ascetic is vulnerable to spiritual imbalance. Balanced spiritual formation is cultivated in the company of like-minded comrades and sensitive confidants. We draw wisdom and comfort from one another; we encourage and are encouraged by the example of our fellow Christians. To pursue spirituality alone is folly, and ultimately it misses the point of being the body of Christ.

Some Biblical Terms for Community

Hebrew ʿēdāh: "Community, Assembly"

The Hebrew term most often glossed "community" is *ʿēdāh*. The noun *ʿēdāh*, "community, company, assembly" (*HALOT* 746; BDB), refers to a group of people as a whole, not as a society at large, but as a cohesive community, sharing a common identity and acting in concert (*THAT* 1:742–48; *TWOT* 1:388).[28] This term always refers to community in an objective sense (homogeneous group), never in a subjective sense (experiential sense of community). Nevertheless, since it depicts the people of God as a solidarity, it naturally forms the basis for the concept of the people of God enjoying a sense of community, albeit an experience not expressed with this linguistic marker.

The term *ʿēdāh* ranges from broad to individual levels of community: humanity as a whole (2 times), Israel as a whole (136 times), the godly

---

25. Lloyd W. Ratzlaff, "Salvation: Individualistic or Communal?" *Journal of Psychology and Theology* 4, no. 1 (1976): 108–17.

26. David Fergusson, "Reclaiming the Doctrine of Sanctification," *Interpretation* 53 (1999): 380–90.

27. Richard J. Goodrich, "John Cassian on Community," *Crux* 38, no. 4 (2002): 23–30.

28. The traditional gloss, "congregation" (KJV, RSV), is a bit misleading, since it conveys a group specifically gathered for a religious service—a sense more appropriate to *qāhal* ("assembly, congregation"). The relationship between *qāhal* ("assembly") and *ʿēdāh* ("community") is seen in the expression, "all the assembly of the community [*qāhal ʿēdāh*] of the Israelites" (Num. 14:5). The term *ʿēdāh* refers to Israel as a society as a whole, e.g., "the whole community of the Israelites," *kol ʿēdāh bĕnê yisrāʾēl* (thirty-five times, e.g., Exod. 12:3). However, when the community (*ʿēdāh*) gathers or assembles together (forms of the verb *qhl*, "to assemble") for corporate functions, such as worship, it is designated as the assembly or congregation (*qāhal*).

within Israel (3 times), a close-knit group of friends (3 times), and family/clan (9 times). As statistical distribution reveals, *ʿēdāh* most often refers to the Israelite community as a whole. In these cases, it does not refer to Israelite society as a whole but is limited to contexts where Israel (or a significant portion) gathers in one location to act in concert as the united people of God (e.g., Josh. 18:1).[29] Thus, the first time Israel was designated by *ʿēdāh* as a community was at the Passover on the eve of the exodus (Exod. 12:3, 6, 19, 47), the decisive event that transformed the descendants of Abraham into the people of God (Ps. 74:2). This term is used most often during the Exodus-conquest period, when Israel lived, moved, and acted as one (128 times). Once dispersed into tribal regions, *ʿēdāh* was reserved for important national assemblies in Jerusalem, in which the gathered assembly symbolized the nation's corporate community (1 Kings 8:5; 12:20; 2 Chron. 5:6).

Israel's cohesiveness as community was not based on mere ethnic homogeneity, but on its identity as the covenant people of God, "the community" (*ʿădāṯ*, Num. 27:17; 31:16; Josh. 22:16, 17) of Yahweh. The boundaries of the community were defined and maintained by obedience to the commands of Yahweh, who said, "Speak to the whole community of the Israelites and tell them, 'You must be holy because I, Yahweh your God, am holy'" (Lev. 19:2, translation mine). The distinction between the rebellious community of Korah and the righteous of the community of Israel (Num. 16:1–35) was archetypal of the moral dichotomy that would arise between the righteous and wicked. In the poetic books, *ʿēdāh* is reserved for the community of the righteous (Pss. 1:5; 111:1; Prov. 5:14), as opposed to the community of the wicked (Pss. 22:16[17]; 86:14; 106:17–18).[30]

Greek *Koinōnia*: "Community, Fellowship"

No term embodies the ideals of Christian community as *koinōnia*. Used but once in the LXX (Lev. 5:21, "pledged contribution"), *koinōnia* as a socio-linguistic marker for community first enters biblical literature in the New Testament, adopted from ancient Greek discourse. In ancient Greek

29. The noun *ʿēdāh* is derived from the verb *yāʿad*, "gather together, meet [with someone]" (*NIDOTTE* §6337), e.g., "all the community [*ʿădat*] which assembled [*hannôʿadîm*]" (Num. 14:35; 16:11; 27:3; 1 Kings 8:5; 2 Chron. 5:6). When collocated, they describe the community of Israel gathering to act in concert (Num. 14:35; 16:11; 27:3), often to meet together in worship before God (Num. 10:3; 1 Kings 8:5; 2 Chron. 5:6). The verb *yāʿad*, "meet [with someone]," is used of God meeting with Israel at the sanctuary: "There I will *meet* with you [the Israelites]" (Exod. 29:42–43).

30. In later Hebrew, *ʿēdāh* not only referred to Israel as a covenant community but also to a gathering for prayer (Marcus Jastrow, *A Dictionary of the Targumim, the Talmud Babli and Yerushalmi, and the Midrashic Literature* [London: Luzac, 1903; repr., Peabody, MA: Hendrickson, 2005] 2:1043). In the Qumran literature, *ʿēdāh* occurs about a hundred times, designating the sect as the true "holy community" in contrast to apostate Judaism (CD 20:2; 1QS 5:20). It also views the earthly community as the counterpart of the heavenly (1QM 1:10; 4:9). See L. E. Frizzell, "The People of God: A Study of the Relevant Concepts in the Qumran Scrolls" (Ph.D. dissertation, Oxford University, 1974), esp. 223–26.

sociopolitical thought, the ideal culture unified the public institutions of society and expression of community among its citizens. The solidarity of cultural identity led to civic participation and corporate engagement in the life of a vibrant community. This elusive ideal, never fully realized in Greek society, provided the conceptual framework for Paul's portrait of Christian community, an ideal within reach by the dynamic energizing of the Spirit.

The term *koinōnia* has a fourfold range of meanings: (1) "community life, fellowship, close mutual relationship" (Acts 2:42; 1 Cor. 1:9; 2 Cor. 8:4; 13:14; Gal. 2:9; Phil. 2:1; 1 John 1:3 [twice], 6, 7); (2) "participation, sharing in [common]" (1 Cor. 10:16; Phil. 1:5; 3:10; Philem. 6); (3) "partnership" (2 Cor. 6:14); and (4) "contribution, gift, sharing of [material goods]" (Rom. 15:26; 2 Cor. 9:13; Heb. 13:16). It is from a root whose derivatives share a set of common concepts: (1) verb *koinōneō*, "to have in common; share, contribute; participate" (Rom. 12:13; 15:27; Gal. 6:6; Phil. 4:15; 1 Tim. 5:22; Heb. 2:14; 1 Peter 4:13; 2 John 1:11); (2) adjective *koinos*, "common, mutual" (Acts 4:32; Titus 1:4; Jude 3); (3) adjective *koinōnikos*, "generous" (1 Tim. 6:18); and (4) noun *koinōnos*, "partner, partaker; participant" (Matt. 23:30; Luke 5:10; 1 Cor. 10:18, 20; 2 Cor. 1:7; 8:23; Philem. 17; Heb. 10:33; 1 Peter 5:1; 2 Peter 1:4).

Used of Christian community, *koinōnia* describes mutual participation in one another's lives and the resulting sense of interpersonal connectedness: first, of believers' fellowship with the triune God (1 Cor. 1:9; 2 Cor. 13:14; Phil. 2:1); and second, of believers' fellowship with one another (Acts 2:42; 2 Cor. 8:4; Gal. 2:9). The latter is derived from and modeled after the former: "What we have seen and heard we proclaim to you also, so that you too may have fellowship with us; and indeed our fellowship is with the Father, and with His Son Jesus Christ" (1 John 1:3 NASB). Sharing in the Christian community is contingent on genuine communion with Christ, demonstrated by obedience (1 John 1:6–7). This communion with God and one another is epitomized in the Lord's Supper, where believers meet together to meet with God (1 Cor. 10:16).

Christian community is based not on what its members have in common in the world, but on what they share in Christ. The community shares a mutual faith (Titus 1:4; Philem. 6), enjoys a common salvation (Jude 3), and drinks from the same Spirit (1 Cor. 12:13). Believers participate with one another in Christ's life (2 Peter 1:4), share in the sufferings of Christ and fellow believers by enduring persecution together (2 Cor. 1:7; Heb. 10:33; 1 Peter 4:13), and will share eschatological glory with one another (1 Peter 5:1). The unity of believers transcends worldly distinctions of race, class, and gender that divide secular society; these are dismantled in the Christian community (Gal. 3:27–29; Eph. 2:11–22).

The concept of *koinōnia* also refers to community life. Believers enjoy a deep sense of connection as they participate with one another in ministry, especially meeting the needs of their poor (2 Cor. 8:4) and proclaiming the gospel (2 Cor. 8:23; Gal. 2:9). The focus of *koinōnia*, however, is not so much an emotional feeling of community, but the experiential practice of community.

As practical expression of *koinōnia* (Acts 2:42), the early church practiced a community of goods (Acts 2:44–45; 4:32–35).[31] The Christian community expresses *koinōnia* by sharing equal partnership in the spiritual, physical, and material benefits of God's beneficence (2 Cor. 8–9; 1 Tim. 6:18), meeting the needs of its poor (Acts 4:32–37; Rom. 12:13; 15:26–27; 2 Cor. 9:13; Heb. 13:16) and supporting the ministry of the gospel (Gal. 6:6; Phil. 1:5–7; 4:14–15).

Obstacles to Building Community: Disconnectedness and Individualism

Unfortunately, Christians today do not always enjoy a close sense of community. The villain that prevents us from building a sense of community is ourselves. Too many of us are ambivalent about our need for community and do not wish to get too close to each other.[32] Researchers identify several obstacles to building community.

Demise of Community Life in Contemporary Society

One casualty of contemporary society is the transformation of traditional forms of community and the demise of community life. Many upwardly mobile Americans rarely put down roots or establish connectedness that comes only with time. With more two-career couples in the workplace and people working longer hours and spending more time commuting, lack of discretionary time takes its toll on their availability to connect with others.[33] Some are community dropouts living self-contained lives. Some unconnected individuals may never have experienced the pleasure of a close sense of community and may even lack a vocabulary to express that void. One prison inmate in Michigan, raised in a single-parent home by an emotionally distant working mother, reports in a touching first-person account that the first sense of interpersonal community he had ever known in his life was among the other residents on death row.[34]

The Exaltation of Individualism in Contemporary Western Civilization

In his recent book, Robert Bellah describes two kinds of individualism that exert a strong influence upon the heart of people in the West: (1) utilitarian individualism, exemplified by Ayn Rand's *The Virtue*

---

31. See D. M. Beck, "Community of Goods," in *The Interpreter's Dictionary of the Bible*, ed. George Arthur Buttrick (New York: Abingdon Press, 1962), 1:666; C. Ukachukwu Manus, "The Community of Love in Luke's Acts: A Sociological Exegesis of Acts 2:41–47 in the African Context," *West African Journal of Ecclesial Studies* 2 (1990): 11–37; and Justin Taylor, "The Community of Goods Among the First Christians and Among the Essenes," in *Historical Perspectives from the Hasmoneans to Bar Kokhba in Light of the Dead Sea Scrolls and Associated Literature*, January 27–31, 1999, ed. David M. Goodblatt and Avital Pinnick (Boston: Brill, 2001), 147–61.

32. Ralph Keyes, "In Search of Community," *National Elementary Principal* 54, no. 3 (1975): 8–17.

33. Patricia Roos, Mary Trigg, and Mary Hartman, "Changing Families/Changing Communities," *Community, Work and Family* 9, no. 2 (2006): 197–224.

34. Tony Chapman, "My Neighborhood," *The Other Side* 39, no. 2 (2003): 44–45.

of Selfishness and Robert Nozick's *Anarchy, State and Utopia*; and (2) expressive individualism, which embraces Kant's interest in autonomy and Nietzsche's insistence on creativity and originality.[35] Yankelovich suggests that expressive individualism has produced five negative effects in Western civilization: (1) decrease in family cohesiveness; (2) decrease in feelings of respect for other people and other moral virtues; (3) a sense that everyday life is becoming more impersonal; (4) loss of a sense of community; and (4) loss of a spiritual dimension to life in the wake of the mundane consumerism and materialism of everyday life.[36] Many American Christians fail to appreciate the value of community due to these two kinds of individualism.

Bowling Alone

In his landmark 2000 book, *Bowling Alone: The Collapse and Revival of American Community*, Harvard professor Robert Putnam makes the case that Americans have become a nation of loners.[37] He cites declining membership in groups like the PTA, Kiwanis, churches, book clubs, garden clubs, political groups, and, yes, even in bowling leagues. Putnam shows that we are increasingly engaging in privatized forms of leisure (like watching TV, surfing the Internet, playing video games) rather than connecting with others. Though our lives are increasingly peopleless, our hardwired need for connections pines away deep within our souls. Technology designed to enhance the quality of our lives is driving us apart. This loss of connectedness with others is not some nebulous intangible but a factor that affects the quality of our lives.

Individualism Is Antithetical to the Values of Community

Proverbs 18:1 describes the person who disconnects himself from community to live in a self-contained universe. Community involves being interested in others, but the self-centered person sees no utilitarian need for such involvement. This isolation, however, is self-destructive since it cuts one off from the shared wisdom of community.

> One who isolates himself seeks his own desires;
> he rejects all sound judgment.
> —(Prov. 18:1, translation mine; cf. NET)

The term *niprād*, "one who isolates himself," describes a person who is anti-social.[38] The Mishnah uses this verse to teach the necessity of being part

35. Robert Bellah et al., *Habits of the Heart: Individualism and Commitment in American Life* (Berkeley, CA: University of California Press, 1985).

36. Daniel Yankelovich, "Trends in American Cultural Values," *Criteron* 35, no. 3 (1996): 2–9.

37. Robert D. Putnam, *Bowling Alone: The Collapse and Revival of American Community* (New York: Simon & Schuster, 2000).

38. This niphal participle conveys a reflexive nuance: this person has intentionally separated himself from community life. Used literally, *pārad* "to separate," refers to geographical

of the life of a community because people have social/moral responsibilities and need each other (*Aboth* 2:4). The second line of Proverbs 18:1 says that the one who isolates himself is a problem for the community since he stands opposed to its collective moral conscience (cf. Prov. 17:14; 20:3). This kind of self-centered individual is the antithesis of the values of community.

I Cannot Be a Rock or an Island

In 1965, Paul Simon touched many lonely souls with the release of his classic pop/folk song, "I Am a Rock" (later rerecorded with Art Garfunkel and rereleased in 1966 as the final track on their album *Sounds of Silence*). This blue solo is the self-declaration of a wounded soul who had been hurt one too many times. He now protects himself by disconnecting from others and, in seclusion, making himself a rock or an island to himself. However, Simon explained, "The loneliest people in the world are those that cannot share their loneliness, through fear, pride, or anger. The ache builds walls, fear populates their dreams, and pride is the jailor of the soul."[39] The song is really a critique of the character's choice to withdraw.

Every time this golden oldie comes on the radio, I enjoy singing it. However, it cannot be the theme song of my life. I cannot be a rock or island unto myself; I must be a bridge reaching out to others. It is risky to open up to others who may hurt me. But the miserable path of self-protected isolation is far worse. Only the comfort of others and the love of a close-knit community can heal the aching heart.

Importance of Christian Community

Community Provides Wisdom

Just as one is what he eats, one becomes like those with whom he associates. Proverbs 13:20 says, "The one who walks with the wise grows wise, but the one who associates with fools suffers harm" (translation mine). An individual will grow wise by participating in a close-knit community of wise people.[40] The point is that one should join the community of the wise, and move in the same direction with them.

Community Provides Sharpening

Proverbs 27:17 is perhaps the best-known passage on the benefits of godly friendships.[41] The best way to sharpen a knife is by the friction from rubbing

---

separation of people (Gen. 13:9) and physical severing of objects (Gen. 30:40). Used figuratively of relationships, it describes the severing of friendship due to conflict (Prov. 16:28; 17:9).

39. Paul Simon, liner notes, *The Paul Simon Song Book* (London: CBS Records, 1965).

40. Used with the preposition *ʿet*, "with," the verb ***hālak***, "to walk," means "to associate with [someone]" (BDB 234.2.3.b; cf. Mic. 6:8; Job 34:8). The term ***hôlēk*** (the so-called *qerê* reading) is a participle that connotes continual, durative action.

41. See Bruce Waltke, "Friends and Friendship in the Book of Proverbs: An Exposition of Proverbs 27:1–22," *Crux* 38, no. 3 (2002): 27–42.

it against another piece of iron. Similarly, the best way to improve one's moral character is by the "friction" of personal interaction with one's friends. "As iron sharpens iron, so one person sharpens his friend" (translation mine).

This proverb is taken in various ways. For example, the Talmud suggests two students sharpen each other in their study of Torah (*b. Taanith 7a*). More likely, the point is simply that constructive criticism from a trusted friend sharpens one's moral character.

Community Provides Accountability

Deuteronomy is a covenant renewal document wherein Moses urges Israel to commit itself to, not only trust, but also obey Yahweh.[42] In the Decalogue, Moses uses singular imperatives and prohibitions (Deut. 5:6–21). However, in the preceding and following hortatory sections, he appeals to the people to watch themselves via plural forms: "Watch out for yourselves (*hiššāmĕrû lākem*) lest you forget the covenant that Yahweh your God made with you!" (4:23, translation mine); "Watch out for yourselves (*hiššāmĕrû lākem*) lest your heart is deceived and you turn away from Yahweh your God!" (11:16, translation mine; cf. NET). This interchange highlights our mutual accountability to God and to one another.

One practical way to build community and accountability is to covenant with a Christian friend or members of a small group to serve as accountability partners. I ask a set of five questions of my accountability partner each week, and he asks the same of me.

1. "Have you *done* anything this week you shouldn't have done?"
2. "Have you *said* anything this week you shouldn't have said?"
3. "Have you *seen* anything this week you shouldn't have looked at?"
4. "Have you *not done/said* anything this week you should have done/said?"
5. "Have you just lied to me four times?!"

Several years ago, one of my friends expressed appreciation for our covenant to hold one another accountable with these questions. He revealed that when he was out of town on a business trip the previous week, an attractive woman propositioned him for a night of unbridled passion. He was tempted, but his commitment to Christ—and knowledge that I would be asking these questions in a couple of days—gave him strength to resist.

Community Provides Support

Ecclesiastes 4:1–6:9 laments various ways people derail their lives.[43]

---

42. K. A. Kitchen, *The Bible in Its World* (Exeter, UK: Paternoster Press, 1977), 79–85; idem, "The Fall and Rise of Covenant, Law and Treaty," *Tyndale Bulletin* 40 (1989): 118–35; John Walton, *Ancient Israelite Literature in Its Cultural Context: A Survey of Parallels Between Biblical and Ancient Near Eastern Texts* (Grand Rapids: Zondervan, 1990), 95–110.

43. See Michael V. Fox, *A Time to Build Up and a Time to Tear Down: A Rereading of*

One of the most lamentable mistakes is trying to go it all alone. In 4:7–12, Qoheleth considers the plight of the loner and commends the close-knit community of family and friends.[44]

> Two people are better than one,
>   because they enjoy better benefit from their labor.
> For if one falls, the other will lift up his companion;
>   but pity the one who falls with no one to help him up . . .
> Although an assailant may overpower one who is alone,
>   two are able to withstand him.
> Truly, a three-ply cord is not easily broken!
> —(Eccl. 4:9–12, translation mine; cf. NET)

The loner is the loser. Life's journey is difficult and sometimes perilous; it is better that one not face it alone.[45] God designed companionship to shoulder life's burdens and to share its pleasures. Friends and family celebrate the good times together and help one another get through the bad. The graded numerical parallelism of "one//two" and "two//three" in verses 9–12 says that there is strength in numbers.[46] If one is bad but two are better, three is best: "a three-ply cord is not easily broken!" (v. 12b). The point of this metaphor is simply that a group of tightly knit souls is like a heavy-duty "three-ply rope." The typical rope is made of two strands twisted together; ropes designed for heavy-duty loads are composed of three strands. A strikingly similar saying appears in the *Gilgamesh Epic*, an ancient Mesopotamian classic celebrating friendship.[47] Describing their camaraderie, Gilgamesh tells Enkidu that there is safety and strength in numbers: " Two men will not die, the towed boat will not sink; a three-ply cord cannot be cut."[48] Qoheleth makes a similar point: people cope with crisis better in the context of a close-knit community of family and friends.[49]

Ecclesiastes (Grand Rapids: Eerdmans, 1999), 1–26; and Ardel B. Caneday, "Qoheleth: Enigmatic Pessimist or Godly Sage?" in *Reflecting with Solomon: Selected Studies on the Book of Ecclesiastes*, ed. Roy B. Zuck (Grand Rapids: Baker, 1994), 81–114.

44. R. N. Whybray, "The Futility of Injustice: Ecclesiastes 4," in *Reflecting with Solomon*, 271–80.

45. C. L. Seow, *Ecclesiastes*, Anchor Bible 18C (New York: Doubleday, 1997), 189.

46. Graham Ogden, "The Mathematics of Wisdom: Qoheleth IV 1–12," *Vetus Testamentum* 34 (1984): 446–53.

47. See Aaron Shaffer, "The Mesopotamian Background of Qohelet 4:9–12," *Eretz Israel* 8 (1967): 246–50; idem, "New Information on the Origin of the 'Three-Fold Cord,'" *Eretz Israel* 9 (1969): 159–60; and B. W. Jones, "From Gilgamesh to Qoheleth," in *The Bible in the Light of Cuneiform Literature: Scripture in Context III*, ed. W. W. Hallo et al. (Lewiston, MT: Edwin Mellen, 1990), 349–79.

48. Cited by Seow, *Ecclesiastes*, 189.

49. For a popular-level exposition of the theme of friendship in Ecclesiastes, see Thomas M. Hart, "Qoheleth Looks at Friendship," *Bible Today* 32 (1994): 79–83.

Importance of Building Community on the Christian College and Seminary Campus

In recent years, educators have begun to recognize the importance of building community on the school campus.[50] Since community is a central feature of spiritual formation, it is particularly important to develop on the campus of the Christian college and seminary, which function as the training ground for future Christian leadership.[51] In 1990, the International Council of Accrediting Agencies for evangelical theological education identified one of the most significant challenges of evangelical seminaries as the need to build a great sense of community on their campuses.[52]After examining demographic and cultural changes over twenty-five years, McKinney concludes that Christian higher education can best minister to its students by building a sense of community and reaffirming the value of sacrifice and service to others.[53]

Building Community as the Antidote to Fostering Competition in Education

Numerous theoretical and empirical studies reveal that the traditional educational approach breeds competition, not community.[54] Rather than

50. See, e.g., Stephen Wright, "Exploring Psychological Sense of Community in Living-Learning Programs and in the University as a Whole" (Ph.D. dissertation, University of Maryland, 2004); Eric Schaps, "Creating a School Community," *Educational Leadership* 60, no. 6 (2003): 31–33; T. Sergiovanni, *Building Community in Schools* (San Francisco: Jossey-Bass, 1994); Robert C. Andringa, "Is There 'Community' in Your Academic Community?" *Journal of the College and University Personnel Association* 25, no. 3 (1974): 40–43; Sue Johnston, "Building a Sense of Community in a Research Master's Course," *Studies in Higher Education* 20, no. 3 (1995): 279–91; John Lounsbury and Daniel Deneul, "Collegiate Psychological Sense of Community in Relation to Size of College/University and Extroversion," *Journal of Community Psychology* 24, no. 4 (1996): 381–94; and Mark A. Royals and Robert J. Rossi, "Individual-Level Correlates of Sense of Community: Findings from Workplace and School," *Journal of Community Psychology* 24, no. 4 (1996): 395–416. See also the essay on building community on the campus in the self-study report by the University of South Carolina, "Ten Ways to Change Undergraduate Education: X. Cultivate a Sense of Community," http://naples.cc.sunysb.edu/Pres/boyer.nsf/webform/X (accessed December 6, 2006).

51. Steve Bohus, Robert Woods, and Caleb Chan, "Psychological Sense of Community Among Students on Religious Collegiate Campuses in the Christian Evangelical Tradition," *Christian Higher Education* 4, no. 1 (2005): 19–40; Alfred P. Rovai and Jason D. Baker, "Sense of Community: A Comparison of Students Attending Christian and Secular Universities in Traditional and Distance Education Programs," *Christian Scholar's Review* 33, no. 4 (2004): 471–89; and Steve G. Fortosis, "Perspectives on Community," *Christian Education Journal* 10, no. 1 (1989): 39–50.

52. Tite Tienou, "The Future of the International Council of Accrediting Agencies," *Evangelical Review of Theology* 19, no. 3 (1995): 287–91.

53. Larry J. McKinney, "Ministering to College Students in the 1990s," *Christian Education Journal* 12, no. 3 (1992): 193–203; and idem, "Ministering to College Students at the End of the Twentieth Century," *Didaskalia* 7, no. 1 (1995): 3–19.

54. For example, M. Deutsch, "A Theory of Cooperation and Competition," *Human Relations* 2 (1949): 129–52; Ellen Weber, "Power to the Pupils: How Group Efforts Can Build Community in Your Classroom (Second of two parts on replacing competition with cooperation)," *Teachers in Focus* 5 (November 1996): 24–26; Royals and Rossi, "Individual-

instilling the social values of cooperation and interdependence—ideals crucial to community in our increasingly fragmented society—traditional educational philosophy instills individualism and elitism. While this promotes academic excellence, it is at the expense of community. Schools need to build community, not just breed competition.

Building Community as Balance Between Academics and Practice

Evangelical theological education is often content oriented, suffering a dichotomy between the affective and cognitive domains. Better balance may come by cultivating a sense of Christian community.[55] While academic excellence is critical in theological education, the Christian campus must not ignore the essential core values of spiritual formation and community.[56] As much as the church needs proficient academicians, the world needs the life and power of Christian community.

Building Community as Remedy for the Inherent Structural Shortcoming in Theological Education

The popular conception of the seminary as an educational institution is akin to a factory that produces a product: a godly preacher factory. While the seminary can sharpen skills necessary for exegesis and exposition, no seminary exists that can, in and of itself, produce spiritual character.[57] Nothing in an academic curriculum or any course syllabus can produce character development; this occurs only in the context of experiencing a strong sense of community within the school life.[58] The cognitive and affective reside in different domains than the spiritual and moral. The fact is that spiritual growth is best cultivated outside the classroom. In recent years, some educational leaders have begun calling on the church to partner with the seminary in cultivating the spiritual growth of their ministers in training.[59] The spiritual formation program on the campus is increasingly seen as an important element in a more holistic approach to theological education and ministry training.[60]

Level Correlates of Sense of Community"; Kenneth A. Strike, "Community: Why Schools Should Be More Like Congregations than Banks," *American Journal of Education* 110, no. 3 (2004): 215–32.

55. Israel Gallindo, "Methods of Christian Education Towards Christian Spiritual Formation," *Review and Expositor* 98, no. 3 (2001): 411–29.

56. Michael Reuscling, "For His Glory," *Ashland Theological Journal* 33 (2001): 17–22.

57. For example, see H. Frederick Reisz, "Assessing Spiritual Formation in Christian Seminary Communities," *Theological Education* 39, no. 2 (2003): 29–40.

58. Eric Schaps, Marilyn Watson, and Catherine Lewis, "A Key Condition for Character Development: Building a Sense of Community in School," *Social Studies Review* 37, no. 1 (1997): 85–90.

59. For example, see Richard Stoll Armstrong, "A Vital Partnership," *Journal of Academy for Evangelicals in Theological Education* 12 (1997): 3–7.

60. See Israel Gallindo, "Methods of Christian Education Towards Christian Spiritual Formation."

Building Community as the Relational Salve for Emotional Distance from God

The seminary experience is a time to focus on studying Scripture in depth, often at the risk of losing one's emotional closeness to God. For many seminarians, moving into the rigors of academic study of Scripture can be a disconcerting experience. For example, it is an emotional shock when the naïve young seminarian is confronted with exegetical evidence that his theological presuppositions lack adequate foundation. It is difficult to lose the sense of Scripture as "God's love letter to me," to begin to exegete the text in the original languages to determine its historical contextual meaning for its original audience. Without knowing why, some seminarians sense that Scripture no longer seems to speak directly to their heart. God suddenly seems far away. Many seminarians misdiagnose this experience as spiritual burnout.[61] It is actually a form of cognitive dissonance—an experience in which a person is confronted with inconsistency between one's original beliefs and the actual reality. It takes a community of students to help one another work through the confusion, disorientation, and disillusionment when one's theological universe comes crashing down, or when God seems distant.

Building Community and Your Choice Between the Good, the Bad, and the Ugly

In 1967, Sergio Leone directed the "spaghetti western," *The Good, the Bad and the Ugly*, the last of three movies featuring the legendary "man with no name." The story line, set against the backdrop of the Civil War, is a simple treasure hunt by two gunmen who team up to find a fortune of gold buried in a graveyard. However, this morality play features a twist on the conventional buddy movie since neither is inclined to trust or share the loot with the other.[62]

The *Good* is Blondie (Clint Eastwood), a wandering gunman who teams up with the *Ugly*, Tuco (Eli Wallach), a wanted Mexican bandit, to defraud local authorities of the bounty on Tuco's head. Blondie turns in his partner for the bounty, shoots the rope around his companion's neck as he is about to be hung, and helps him make his escape. They split the bounty and travel on to repeat their stunt. However, theirs is an uneasy partnership because each regularly tries to take advantage of the other.

At one point, the two encounter a group of dead and wounded soldiers; before the last one dies, he tells about a treasure buried in a graveyard. In a turn of fate, Tuco learns only half of the story and Blondie the other half.

---

61. M. McCarthy, G. H. Pretty, and V. Catano, "Psychological Sense of Community and Student Burnout," *Journal of College Student Development* 31 (1990): 211–16.

62. This plot summary is partially indebted to *Wikipedia*, s.v., "The Good, the Bad and the Ugly," available at http://en.wikipedia.org/wiki/The_Good,_the_Bad_and_the_Ugly (accessed June 26, 2006).

Now the two need each other and must work together, since each has a different piece of the puzzle. But teamwork does not come naturally to such strong-willed outlaws. They soon learn that their greatest challenge in finding the hidden gold is to learn to trust each other and work together. The two are forced to trust each other only when they must team up to survive the threat of a wicked killer—Angel Eyes, the *Bad* (Lee Van Cleef)—who learns they have the information he wants.

When they finally arrive at the graveyard, their tenuous alliance is abandoned as each tries to find the buried gold before the other. Tuco succeeds in digging up the gold only to find himself staring down the barrel of Blondie's gun. After placing Tuco's neck in a noose, fastening it to a nearby tree, and making Tuco stand on the unstable wooden cross of one of the graves, Blondie takes half the gold and rides away, leaving Tuco with his half of the gold on the ground. In a dramatic twist, Blondie turns around to shoot the rope above Tuco's head, as he used to do in their times of partnership, freeing him one last time before riding off as Tuco screams in rage in his wake. The two succeeded in reaching their goal but at the cost of their "friendship."

One of the themes in this film is that each person must make life choices that shape one's moral character. The opening scenes, which introduce the audience to each character, are accompanied by captions identifying the Good, the Bad, and the Ugly. In a similar sense, I think the Christian college or seminary experience can be "the good, the bad, or the ugly." It all depends on whether or not we work as a team to find the treasure of spiritual formation. Seminary and Bible college can be a once-in-a-lifetime opportunity to build a community of friends for the rest of your life. Failing to do so, it can be a hauntingly lonely place for an unbearably long time.

Building a Community of Practice on the Campus Through Spiritual Formation Groups

One of the best ways to build community on the Christian college and seminary campus is through a spiritual formation group program. The typical piritual formation group is composed of a small number of dedicated believers meeting together to pursue the mutual goal of spiritual growth, while at the same time building a sense of Christian community.[63] However, this is more than a superficial touchy-feely experience. It is the comraderie and esprit de corps that a tightly knit fellowship of like-minded believers enjoy as they spur one another on to Christian love and good deeds (Heb. 10:24).

---

63. For recent examples of resources for spiritual formation in small groups, see James Bryan Smith, *A Spiritual Formation Workbook: Small Group Resources for Nurturing Christian Growth* (San Francisco: Harper, 1993); Michael C. Gemignani, *To Know God: Small-Group Exercises for Spiritual Formation* (Valley Forge, PA: Judson Press, 2001); Gerrit Scott Dawson, *Companions in Christ: A Small-Group Experience in Spiritual Formation* (Nashville: Upper Room Books, 2001); and Barb Nardi Kurz, *The Heart's Journey: Christian Spiritual Formation in the Life of a Small Group* (Nashville: Discipleship Resources, 2001).

Researchers studying the dynamics of community life typically distinguish two main types of communities: (1) geographic or territorial communities, which build a sense of community through physical rootedness; and (2) relational communities, which build a sense of community through social bonding.[64] A subset of the latter is the community of practice. The spiritual formation group is a relational community of practice. It may be helpful to compare and contrast this kind of relational community with an ordinary geographic or territorial community.

A geographic or territorial community is marked primarily by the physical proximity of its members (neighborhoods, villages, towns, cities). The campus of the college or seminary is a geographic community since its students, faculty, staff, and administration all congregate in the same location. On the other hand, a relational community is composed of a group of people who are bound together through interpersonal contact and quality of interaction but may live and work in disparate locations.[65] Close friends who enjoy tight social bonding but live in different neighborhoods or even different cities are a relational community. The raison d'être of a relational community is simply enjoyment of being with one another, encouraging one another, and meeting mutual emotional/social needs. A small group of friends on a college or seminary campus is a relational community; its members enjoy much closer bonding and connectedness than the mere geographic community of the campus itself.

The community of practice is a subtype of relational community.[66] It is more than a network of contacts or group of close friends. This is a group of people who engage in a process of collective learning and skill development that creates interpersonal bonds between them.[67] In pursuing their goal of competence in their domain, members engage in joint discussions and activities, help each other, and share information. Members of a community of practice develop a shared repertoire of resources: experiences, stories, tools, ways of addressing recurring problems—in short, a shared practice. The impressionists, for example, met in cafes and studios to discuss the style of painting they were inventing. Their regular interactions made them a community of practice, even though they usually painted alone. This provides an apt model for the spiritual formation group; it is a relational community of practice.

Participation in a community of practice may be conscious or uncon-

64. J. R. Gusfield, *The Community: A Critical Response* (New York: Harper Colophon, 1975). Also see S. Riger and P. Lavrakas, "Community Ties Patterns of Attachment and Social Interaction in Urban Neighborhoods," *American Journal of Community Psychology* 9 (1981): 55–66.

65. C. Fischer, *To Dwell Among Friends: Personal Networks in Town and City* (Chicago: University of Chicago Press, 1982).

66. A. Strauss, "A Social-World Perspective," *Studies in Symbolic Interaction* 1 (1978): 119–28.

67. E. Wenger, "Communities of Practice," in *International Encyclopedia of the Social and Behavorial Sciences*, ed. N. J. Smesler and P. B. Baltes (New York: Elsevier, 2001), 4:2339–42.

scious; however, the more intentional the participation is, the more likely the sharing and interaction will increase the competences of its members. The "windshield wipers" community of practice at an auto manufacturer makes a concerted effort to collect and document all the tricks and lessons they have learned into a knowledge base.[68] Nurses who meet regularly for lunch in a hospital cafeteria may not realize that their lunch discussions are one of their main sources of knowledge about how to care for patients, but in the course of all their conversations, they have developed a set of stories and cases that become a shared repertoire for them to think about and discuss new cases.

The prime example of a community of practice is the system of apprenticeship involving one master (Journeyman) and several apprentices.[69] This kind of community functions as a living curriculum for the apprentice. It is the competence of the master and the growing competencies of the other apprentices that pull the novice along until he has a well-rounded training experience and is competent in his art. Many corporations in the modern business world employ the model of a community of practice in developing the professional skills of its executives and employees.[70]

Many in higher education have begun to use the community of practice model to transcend traditional approaches to education through cohort groups who move through the curriculum of a specialized program together.[71] I believe that the community of practice is a helpful model for understanding the purpose, formation, structure, and dynamics of a Christian spiritual formation group. However, the spiritual formation group transcends the business and educational models since it seeks to develop, not only professional skills and a body of knowledge, but also spiritual/moral growth within the context of a spiritual community.

Spiritual Factors in Building Community

One of the most ubiquitous topics in contemporary Christian literature is that of "building community."[72] So it comes as something of a surprise

---

68. For example, P. Willis, *Learning to Labour: How Working-Class Kids Get Working-Class Jobs* (Cambridge, UK: Cambridge University Press, 1977).

69. J. Lave and E. Wenger, *Situated Learning: Legitimate Peripheral Participation* (Cambridge, UK: Cambridge University Press, 1991).

70. J. Brown and P. Duguid, *The Social Life of Information* (Harvard: Harvard Business School Press, 2000); and E. Wenger, R. McDermott, and W. Snyder, *Cultivating Communities of Practice: A Guide to Managing Knowledge* (Harvard: Harvard Business School Press, 2002).

71. E. Wenger, *Communities of Practice: Learning, Meaning, and Identity* (Cambridge, UK: Cambridge University Press, 1998).

72. For example, Nelson R. Reppert, "Develop a Sense of Community," *Christian Ministry* 13, no. 4 (1982): 29–31; Sondra Mattael, "Transcripts of the Trinity: Communion and Community in Formation for Holiness of Heart and Life," *Quarterly Review* 18, no. 2 (1998): 123–37; Francis Bridger, "Ministerial Formation and Community: A Case Study from the Church of England," *Journal of Christian Education* 44, no. 3 (2001): 53–64; Robert Watson and Michael Nanqis, "The Contribution of the Desert Tradition to a Contemporary

that this expression does not actually appear in Scripture. This linguistic marker has come into Christian discussion from the discipline of sociological studies in community dynamics.[73] Nevertheless, the concept of building community is universal in human experience. Even if the precise expression, "building community," may not occur anywhere in the Bible, the concept itself permeates Scripture. Let's consider a few biblical examples.

Paul repeatedly exhorts believers to build up the Christian community. A strong sense of Christian community is "built up" when all of its members participate in the work of ministry to one another (Eph. 4:12, 16), pursue what makes for peace (Rom. 14:19), please their neighbors for their good (Rom. 15:2), encourage one another (1 Thess. 5:11), moderate their Christian liberty out of love (1 Cor. 8:1; 10:23), exercise their spiritual gifts in a way that builds community rather than exalts self (1 Cor. 14:12, 26), and speak only what is beneficial to others (Eph. 4:29).

The New Testament frequently uses the expression "one another" (*allēlous*) to describe positional and experiential aspects of Christian community. We belong to the body of Christ in which we are members of one another (Rom. 12:5; Eph. 4:25), and God works in our lives to give us unity with one another through Christ (Rom. 15:5). Building community is often expressed by an imperative governing the accusative *allēlous,* "one another." There are twenty-five categories of commands that believers:

1. love one another (John 13:34; 15:12,17; Rom. 13:8; 1 Peter 1:22; 1 John 3:11, 23; 4:7, 11; 2 John 1:5)
2. be devoted to one another (Rom. 12:10a)
3. have mutual concern for one another (1 Cor. 12:25)
4. serve one another (Gal. 5:13)
5. carry the burdens of one another (Gal. 6:2)
6. honor one another (Rom. 12:10b)
7. encourage one another (1 Thess. 4:18; 5:11)
8. bear patiently with one another (Eph. 4:2; Col. 3:13a)
9. be kind and compassionate to one another (Eph. 4:32a)
10. confess sins to one another (James 5:16)
11. forgive one another (Eph. 4:32b; Col. 3:13b)
12. show hospitality to one another (1 Peter 4:9)
13. accept/receive one another (Rom. 15:7)
14. warmly greet one another (Rom. 16:16; 1 Cor. 16:20; 2 Cor. 13:12; 1 Peter 5:14)
15. submit to one another (Eph. 5:21)

Understanding of Community and Spiritual Intersubjectivity," *Journal of Psychology and Christianity* 20, no. 4 (2001): 309–23; L. S. Cahill, "Christian Character, Biblical Community, and Human Values," in *Character and Scripture: Moral Formation, Community, and Biblical Interpretation*, ed. W. P. Brown (Grand Rapids: Eerdmans, 2002), 29–54.

73. For example, see S. B. Sarason, *The Psychological Sense of Community: Prospects for a Community Psychology* (San Francisco: Jossey-Bass, 1974).

16. treat one another as more important than one's self (Phil. 2:3)
17. instruct and exhort one another (Rom. 15:14; Col. 3:16a; Heb. 3:13)
18. speak to one another in psalms, hymns, and spiritual songs (Eph. 5:19; Col. 3:16b)
19. spur on one another to love and good works (Heb. 10:24)
20. wait for one another in worship (1 Cor. 11:33)
21. live in harmony and unity with one another (Rom. 12:16; 15:5)
22. show humility toward one another (1 Peter 5:5)
23. pursue what is good for one another (1 Thess. 5:15)
24. build up one another (Rom. 14:19; 1 Thess. 5:11)
25. follow Jesus' example of "washing the feet" of one another (John 13:14)

Believers are also exhorted not to pass judgment on one another (Rom. 14:13), not to "bite and devour" one another in interpersonal conflict (Gal. 5:15), not to provoke one another (Gal. 5:26a), not to be jealous of one another (Gal. 5:26b), not to lie to one another (Col. 3:9), not to repay evil to one another (1 Thess. 5:15), not to speak against one another (James 4:11), and not to grumble against one another (James 5:9).

A close-knit community enjoys a deep sense of interpersonal bonding. This formation of a close emotional tie between people links their lives together. A mother and her newly born infant, for example, naturally experience close bonding. In an ideal family, children enjoy a close bond with one another, but in dysfunctional families they tear one another part. Christian community is like a family. Our heavenly Father has given us birth into his family, and he urges us to bond with one another: "Make every effort to keep the unity of the Spirit through the bond of peace" (Eph. 4:3); "Add love, which is the perfect bond" (Col. 3:14 NET). In both these passages, the term "bond" (*sundesmos*) is a metaphor picturing an object such as a rope, band, or chain that binds somebody to something (cf. Job 41:15 [LXX]; Isa. 58:6, 9 [LXX]; Col. 2:19).

In the garden of Gethsemane, Jesus prayed that through his death, all believers would become "one" in him (John 17:11, 21–23). God has initially answered this prayer through making all believers—Jews and Gentiles, slave and free, male and female—members of the "one" body of Christ (Rom. 12:4–5; 1 Cor. 10:17; 12:11–13, 20; Eph. 2:11–22; Col. 3:15). Believers experientially express this oneness by being united in one spirit, having one mind, being knit together in one heart, and glorifying God with one voice (Acts 1:14; 4:32; Rom. 15:6; Col. 1:27; 2:2–3).

Personal Factors in Building Community

Researchers in the dynamics of community agree that one of the keys to building a sense of community is *esprit de corps* derived from a "spark of friendship."[74] Building strong ties to a group of close friends is an essential

74. D. W. McMillan, "Sense of Community," *Journal of Community Psychology* 24, no.

element of Christian community.[75] Let us consider two biblical concepts that deal with building a community of friendships.

To Have Friends You Must Be a Friend

Friendship is an important theme in Scripture. This is perhaps best exemplified by the Hebrew term *rēaʿ*, "friend, comrade, companion" (BDB 946.1; *HALOT* 1254.1–3), which appears in numerous passages describing a true friend. A person who is generous (Prov. 19:6), as well as gracious of speech and pure in heart (Prov. 22:11), will win friends. Friends enjoy spending time with each other in their homes (Zech. 3:10) and help one another with personal chores (Deut. 19:5). Close friends confide in one another (Ps. 55:13-14). The epitome of interpersonal communication, after which Moses compared Yahweh's self-revelation to him, is that of true friends (Exod. 33:11). Good friends provide sound counsel to one another (Prov. 27:9), sharpen one another's moral character (Prov. 27:17), and are willing to let one another know when one of them is sinning (Prov. 27:6). A friend demonstrates loyalty (2 Sam. 3:8; Prov. 17:17), can be trusted (Ps. 41:9), and may even be closer than a brother (Prov. 18:24). A true friend sides with his companion in the face of personal opposition (2 Sam. 16:17) and does not dissolve the relationship over misunderstanding (Prov. 27:10). When one friend suffers, a true friend feels his or her pain (Ps. 35:14), provides the comfort of one's presence (Judg. 11:37–38; Job 2:11), shows kindness and comfort (Job 6:14), and prays for his or her friend (Job 16:20–21). The test of true friendship is how one responds to his or her companion when others criticize that friend (Prov. 16:28), when one's friend suffers calamity (Job 19:14, 19, 21; Pss. 38:11; 88:18), and when one friend inadvertently offends the other in some way (Prov. 17:9). A friend does not break his or her promises (Ps. 55:20). While a person may enjoy numerous friendships, one's closest friend is called "your friend who is as your own soul" (Deut. 13:6 NASB).

True Friendship Is Rare and Requires Dedication

Proverbs 18:24 offers valuable insightful about friendship. It contrasts two kinds of friendships, namely, superficial acquaintances and true friendships: "Some people play at friendship, but a true friend sticks closer than a brother" (translation mine). The key to cultivating and maintaining a genuine friendship is a willingness to work—not just play—at the friendship, and to be loyal to one's friend through thick and thin.

The first line is notoriously hard to translate; the syntax is difficult, the meaning of the terms is ambiguous, and the text is uncertain.[76] The expression

---

4 (1996): 315; see also Heather Chipeur, "Dyadic Attachments and Community Connectedness," *Journal of Community Psychology* 29, no. 4 (2001): 429–46.

75. J. Stephen Rhodes, "The Church as the Community of Open Friendship," *Asbury Theological Journal* 55, no.1 (2000): 41–49.

76. For example, the first line has been taken as: (1) a warning about those who make a pretense of friendship but are not loyal: "There are friends who pretend to be friends" (RSV);

ʾîš rēʿîm may be taken as (1) genitive of characteristic: "man of friends," a friendly person;[77] or (2) introductory assertion: "some friends are . . ."[78] The plural *rēʿîm* is from *rēaʿ* II, which may refer to anyone from a close friend (BDB 946.1; *HALOT* 1254.1–3) to a loose acquaintance (BDB 946.2; *HALOT* 1254.4–5). The term *ləhitrōʿēʿa* is a prefixed infinitive that functions in a verbal sense here (cf. Isa. 60:21). It comes from the verb *rāʿaʿ* "to smash, shatter, break" (Job 34:24; Ps. 2:9; Prov. 25:19; Jer. 11:16; 15:12). The lexicons debate whether the hithpael form conveys (1) a reciprocal sense, "to smash one another" (*HALOT* 1270.2); or (2) a passive sense, "to be broken to pieces" (BDB 950). The first depicts the destructive effect of interpersonal conflict: "Some friends tear one another apart." The second describes the destruction of the friendship itself: "Some friends are torn apart." The latter seems to provide a tight parallel with the second line. On the other hand, the *Biblia Hebraica Stuttgartensia* editors suggest emending MT to *hitrāʿot*, with the idea that some only play at friendship halfheartedly: "Some people play at friendship."[79]

---

(2) an observation that some make only halfhearted efforts at friendship: "Some friends play at friendship" (NRSV); (3) a caution that friends sometimes hurt one another: "A person who has friends may be harmed by them" (NET); (4) advice to not pursue too many friendships since some will not be loyal: "A man of too many friends comes to ruin" (NASB; cf. NIV); (5) counsel to be friendly to one's friends: "A man who has friends must himself be friendly" (NKJV; cf. KJV); and (6) a declaration that friends are good for company, but one still needs a true friend: "There are companions to keep one company" (*Tanakh: The Holy Scriptures: The New JPS Translation According to the Traditional Hebrew Text* [Philadelphia: Jewish Publication Society, 1984]).

77. Many interpreters take *ʾîš* as the noun *ʾîš* I "man" (BDB, 35–36) and understand *ʾîš rēʿîm* as a genitive construct: "a man of friends." Construct expressions in which the genitive follows *ʾîš* often highlight someone's prominent characteristic, e.g., *ʾîš dəbārîm*, "man of words," is an eloquent man (Exod. 4:10); *ʾîš elōhîm*, "man of God," is a prophet (1 Sam. 2:27); *ʾîš milḥămôt*, "man of battles," is a warrior (2 Sam. 8:10); *ʾîš haddāmîn*, "man of bloodshed," is a murderer (2 Sam. 16:7); *îš ḥămāsîm*, "man of violences," is a violent man (2 Sam. 22:49); *îš habbəliyyāʿl*, "man of worthlessness," is a scoundrel (2 Sam. 16:7). Thus, *ʾîš rēʿîm* may be interpreted as an idiom for someone who has friends: "a man who has friends" (cf. KJV, NET); or less likely, someone who has too many friends: "a man of many friends" (cf. ASV, NASB, NIV).

78. The Hebrew lexicons consistently take *ʾîš* here as the particle *ʾîš* II, "there is" (*HALOT*, 44), which is a poetic variant of *ʾîš*, "there is" (2 Sam. 14:19; Mic. 6:10) (*HALOT*, 92; BDB, 442.2). The long form *ʾîš* and short form *ʾiš* are both attested in related terms, e.g., Aramaic *ʾît* and Ugaritic *ʾit*, both meaning "there is." This is supported by the parallelism in the first and second lines between *ʾîš* II, "there is," and the synonymous particle *yēš*, "there is" (*HALOT*, 92). This pairing of *ʾîš* and *yēš* finds analogy in the equivalent pairing of *yēš* and *yēš* elsewhere (Eccl. 7:15). This approach is reflected in several ancient versions (Aramaic Targum, Syriac Peshitta, Greek recensions), is adopted by several translations (RSV, NRSV, CEV, *Tanakh*), and is advocated by some commentators (C. H. Toy, *The Book of Proverbs*, ICC [New York: Charles Scribner's Sons, 1899; repr., Edinburgh: T & T Clark, 1988], 366). The particle *ʾîš* II may function in one of two ways here: (1) in a positive sense, e.g., "There are companions to keep one company" (*Tanakh*); or (2) in a pejorative sense, e.g., "Some friends play at friendship" (NRSV).

79. The suggested emendation of *ləhitrōʿēʿa* to *hitrāʿôt* results in a hithpael infinitive construct from *rʿh* ("to associate") that means "to be a companion" (BDB, 945; cf. Prov. 22:24; Isa. 11:7). The preposition *rʿh* may denote purpose, indicating that the purpose of

The second line describes genuine friendship: "but a true friend sticks close like a brother" (v. 24b). Popular exposition often adopts a christological approach, identifying the "true friend" as Jesus. However, *ʾōhēb* probably refers to a close personal "friend" (Judg. 5:31; 2 Sam. 19:6; Pss. 5:11[12]; 38:11[12]; 69:36[37]; 88:18[19]; 119:132; Prov. 14:20; 17:17; 27:6; Isa. 41:8; Jer. 20:4, 6; Lam. 1:2; Esther 5:10, 14; 6:13; 2 Chron. 20:7). When used concretely, *dāḇēq*, "cling to [someone/thing]," refers to something that adheres/sticks to the surface of an object, e.g., bone clinging to skin (Job 19:20), a hand grasping a sword (2 Sam. 23:10), a belt tight against one's waist (Jer. 13:11), the tongue cleaving to the roof of the mouth (Ps. 22:15[16]; cf. Job 29:10; 38:38; Pss. 44:25; 137:6; Lam. 4:4; Ezek. 3:26; 29:4). Used figuratively, it refers to a commitment to another person: "be loyal to [someone]" (Deut. 10:20; 11:22; 13:4; 30:20; Josh. 22:5; 23:8; 2 Sam. 20:2; 2 Kings 18:6) (BDB 179–80). Its collocation with *ʾōhēb*, "friend," suggests the loyalty shown by a true friend: "sticks closer than a brother" (cf. KJV, ASV, NASB, RSV, NRSV, NET), "more loyal than brothers" (TEV), "closer than your own family" (CEV), "more devoted than a brother."[80] The purpose of comparing a true friend to one's sibling is not to denigrate the typical sibling relationship but to magnify the loyalty of a true friend (cf. Prov. 17:17; 27:10). It is desirable to enjoy many acquaintances for social enrichment, but it is critical to have at least one true friend who will stand by you in your darkest days and most difficult moments. Thus, Proverbs 18:24 pictures two kinds of relationships: some are fair-weather friends; others are stout and faithful soul mates. Interpersonal commitment such as this is the essence of true community.

Practical Factors in Building Community

Common sense, intuition, and personal experience suggest that building a sense of community is contingent on some very practical factors. Most people have some vague ideas about what it takes to cultivate a sense of community. Academic researchers who study the dynamics of community, both on theoretical and empirical levels, have discovered what seem to be universal principles in the dynamics of a close-knit sense of community. Their findings seem consistent with biblical descriptions of the dynamics of human

---

friendship is enjoyment of interpersonal relationships: "Friends are for companionship" (Targum). However, some take the hithpael in the so-called "Hollywood" sense: (1) "There are friends who *pretend to be friends*" (RSV), "There are friends who *play at friendship*" (cf. NRSV); or (2) "A man who has friends *must show himself friendly*" (cf. KJV). This may be reflected in Ben Sirach: "There is a friend who is a companion at the table, but he will not continue in the day of your affliction" (*Ecclus* 6:10). Elsewhere in Proverbs, the construction *yēš*, "there is," followed by a hithpael verb describes someone who pretends to be what he is not: "Some pretend to be rich and yet have nothing; others pretend to be poor and yet possess great wealth" (13:7, translation mine). This approach provides a tight parallel with the second line, contrasting those who merely play at friendship halfheartedly with the true friend who is dedicated to his friend.

80. *Tanakh: The Holy Scriptures: The New JPS Translation According to the Traditional Hebrew Text* (Philadelphia: Jewish Publication Society, 1985).

community and true to everyday life experience.[81] While a spiritual formation group is a uniquely Christian community, it shares many of the universal features of any human community. Paying attention to these universals may help build a sense of community even in a spiritual formation group.[82]

Since Sarason published his seminal work in 1974, research in the discipline of community psychology has focused on the dynamics of what contributes to a "sense of community."[83] Sarason defined a sense of community as "the perception of similarity to others, an acknowledged interdependence with others, a willingness to maintain this interdependence by giving to or doing for others what one expects from them, and the feeling that one is part of a larger dependable and stable structure."[84] More recently, McMillan and Chavis defined a sense of community as "a feeling that members have of belonging, a feeling that members matter to one another and to the group, and a shared faith that members' needs will be met through their commitment to be together."[85]

Scholars generally regard the theoretical framework and empirical analysis of McMillan and Chavis as the starting point for any research in a sense of community.[86] McMillan and Chavis identify five major factors that contribute to a strong sense of community: (1) sense of belonging to a community; (2) boundaries and symbols of the community; (3) participation and influence in the community; (4) fulfillment of needs through the community; and (5) shared emotional connection.[87]

---

81. According to the so-called Wesleyan quadrilateral, Christian theology is built on: (1) Scripture, (2) tradition, (3) reason, and (4) experience.

82. Paul Dokecki, J. R. Newbrough, and Robert O'Gormon, "Toward a Community-Oriented Action Research Framework for Spirituality: Community Psychological and Theological Perspectives," *Journal of Community Psychology* 29, no. 5 (2001): 497–518.

83. S. B. Sarason, *The Psychological Sense of Community: Prospects for a Community Psychology* (San Francisco: Jossey-Bass, 1974); and idem, "Commentary: The Emergence of a Conceptual Center," *Journal of Community Psychology* 14 (1986): 405–7.

84. Sarason, *Psychological Sense of Community*, 157.

85. D. W. McMillan and D. M. Chavis, "Sense of Community: A Definition and Theory," *American Journal of Community Psychology* 14, no. 1 (1986): 6–23.

86. Ibid.; D. M. Chavis, J. H. Hogge, D. W. McMillan, and A. Wandersman, "Sense of Community Through Brunswick's Lens," *Journal of Community Psychology* 14, no. 1 (1986): 24–40; D. W. McMillan, "Sense of Community," *Journal of Community Psychology* 24, no. 4 (1996): 315–25; D. M. Chavis and G. Pretty, "Sense of Community: Advances in Measurement and Application," *Journal of Community Psychology* 27, no. 6 (1999): 635–42. McMillan and Chavis also have constructed a questionnaire index to assess the degree of SOC of individuals in any particular community. For critical evaluations of the SOC Index, see Patricia L. Obst and Katherine M. White, "Revisiting the Sense of Community Index: A Confirmatory Factor Analysis," *Journal of Community Psychology* 32, no. 6 (2004): 691–705; Heather M. Chipuer and Grace M. H. Pretty, "A Review of the Sense of Community Index: Current Uses, Factor Structure, Reliability, and Further Development," *Journal of Community Psychology* 27, no. 6 (1999): 643–58; and D. Adam Long and Douglas D. Perkins, "Confirmatory Factor Analysis of the Sense of Community Index and Development of a Brief SCI," *Journal of Community Psychology* 31, no. 3 (2003): 279–96.

87. Subsequent research builds on the McMillan-Chavis model: John E. Puddifoot,

Cohesiveness: Sense of Belonging to a Community

According to McMillan and Chavis, a main factor in building a sense of community is the subjective assurance that one belongs to and is accepted by a particular group.[88] Even in educational contexts, people have an inherent need to feel that they "belong" to and are accepted by a group.[89] Christians writing on the role of community in spiritual formation also emphasize that individuals long for a sense that they "belong" to the group.[90] Christians do not just attend church; they see themselves as belonging to a Christian community. People want to belong, not just believe.[91]

Constraints: Boundaries and Symbols of a Community

Boundaries are external social and/or moral markers that define and protect the cohesiveness of a community. They comprise a shared set of moral norms, social mores, traditional values, and beliefs about appropriate behavior by the members of the community. In formal communities, boundaries are published to articulate the standards for the community. In informal

---

"Dimensions of Community Identity," *Journal of Community and Applied Social Psychology* 5, no. 5 (1995): 357–70; Jean L. Hill, "Psychological Sense of Community: Suggestions for Future Research," *Journal of Community Psychology* 24, no. 4 (1996): 431–38; Christopher C. Sonn and Adhon I. Fischer, "Sense of Community: Community Resilient Responses to Oppression and Change," *Journal of Community Psychology* 26, no. 5 (1998): 457–72; Mark Rapley and Grace M. H. Pretty, "Playing Procrustes: The Interactional Production of a Psychological Sense of Community," *Journal of Community Psychology* 27, no. 6 (1999): 695–713; Anne E. Brodsky, Patricia J. O'Campo, and Robert E. Aronson, "PSOC in Community Context," *Journal of Community Psychology* 27, no. 6 (1999): 659–79; Anne F. Brodsky and Christine M. Marx, "Layers of Identity: Multiple Psychological Senses of Community Within a Community Setting," *Journal of Community Psychology* 29, no. 2 (2001): 161–78; Patricia Obsr, Sandy G. Smith, and Lucy Zinkiewicz, "An Exploration of Sense of Community," *Journal of Community Psychology* 30, no. 1 (2002): 119–33; and Stefano Tartaglia, "A Preliminary New Model of Sense of Community," *Journal of Community Psychology* 34, no. 1 (2006): 25–36.

88. McMillan and Chavis identify several significant attributes of a sense of belonging (membership) to a relational community: (a) conscious identification with the purpose of the community; (b) perceived similarity to others: homogeneity between members of the community; (c) a common symbol system shared between individual and community; (d) integration into the group; (e) a shared emotional connection among its members; and (f) a spirit of community (esprit de corps). See McMillan and Chavis, "Sense of Community: A Definition and Theory," 6–23; and McMillan, "Sense of Community," 315, 322). Also see Anne Brodsky and Christine Marx, "Layers of Identity: Multiple Psychological Senses of Community Within a Community Setting," *Journal of Community Psychology* 29, no. 2 (2001): 161–78.

89. Constance M. Perry, "Caring in Context: Sense of Community and Belonging," *School Community Journal*, 6:2 (1996) 71–78.

90. Joseph R. Myers, "The Search to Belong: Four Spaces, Many Possibilities," *Christian Standard* 139 (May 9, 2004): 292–93; Tim Parsley and Russ Howard, "The Search to Belong: Rethinking Our Strategy," *Christian Standard* 139 (May 9, 2004): 293–95; Myron D. Williams, "How Do We Define Belonging?" *Christian Standard* 139 (May 9, 2004): 296–97.

91. R. Baumeister and R. Leary, "The Need to Belong: Desire for Interpersonal Attachments as a Fundamental Human Motivation," *Psychological Bulletin* 117 (1995): 497–527.

communities, boundaries are communicated by word-of-mouth social channels. Group symbols are traditions, rituals, ceremonies, rites of passage, even forms of speech and dress, that preserve a sense of community history and create a group identity around which to develop an esprit de corps.[92]

Contact: Participation and Influence in the Community

According to McMillan and Chavis, a sense of community is also built when the individual participates in the life of the community.[93] Participation takes various forms, from opening up in transparent communication to performing acts of service or making charitable contributions to the community. Individuals are more likely to participate when they are provided opportunities, receive assurance that they are competent to perform, and are socially rewarded for their participation. When this occurs, the participant is viewed as a full-fledged member, thus integrating him/her into the group. The technical literature describes this as "person-community fit," but it is more commonly known as simply "fitting in."[94] In addition, a sense of community is built when each individual has a sense that his or her voice is heard and valued by the community. On the other hand, when one or more individuals try to exert more influence or control over the group than is appropriate, community cohesiveness diminishes.

Care: Fulfillment of Needs Through the Community

A sense of community also is built when the group meets the needs and/or fulfills the desires of its members. McMillan notes that the needs and desires that a group is prepared to fulfill are largely contingent on the shared values and goals of its members and on the nature of its homogeneity.[95] When members meet the needs of one another, they create an "economy of social trade," that is, a reciprocity of meeting one another's needs. The fulfillment of the needs of individual members is often based upon an interdependence of the members with one another and a willingness to maintain this interdependence by serving others.[96]

Camaraderie: Shared Emotional Connection

According to McMillan and Chavis, the definitive element in building a sense of community is shared emotional connection among its members.[97] A spirit of community, or esprit de corps, develops from the "spark of friendship" among its members. The development of friendship is

---

92. R. Nisbet and R. G. Perrin, *The Social Bond* (New York: Knopf, 1977), 47.

93. McMillan and Chavis, "Sense of Community: A Definition and Theory," 11.

94. J. Rappaport, *Community Psychology: Values, Research, and Action* (New York: Rhinehart and Winston, 1977).

95. McMillan, "Sense of Community," 322.

96. S. B. Sarason, *The Psychological Sense of Community*, 157.

97. McMillan and Chavis, "Sense of Community: A Definition and Theory," 14.

certainly a subjective experience; however, theoretical research and empirical analysis suggests that interpersonal bonding is typically based on a set of very concrete factors, such as amount of contact, quality of interaction, shared experience, shared history, personal investment, and personal commitment.[98]

Gender Factors in Building Community

Spiritual formation is an important part of the Christian life for males and females alike. However, Hall suggests an effective spiritual formation program must appreciate the subtle differences in how men and women build friendships and express community. On the other hand, spiritual formation also may be hindered if a program adopts a model of community building that is patterned on overly rigid feminine and masculine stereotypes. An effective program must provide balanced formation for both sexes.[99]

The Friendless American Male

In his book, *The Friendless American Male*, David Smith says, "Women seem to have a monopoly on meaningful, intimate relationships. . . . Men have friendships which relate to work or play, but seldom go beyond the surface."[100] Smith observes that most men have buddies, not deep friendships. They spend time with one another but do not share themselves. They talk about problems outside themselves but do not open themselves up. Smith suggests that American males do not share themselves with others because they have been trained to be competitive, not to be friends. They compete with one another from Little League to the adult world of business. Men tend to rate one another by their degree of success. However, friendship demands vulnerability, sharing, and openness—the very opposite of competition. One of the challenges in helping men build Christian community is simply to help them see the importance in doing so.

Sexually/Emotionally Abused Females

A recent empirical study revealed that adult Christian women who had been sexually abused as children demonstrated significantly lower long-term spiritual functioning than non-abused counterparts. The study revealed that sexual abuse adversely impacts spiritual functioning in three areas: (1) a sense of being loved and accepted by God, (2) a sense of community with others, and (3) trust in God's plan and purpose for the future.[101] Since nearly one in five women in America suffer sexual abuse as children,

---

98. McMillan, "Sense of Community," 320–22.

99. Terese Hall, "Gender Differences: Implications for Spiritual Formation and Community Life," *Journal of Psychology and Christianity* 16, no. 3 (1997): 222–32.

100. David W. Smith, *The Friendless American Male* (Ventura, CA: Regal Books, 1983), 103.

101. Terese A. Hall, "Spiritual Effects of Childhood Sexual Abuse in Adult Christian Women," *Journal of Psychology and Theology* 23, no. 2 (1995): 129–34.

any spiritual formation program must be sensitive to this unique obstacle to building community. Another recent case study explores effects of transgenerational exposure to intense suffering by women of Nicaragua. It observed how Christian women were able to overcome personal tragedy and injustice through cultivating a deep spirituality, enjoying close relationship with extended families, and building a strong sense of community with other Christian women.[102]

Conclusion

Community is an essential element of spiritual formation. Indeed, the degree of our success or failure on the pathway of Christian discipleship depends upon the depth of community that we cultivate with one another. In this vein, I like to remind myself of the importance of building Christian friends and community by recalling the words of Clarence the angel to George Bailey in the now classic movie, *It's a Wonderful Life*: "Remember, no man is a failure who has friends!"

102. Brenda Consuelo Ruiz, "Pastoral Counseling of Women in a Context of Intense Oppression," *Journal of Pastoral Care* 48, no. 2 (1994): 163–68.

Chapter 4

New Testament Community and Spiritual Formation

Darrell L. Bock

> Finally, brethren, we beseech and exhort you in the Lord Jesus, that as you learned from us how you ought to live and to please God, just as you are doing, you do so more and more.
>
> —1 Thessalonians 4:1 RSV

No Christian is an island. God does not bring us into fellowship with him and make us a part of his people to function in isolation.[1] We can see this from the very beginning, when God creates man and woman in his image, indicating that fellowship is a key purpose for our creation. That involves both fellowship with God and fellowship with each other.

Spiritual formation means that God is in the business of forming us into his likeness so that we can have deeper fellowship with him and reflect the virtues of righteousness in our lives. Spiritual formation as seen in the New Testament has four key components. Spiritual formation possesses (1) an agent—the Spirit; (2) a dynamic—growth in the context of community identification; and (3) a goal—holiness in the context of mission. It also requires (4) an open and responsive heart that pursues formation as a key purpose in life.

My responsibility is to show how the New Testament portrays these major themes associated with spiritual formation. A great tendency exists, especially in Western culture, to privatize the spiritual experience and make

1. The following is an update of an article I did for the original Spiritual Formation conference held at Trinity Evangelical Divinity School in 2000. Its updated form was presented as part of a workshop at the 2006 Spiritual Forum Conference in 2006 at Long Beach, California.

it a "personal" matter between the believer and God. In correctly emphasizing disciplines and personal time with God, we risk forgetting the whole equation for the sake of recovering something important that spirituality has lost. In the process, numerous mechanisms God has placed in his plan to form us spiritually often are ignored or underutilized. As much as we need to recover the elements of a personal walk that often are neglected in the rush of today's life, we dare not lose other components of spiritual formation that God has revealed are key parts of the spiritual process. God does not form us to turn us into being inwardly focused people. He forms us for fellowship and mission.

We write in the hope that as Paul exhorted the Thessalonians, we should seek to grow and excel still more, realizing that spiritual formation is a process that is never over until God glorifies us. My essay has four units: (1) The Spirit as the Agent of Formation: What We Have; (2) Spiritual Identity: Who We Are and How We Are Enabled; (3) What We Are to Bring: An Open and Seeking Heart; and (4) The Goal of Formation: Holiness and Mission in the Community and to a Needy World—What Does It Look Like? Before surveying these themes, I will lay out some definitions that are a key part of this discussion and explain the difference between spiritual formation and discipleship.

Much of what I hope to say will overlap with points made in the previous chapter about spiritual formation in the Old Testament.[2] After all, the Spirit of God is the major player in spiritual formation. His Spirit works in our spirit to enable us to be spiritually formed, a process that is a central part of our journey of fellowship with God. Spiritual formation should result in testimony to him as our lives form an incarnate doxology to the grace and presence of the living God within us. Let us examine some of the key themes tied to formation and the underlying New Testament theology for it.

Definitions: Spiritual Formation and Discipleship

If one uses the term *spiritual formation*, the first question that often follows is, "What is the difference between spiritual formation and what we have called in the past discipleship?" It is an important and fair question.

Discipleship is about following Jesus. The term comes from the Greek word μαθητής (*mathētēs*), translated "disciple." It means a learner or follower. In the Greek lexicon BDAG (609–10), its meanings include one who engages in instruction through another, a pupil; and one who is associated

2. At the 2000 conference, Richard Averbeck and I presented a joint plenary session to report on the combined results of our respective essays, having initially worked separately on the topic of spiritual formation in the Old and New Testaments. Our goal was to illustrate the very interactive community emphasis both of us had. What surprised us both in our study and subsequent preparation for the plenary was how complementary the emphases in the Testaments are. Since that time, the idea that spiritual formation should be done in community and lead into mission has become a given in discussions of where spiritual formation should lead. Virtually every plenary speaker at the 2006 conference made these points.

with someone who has a pedagogical reputation, a disciple. In practice, discipleship focuses upon edification programs we undergo and undertake, often with a mentor to lead us. Usually a more mature person in the Lord takes on the task of "discipling" others in their walk. So discipleship is about following. It focuses on what we do in following Jesus and growing in the Lord.

Spiritual formation is a broader concept. *Spiritual formation* is a composite term not found explicitly in the Bible. It refers to all God undertakes and undergoes for us to bring us to maturity. It points to the resources he brings to the task of forming us into his likeness, as well as to what we do in the pursuit of this goal. The closest single term to this idea in the New Testament is found in 2 Corinthians 3:18, where Paul says we as believers are being "transformed" (μεταμορφούμεθα, *metamorphoumetha*) into the image of God and from one glory to another by God's Spirit. This verb means "to be changed," "be transformed" (BDAG, 639). In this 2 Corinthians text, this change takes place inwardly and is visible outwardly in a changed life. Thus, spiritual formation is what God does to and for us, along with all he makes available to make this transformation possible, a process that never ends until he brings us to himself.

In sum, God uses discipleship programs and disciplines to aid in bringing us to maturity, but his program of spiritual transformation and the resources he brings to that task are much broader than we realize if we speak only about discipleship. So it becomes important to focus on the resources and identity God gives us to form us into people who walk in his paths. It is to the four key elements of that provision that we now turn.

What We Have: The Spirit as the Agent of Formation

Underlying the biblical images of spiritual formation is the Spirit's association with the concept of wind blowing where it wishes. The work of the Spirit is not reducible to a formula, nor can it be bottled like a prescription. The spiritual life is too dynamic a process to be handled like building a car on an assembly line. God is not in the business of just making Hondas. Rather each person is being crafted for a unique role as a child of God in unique places that God also brings into one's life. Another way to say this is that though God is in the business of replicating his character in his children, each copy is a special edition. More than that, such formation takes place *in the natural flow of life*. It is organic to our daily activities, taking place spontaneously with them. This means that formation cannot be pursued as a class. Formation takes place in the context of living, although it is important that the believer be intentional about it, which is where practices like the spiritual disciplines come in, helping us to gain our proper focus each day. Whether we pray, study Scripture, take some time off for silence before God, or take time now and again for a retreat, the goal is always to re-center our relationship to God in a manner that prepares us for daily life and engagement. We can do this with confidence that God will aid us in this pursuit, both through what he does with us in the quiet moments and through what he does with us in our daily activities.

One of the great promises contained in 1 Corinthians 2 is that in the process of spiritual growth, God is doing an "inside" job. He invades us with his Spirit, interpreting spiritual things with a Spirit who knows his mind and heart (2:13). In fact, so confident is Paul of this truth that he speaks of himself possessing the "mind of Christ" in verse 16. Having the mind of Christ means being so in tune with the Spirit that spiritual discernment is a given as a character trait. The result is an embrace of the gospel in a way that is the opposite of the jealousy currently being displayed among the carnal Corinthians. This look at what we have been given in the Spirit highlights a major point of our entire study. Spiritual formation demonstrates its presence not only in how we relate to God, but also especially in how we relate to others, particularly those in our community. In fact, without such reliance on and direction from the Spirit, we will respond instinctively in a way that breaks down relationships, which is what was happening in Corinth.

The key concept of realizing what a central resource we have in the Spirit has deep roots in the New Testament. No book states it more powerfully than Romans, where it is at the core of what it means to experience the gospel. The key text here is Romans 1:16–17. There Paul states that he is not ashamed of the gospel for it is the *power* (δύναμις, *dunamis*) of God unto salvation for those who believe. I used to think that verse 16 was mistranslated, for I wanted it to read, "I am not ashamed of the gospel, for it is the salvation of God for those who believe." In other words, for the longest time I could not figure out why Paul highlighted power as the key core concept of the gospel rather than salvation. I thought getting saved is what excited Paul. This text tells us, however, that it was "getting enabled" that was at the core of Paul's enthusiasm for the gospel.

It took reading through Romans as if it were a narrative and understanding its message to appreciate what Paul was saying. You see, Paul was arguing that humanity functions without the Spirit and is tarred by sin. So people were impotent in being able to serve God and reflect righteousness, and this left them eternally culpable before God (Rom. 1:18–3:20). In other words, they were powerless to live spiritually in a way that was honoring to God. So God went to work in justifying them through the work of Christ on the cross and the resurrection-ascension (Rom. 3:21–4:25). However, Paul's gospel does not stop at God forgiving sin and declaring those who trust in Christ justified. The gospel does not go up merely through Romans 4. It proceeds on through Romans 8. Here is where the power and potency for righteousness enters in, for Paul goes on in Romans 5–8 to discuss sanctification and the entry of the Spirit into the life in such a way that righteousness is now possible. In fact, it is even characteristic of the one who experiences the new birth. Here is where the gospel is *power*. That power is the enabling presence of the Spirit, who in turn directs us into righteousness. The reason the gospel was good news to Paul was not just because it "saves" us but also because it frees us and enables us to live a life that can honor God. The gospel, then, is not about a momentary transaction, as important as God's declaring us righteous through Christ is. Rather, the gospel for Paul is about a permanently enabled relationship with God rooted in the Spirit that is the essential gift of the gospel indicating that we are truly children of God. We are enabled from the heart and from head to toe. People who, because of sin, could not honor and worship God, can now have a life of responsive worship to God, a worship rooted in righteousness (Rom. 12:1–2).

A moment's reflection on the Old Testament and its images of purity help us here. When one is either unclean or has sinned (the two concepts are not the same), one needs cleansing. This involved either a washing or a sacrifice that cleansed. However, the point of the cleansing or the sacrifice was that the impurity or sin was removed, so that one was now forgiven or cleansed, freed from that impurity so that service for God and the nearness of his presence became possible again. So one is washed or forgiven so that fellowship with God can begin anew. This pictures salvation as well. We are a dirty and powerless vessel that God through Christ both cleanses and forgives. Now that the vessel is washed and clean, God's Spirit can enter in to do his work. This is very much what is pictured in the baptism of the Spirit depicted in Romans 6:2–4. We are raised out of death into new life, a new life that God makes provision for through his Spirit.

Jesus made the same point in his Sermon on the Mount (Matt. 5–7), and the ministry of John the Baptist makes this same point in a slightly different way. Disciples are called to be righteous and reflect sonship with God. Only one ruled by God and participating in the effective presence of his kingship can live this way. This is what being a follower of Jesus, a disciple, means. John the Baptist prepared for Jesus' coming and the coming of this kingdom and its dynamic rule by preaching its approach and telling his audience that while he only baptized with water, one coming after him was greater. That greater one to come would baptize with the Spirit and fire. In other words, the sign of the arrival of the Promised One would be the arrival of the Spirit through the Messiah (Luke 3:15–16). Of course, the Baptist was pointing to Jesus. Thus, the righteousness of the kingdom called for in disciples through the Sermon on the Mount (and its parallel of the Sermon on the Plain in Luke 6:20–49) becomes possible because his disciples have access to the Spirit. This point is illustrated in Luke 24:49, Acts 1:8, and 2:14–41, where the promised Spirit coming down on God's people enables them to witness effectively for God. It is reaffirmed in Acts 11:15–17, where Peter calls the coming of the Spirit the beginning (v. 15), and he cites the promise of John the Baptist about the bringing of the Spirit through Messiah, a gift that comes through faith in the Lord Jesus Christ.

Not only is this an emphasis of Paul and of Jesus in the Synoptics, but Jesus teaches it again to us in John's gospel. One of the most important themes of the Upper Room Discourse is that Jesus' approaching departure will enable him to send to them the Paraclete, yet another reference to the Spirit. His presence will free them up to do what God's people are called to do. The Spirit's presence is the basis for Jesus' exhortation to abide in him and bear fruit, abiding in his love. Once again, the gift of the Spirit is what enables righteousness, obedience, and love. The Spirit is given and enables us in our relationships. Thus evidence of spiritual formation will show itself in the quality of our relationships: "By this everyone will know that you are my disciples, if you have love for one another" (John 13:35 NRSV).

Now anyone familiar with the Old Testament would recognize that these themes are not new, for built into the hope of the new covenant was the offer of the forgiveness of sins and the idea that God would place his law on his people's hearts (Jer. 31:31–34), that is, God would do a spiritual work from within the person. The result is that people will know God and will not need to be taught. The picture here is not that there will be no need for teaching and teachers but that those who are spiritual respond to and are drawn to God's teaching (John 6:44–45). Ezekiel pictured the result from the standpoint of purity, a point we made above. For him, a corrupt vessel is washed and cleansed (forgiveness), which in turn frees up that washed, now clean vessel to be indwelt by God's Spirit (36:24–27). The result is a people who follow God's statutes. It is this imagery Jesus discussed with Nicodemus, though the rabbi did not understand him (John 3).

The sum of all these allusions is that the Spirit of God empowers us, not for miracles, but for a righteous, God-honoring life lived out in the context of community and healthy relationships (Titus 2:11–14). The gospel is about a renewed, unending, enabled relationship with God, which liberates us to live well with others. It is eternal, not just in duration but in quality (John 10:10). That is why it is called the abundant life. That is why Jesus defines eternal life as knowing the Father and the Son in John 17:3.

Formation is simply drawing on the resources the Spirit provides because he has invaded our space and made it holy for God. In sum, spiritual formation not only allows us to know and worship God, but it also does so in such a way that we live authentically with integrity. The Spirit takes us in this direction. He is committed to transforming us so that growth results. God does that through the events of our lives. We are liberated to participate in healthy community (Eph. 2:1–22) and to incarnate how God relates to humanity by reflecting our sonship in how we relate to those who do not know him (Matt. 5:14–16; Luke 6:27–36).

Who We Are and How We Are Enabled: Spiritual Identity

The image of God filling a vessel is also prominent in the New Testament. There are texts that describe both the individual (1 Cor. 6:19) and the resulting corporate body of believers as a holy dwelling place of God (1 Cor. 3:16; Eph. 2:11–22; 1 Peter 2:5). Interestingly, it is the community that is described this way more often than the individual. For God, it is our position together and our task together that stands at the core of spiritual formation.

No text brings this out more vividly than Ephesians 2:11–22. Here people formerly at odds with each other, Jews and Gentiles, are united into a new holy place God is building. Through the entire passage, the themes of peace and reconciliation sing out a peace that is not only with God but also with others in the community (2:14–17). And in 2:19–22, the Greek prefix σύν (*syn*) appears attached to several terms to convey the ideas of being *fellow* citizens with the saints and of being built *together* and joined *together.* These make the point that God works especially through community. The individualism that pervades our culture and that works against community and having a commitment to it also works against developing spiritual growth.

In terms of personal integrity, 1 Corinthians 6:12–20 is an important passage. Our individual physical bodies have been made holy by God, by his indwelling. Our promised, future resurrection means that even our flesh has spiritual significance and should be treated as holy as well.

Our identity as children before God allows him "to form" our thinking about who we are and what we engage in. Certain practices do not fit with who God has made us to be. But beyond a cognitive understanding is a relational dimension to formation, for it is our sense of relationship with and connectedness to God that reinforces the identity God has given us with his Spirit. It is not only because we understand in our minds that we are a children of God set apart to honor him but also because we sense that allegiance deep in our hearts that we move in the direction of holiness he calls us to take. This heartfelt connection to God is what Jonathan Edwards called "religious affections." This is why disciplines in which we spend time with God are so important. They serve to reinforce our relational connection with God and affirm our continued allegiance to him. These disciplines, as well as our association with the holy community, serve to ground and remind us that we are his. We are not, as our culture repeatedly teaches us, independent agents free to live and do whatever we choose.

The transformation God has formed within us is detailed when one reviews the conceptual backdrop to the togetherness expressed in Ephesians 2:11–22. That backdrop is Paul's prayer for the believer's appreciation of God's hope, riches, and power in Ephesians 1:15–2:10. On behalf of those he has saved, God has exercised spiritual power like that which raised Jesus from the dead. Just as Jesus is raised above all rule, authority, power, and dominion, and every name that has been named, both in this age and in the one to come (Eph. 1:20–21), so also God in his love and mercy has made us alive *together*, raised us *together*, and seated us *together* in the heavenly places with Christ (2:4–6). In this passage, as in Ephesians 2:11–22, the key prefix σύν (*syn*, "with, together") reappears.

However, there is yet another key point made here that goes beyond our being made into a community. This prayer says we are seated with Christ in heaven, which is part of what makes us heavenly citizens according to Philippians 3:20. This means that we also are seated above all rule and authority. The power that we have access to as a result of our position in Christ and the gift of the Spirit is greater than any sinister force that stands opposed to us. "Greater is He who is in you than he who is in the world" (1 John 4:4 NASB). This means that the empowerment for spiritual victory resides in the resources God has given to us. All we need to be formed he has made available to us. Ephesians 1:3 describes it as being blessed with every spiritual blessing from heaven.

However, one other point in this text should not be missed. The raising God has performed is of *us together*. The resources we are to draw on are best used when they take place in the context of our connectedness to each other. In other words, Paul's point is not that God raised each one of us one at a time, but that our empowerment came as a corporate entity. *This connectedness was designed so that we work in concert with each other.* Any doubt of this is erased when one thinks of Jesus' last prayer before he faced the cross in John 17, a prayer for unity among believers. This point is also seen in Ephesians 4:1–16 when one examines the reason for the spiritual gifts Christ gives in the community. It is for our mutual edification. The assumption of all of these texts is that spiritual formation is a very public, corporate exercise. Unlike a diet or an exercise program, God's program for getting us into spiritual shape requires our working out alongside others. Those believers who dislike assembling with the church or who shun small groups are missing one of the great means God uses to form us (Heb. 10:19–25). Those ministries that think only of what they should be doing and are hesitant to work with other like-minded believers are missing a key element of what empowers ministry and growth.

Texts like Ephesians 2:4–6 present this fundamental identity. This identity is crucial to a healthy spiritual formation. Many believers see themselves as fundamentally conflicted. They see their walk in terms of a great daily battle between their old, sinful self and the new, spiritual self, a kind of spiritual WWE battle of the good guy and the bad. Each day is a battle to see who pins whom. It is a life of conflict and tension. They are like a neutral rope in this tug-of-war, being constantly pulled to and fro. Now Scripture does portray such a conflict using the imagery of our flesh to make the point, but Paul would argue that this portrait *is* fundamentally flawed in describing who we really are in Christ. It sells short what God has made of us in Christ. His point would be, "Do you not see what God has made you to be and what resources he has provided for you? You are an exalted, holy child of God who sits above any force trying to bring you down. Your line of descent is now rooted in God, not in your flawed humanity. Drawing on what he has provided, you have the mind of Christ and can live in righteousness." The difference is important, for in the conflict self-portrait, when I sin I tend to excuse it by saying, "I am only a weak, sinful human. It is only natural." However, Paul would say, "No, that is not right. What sin is represents a fundamental betrayal of your new identity and enablement in Christ, a failure to draw on the rich resources of grace and a failure to be responsive to the Spirit's leading and presence. You can now live for God and not sin" (Rom. 8:1–14). That is being spiritually formed because all the elements for success have already been provided. This is now who you are.

This is not to argue that we are perfect or that Paul is presenting an unrealistic idealism. Sin still intrudes into our walk, but it does so when we respond unnaturally and unspiritually, failing to be responsive to God. God graciously has provided for such moments of spiritual failure as well, granting us the forgiveness we need to be restored into relationship. However, what God wishes us to appreciate about his promise is that our most fundamental identity is inclined to him, because his Spirit is a mark of our sonship. The believer who truly identifies with God and being a part of his community seeks to honor and represent God and that community in a manner that pleases the Lord. What this also means is that failure in the spiritual life is our fault and responsibility.

This sonship is also not to be seen merely in individual terms. Another important text comes later in Ephesians 4:17–24. Here the spiritual exhortation is to not walk like the world, or as Paul puts it, like the Gentiles. As Ephesians 2:10 already said, God has made us a new creation, created for good works that God designed so that we could walk in them.[3] Thus, the Ephesians 4 passage goes on to urge us to put off the old man, be renewed in our minds, and put on the new.[4] Most who read this text inject the already discussed old nature/new nature elements into this passage for the old man and new man. Some translations compound the problem by translating the text this way, referring incorrectly to putting off and putting on the old and new *nature*. However in Ephesians 2:15, the new man was defined already as the "new community." It is a corporate image to describe a group, not an internal individual trait. A glance at Galatians

3. See also Titus 2:14, which in explaining the grace of God makes it clear that Christ died to provide forgiveness *and* "to purify for himself a people who are truly his, who are eager to do good" (NET).

4. An interpretive issue creeps in here. In Greek the exhortations in verses 22–24 are given through infinitives, which means that their force is disputed. Are they to be read as indicatives, making statements that we have put off the old man, are being renewed, and have put on the new man? Or are they to be read as imperatives, exhorting us to put off the old man, be renewed, and put on the new man? It is hard to be certain. If indicatives are meant, then everything said above about designed identity is also the point here. God has made you so that you need not walk as the world. However, I prefer the reading that sees an imperatival force. I would argue that the sequence is for imperatives. For if God has put off our old man and put on the new as a past act, then the ongoing renewal of the mind, expressed in a present tense, should have been last in a list of what God is doing. In the new man I am now renewed daily. But the renewal of the mind is second in the sequence. So I read the text to be calling us to "change clothes." Put off the old man, engage in the process of renewing the mind, an ongoing spiritual exercise, and put on the new man.

3:28 confirms this reading. For in the new man, there is neither Greek nor Jew, Barbarian nor Scythian, slave nor free person. These descriptions show that a community made up of such people groups is what the "new man" is.

So what does this mean for our exhortation? I am not to walk like the world, because I am being called to "put off" my association with the world and its practices as a matter of who I am. The clothes I wear will not be as a citizen of the world. I am to engage daily in the renewal of my mind and put on my clothes as a representative of the new community of Christ to which I now belong. My spiritual identity is that I now belong to *and represent* him. This means certain activity is beneath my identity, while other character traits reflect him and his people. Just like one engaged in a war does not fight for the enemy, so too the believer identifies with his side and seeks to represent his community faithfully in the great spiritual cosmic conflict. This identity element in spiritual formation means commitment to Christ means appreciating our relatedness to his children and community.

One other point in Ephesians 4 is important. In 4:20–24, there are two references to truth, which in turn look back to an expression in 4:15, which literally should be translated "truthing in love." This last phrase is often translated "speaking the truth in love." This decidedly waters down the idea. What Paul is noting is that truth, as he is describing it here, permeates the entirety of life. It is more than speech. To live a spiritual life of moral integrity and righteousness before God is to be "truthing" one's way through life. It was in this way that the Ephesians had been taught that "truth was in Jesus" (v. 21) and that they had been created "according to God in the righteousness and holiness of the truth" (v. 24, translation mine). Thus, the truth expressed here is not merely the right teaching of Christian doctrine but an incarnated truth reflective of the very character of God. It is to live a spiritually formed and informed life. Spiritual formation at its essence is the process by which God in Christ through the Spirit forms his effective presence and character within our spirit. Paul is saying that such truth cannot be formed apart from an identity with and engagement of him and his community.

This community identification is also seen in how Jesus taught his disciples how to pray. The Lord's Prayer, which really is the prayer the Lord gave to his disciples to pray, shows this same emphasis. I am not called to pray for my daily bread, for the forgiveness of my sins, and so that I should not be led into temptation; rather we are called to intercede for the body as a spiritual exercise: Give us *our* daily bread; forgive *our sins*; lead *us* not into temptation. Once again we see how spiritual formation is not a private affair but a corporate exercise, designed to be carried out in community, a community of holiness that is remade by God and actively engages in mutual intercession.

Spiritual formation is about a divine work of transformation of heart and character, but it also aims at an engagement with others. When a person comes to new life in Christ through faith, God provides all the elements necessary for spiritual growth. The Spirit is certainly the major component, but also important is the community, both in terms of encouraging the believer in growth and as a point of identification and representation. My identity and calling as a believer is inseparably bound to this community because it is Christ's body, just as I am. All of these texts assume that we share in the task God has called us to share in and that we need one another. When we identify with him, we identify with one another. When we find our identity in him, we share in that identity with other members of the body. Thinking spiritually means appreciating this divine bond that God has given us by seating us together with him. It is to recognize how fundamental our sense of identity is to our spiritual well-being. We are his children, able to represent him in the world faithfully. We are enabled by his Spirit and are motivated in that enablement through the association we have with his body and the representation (witness and reflection in our way of living) we are to make of him and them.

What We Are to Bring: An Open and Seeking Heart

An essential component of this relationship with God is what we bring to it. We must have an open and seeking heart: a heart that seeks him and the communal fellowship he desires for us. The Old Testament states this simply when it says, "The beginning of wisdom is the fear of the LORD" (Prov. 1:7, translation mine). More pictorially is the image from Proverbs 2:1–5, which reads:

> My child,
> if you receive my words,
> and store up my commands within you,
> by making your ear attentive to wisdom,
> and by turning your heart to understanding,
> indeed, if you call out for discernment,
> and raise your voice for understanding,
> if you seek it like silver,
> and search for it like hidden treasure,
> then you will understand how to fear the LORD,
> and you will discover knowledge about God. (NET)

Here is the explanation for how to find wisdom and the fear of God. It is to be received within us. It is to be sought by being called out for. It is to be pursued as the world pursues silver and gold. This last image is the powerful one. How many of us give the same amount of attention to our spiritual lives as we or the world gives to the pursuit of wealth or any other key life goal? What is called for here is a seeking and open heart that is receptive to the things of God. Thus, in a similar vein, Jesus calls for us to have ears to hear (e.g., Matt. 11:15; Mark 4:23; Luke 8:8). Paul calls on us to have our minds transformed so that we can know God's will (Rom. 12:2).

The most important element we bring to the spiritual table is our open and receptive heart for the things of God.

The Goal of Formation: Holiness and Mission in the Community and to a Needy World—What Does It Look Like?

The roles we undertake as we are spiritually formed are also important to consider, for the goal of formation is that we carry out the will of God. Our sanctification is a major concern of God (1 Thess. 4:4; Titus 2:11–14). Perhaps no passage summarizes this concern as well as Galatians 5:2–6:10. In 5:5, Paul notes that it is for the hope of righteousness that we were given the Spirit by faith. This is certainly more than merely being declared righteous in the future. The hope is that God will make us righteous. What is significant is a faith working through love. This involves a living trust that is responsive to God, to his leading and provision. Fulfilling the calling of God is summarized in 5:14, where the call is to love one's neighbor as oneself.

The walk of the Spirit is a walk by means of the Spirit following what Paul calls the desires of the Spirit and not the desires of the flesh (5:16–17). The one who walks in this way bears the fruit of the Spirit, a series of characteristics that are relational in thrust: love, joy, peace, patience, kindness, goodness, faithfulness, gentleness, and self-control (5:22–23). What is so important to note about the fruit of the Spirit is how relational these virtues are. They cannot be worked out in isolation from others. They assume engagement with the community and even the world.

Those who belong to the Spirit have crucified the flesh (5:24). Paul's point here is the one made above. More fundamental than any conflict the believer has with the flesh is the fact that a victory over the flesh and a severing of relationship to it has taken place in Christ.

Everything about this passage argues that spiritual formation yields a character that seeks God's desires, responds to him, and then relates well to others. The passage ends in 6:9–10 with an exhortation that calls us to not "grow weary in doing good" and "let us do good to all people, and especially to those who belong to the family of faith" (NET). The holiness God calls believers to possess is never designed to be exercised in a private, withdrawn, or disengaged way. The expectation is that our holiness will reach out to those around us, a fragrant aroma to God and before humanity (2 Cor. 2:15).

As God's representatives we are called to proclaim his way in word and deed. It is a "prophetic" role, not in the technical sense of giving revelation, but in the sense of setting forth to a needy world an explanation and illustration of God's way. Numerous images drive home the point that we are equipped for this mission.

Whether one thinks of Mark 10:35–45; Luke 24:49 with Acts 1:8; or Acts 13:47, the call is to be a servant who, being empowered by God, is to serve as light before the world. Acts 13 is particularly significant. Here Paul and Barnabas describe their call in terms of the Servant who is a light to the Gentiles. One would think that a text describing Isaiah's servant would refer to Jesus, but Paul's point here appears to be that Jesus' task is taken up by those who follow him. So Ephesians 5:7–14 calls us to walk as children of light in holiness. Our walk should be such that we are able to offer an invitation to others to awake and experience the light that Christ provides.

Sometimes such an outreach will involve risk, persecution, and suffering (2 Cor. 4:17–18; Heb. 12:1–11). The assumption is that God's people are engaged, challenging the world and its ways through the character the Spirit produces. This emphasis on engaging is against any kind of community withdrawal or spiritual isolationism, a danger the church always faces in a hostile world. Often, the church opts to withdraw and play it safe. But this is not reflective of God's call for engagement in mission. Whatever disciplines we pursue in private to get right with God should bring us out into the public square to love, pray, and care for others.

This is why another common image for believers is that of priests, who also are alien ambassadors (1 Peter 2:9–12). The end of this text is also revealing as it reads, "Maintain good conduct among the Gentiles, so that in case they speak against you as wrongdoers, they may see your good deeds and glorify God on the day of visitation" (RSV). This image highlights how our citizenship is now a heavenly one, where we represent God. Our actions are designed to speak to and for him (Phil. 3:20–21; 2 Cor. 5:14–21). Colossians 3, also pointing to the character that emerges from being renewed, stresses how we should be so "heavenly minded" and grounded that we are "earthly good." This is accomplished by putting on "as God's chosen ones, holy and beloved, compassion, kindness, lowliness, meekness, and patience, forbearing one another and, if one has a complaint against another, forgiving each other; as the Lord has forgiven you, so you also must forgive. And above all these put on love, which binds everything together in perfect harmony" (vv. 12-14 RSV). Once again the presence of spiritual enablement translates into healthy relational engagement with others, especially within the community.

Thus, spiritual formation is far from a private exercise between God and myself as an individual believer. Though he does the work in me, it is never just for my own benefit. God renews us, so that we can be ambassadors of renewal for others, whether as encouragement for the edification of other believers or as witnesses of light to those who sit in darkness.

I close with three practical examples, one negative and two positive. These could be multiplied in a wide variety of ways at a myriad of churches around the world. I believe each illustrates how spiritual formation calls us to challenging engagement in a way that stretches our community to rely on the Spirit and challenges the world with a contrary example.

The negative example was an effort by our community and other churches to show how the compassion of Christ addressed the tragic situation caused by AIDS. In the late eighties our church banded together with several other churches to form an organization known as AIM (Alternative Identity Ministries). The goal was to provide outreach, friendship, fellowship, and counseling to those who had been struck by this killer disease. The goal was to minister and reach out to the alternative lifestyle community. Part of the cost of supporting such a ministry involved providing the counseling and support necessary to those trying to leave that lifestyle. With much hope we launched out in this cooperative church effort, with the hope that our spiritual growth had come to the point that we could take on the risk. Sadly, the ministry could not be sustained. What happened is that many in some of the church communities began to worry what would happen if many of those we ministered to showed up in their communities. In short, they panicked when they saw the risk of engaging and reaching out. Social pressures and fear caused enough to withdraw that we could not keep the ministry going. The effort was not a waste, however, as some were reached and in the process we learned much about our own spiritual health as a community.

More positively, our first church plant was intentionally planned for the poorest part of our city. We figured that enough churches had moved out of the city and that suburban church plants already had been covered by others. It required an ethnic crossover and racial cooperation. Fortunately we had an African-American who felt a call to go back into the inner city and minister in his childhood neighborhood. What followed was a spiritually instructive exercise that had several churches cooperating again. After a decade, the church was self-sustaining. It had built a gymnasium-sanctuary that was reaching out into the community. There was a school formed. Our church membership had numerous women who regularly went together down to the church to offer tutoring for the children. Spiritual support for African-American families was provided so that today there are many healthy families, whose life profiles stand out in contrast to the world around them, shining as spiritual lights in one of the darkest areas of the city. Many children have graduated from the school and gone to college. Some have come back to teach at the school to provide for another generation. The work is now self-sustaining. The progress has been so amazing and contrastive to most other more tense, racial realities in our city that it has been the subject of newspaper editorials with titles like "Angels for Christ."

Similar in impact was the churchwide response to Hurricane Katrina in 2005. What the government could not do with millions of dollars behind it, the church, working with others in the community, provided. No other organization could amass such a support group in a dire emergency. This input was so valuable that papers like the *New York Times* wrote editorials about the values of the contribution made by people of faith. Sometimes carrying out the mission brings with it a clear message that the church can and does care.

Here is a spiritual formation that has translated into community terms. The incarnation of spiritual virtues is so powerful that effective outreach has taken place. God is honored and the world sees the compassionate face of the church. None of this could take place without people thinking that spiritual formation means being able to risk depending on God in faith and seeking to have that faith work in surprising ways. Without a spiritually functioning, divinely dependent, praying community, none of this would be possible.

Conclusion

We have argued that spiritual formation possesses (1) an agent—the Spirit; (2) a dynamic—growth in the context of community identification; (3) a requirement—an open and seeking heart; and (4) a goal—holiness in the context of mission. There is no magic formula for how it takes place other than that people seek to draw upon provisions God has given them. Spiritually formed people possess a desire and a heart that says, "Thy will, not my will, be done." In the process, the Spirit does his transforming work, shaping us into the likeness of God. Those character traits lead into the expression of holiness and the pursuit of community. Engagement and mission follows, for as the Father reaches out to the lost, so also his children are formed to reach out to the world. Spiritual formation seeks to let God make us to be like him. God sent his Son to engage the world through a life and death of service and dependence on God. In making us his children, he makes it clear that his Son is not alone in pursuing the task. Only appreciating what it means to be spiritually formed and acting on it will allow us to accomplish the call God has given us to go into the world and share the gospel. Surely a key component of sharing the gospel is giving evidence of being spiritually transformed by that which comes with it.

Part 2

Practicing the Elements of Spiritual Formation

CHAPTER 5

THE SOUL AND SPIRITUAL FORMATION

Klaus Issler

> The good man brings good things out of the good stored up in his heart, and the evil man brings evil things out of the evil stored up in his heart. For out of the overflow of his heart his mouth speaks.
>
> —Luke 6:45

Recently, I was in a line of cars stopped at an intersection waiting for a red light when the railroad-crossing signal sounded off. The long mechanical arm lowered across the road to prevent my way forward. I happened to look in my rearview mirror and noticed a man in the car directly behind me. He was engaged in an animated conversation with someone, but I didn't see anyone else in the car. Then I realized he wasn't happy about waiting for the train to pass. Perhaps he was late for a business appointment. Maybe his wife was in labor at the nearby hospital. In the mirror, I was watching this man fully bursting with rage, yelling obscenities nonstop at the top of his lungs, while the train passed. He went from Silent Sam alone in his car to Raging Roger in ten seconds flat. But I chuckled—not at him but at myself. Before my own self-acknowledgment of sin in this same area, I would have been overwhelmed by feelings of contempt for this performance behind me. Although I'm far from being out of the woods on this, I'm still finding more peace inside. I'm becoming more aware of the dark side of my heart and of God's grace, which is healing more and more of my self-righteousness. So my chuckle was one of identification rather than judgment.

When life is moving along well, it seems it's much easier to be loving and joyful and peaceful. But when we hit the speed bumps of life, we often give evidence to a much different side of our character. Jesus tells us, "The good man brings good things out of the good stored up in his heart, and the evil man brings evil things out of the evil stored up in his heart. *For out of the overflow of his heart his mouth speaks*" (Luke 6:45, emphasis mine). For the man in the car behind me, I observed a heart or inner life that had formed a readiness to erupt in an overt, angry tirade given certain circumstances. I get a bit short with my wife when I'm into my "on-task" mode at home or when I'm behind on a project that has come due and I'm trying to do some last-minute touch-up on that project before leaving for work. Can you remember a time recently when you were a bit short with family or roommates? Or perhaps someone was a bit short with you and you responded in kind. Or, if the stress was increased, consider your "worst" nightmare, twenty-four-hour period, when everything seems to go badly. How do you or I handle that? How do we respond to those around us? The question of this chapter confronts us: "Is it possible that a heart can be so formed that we infrequently or rarely bear such bad fruit, despite the circumstances?"

Jesus Shows Us the Way

The last twenty-four hours of Jesus' life, before his tortuous death on the cross, was an extensive trial and test of the formation and rootedness of his heart. Imagine the wide range of thoughts and emotions that Jesus experienced, including the excruciating physical abuse. What is remarkable is that Jesus endured these extreme trials without ever sinning (Heb. 2:14; 4:15)! And I don't think we should explain away this triumph by saying that Jesus' perfectly formed heart was the result of Jesus' tapping into his own divine powers. That would cheapen the victory and Jesus' example for us.[1] Let us, then, ponder some of the difficult events of his last twenty-four hours.

In the upper room, thirteen men had gathered for the Passover Feast, all with dirty feet. Since no one had volunteered to do this menial task, reserved for the lowliest of slaves, Jesus humbled himself and slowly washed each foot (John 13:4–17). Later (or before) another dispute arose among the disciples as to who was the greatest among them (Luke 22:24–27; cf. Luke 9:46–48 for a previous dispute), an event that may have prompted Jesus' example of humility. He concluded his comments to them on humility with the words, "But I am among you as one who serves" (Luke 22:27). When the thought of his betrayal crossed his mind, Jesus became troubled in spirit and announced, "I tell you the truth, one of you is going to betray me" (John 13:21). A few minutes later Jesus sent Judas off to betray him, saying, "What you are about to do, do quickly" (John 13:27).

Jesus also warned the disciples, telling them, "Satan has asked to sift you [all] as wheat" (Luke 22:31). Then, addressing Peter, Jesus said, "But I have prayed for you, Simon, that your faith may not fail. And when you have turned back, strengthen your brothers" (Luke 22:32). But Peter

1. For further study of the example of Jesus' life, see my chapter, "Jesus' Example: Prototype of the Dependent, Spirit-Filled Life," in *Jesus in Trinitarian Perspective: An Introductory Christology*, ed. Fred Sanders and Klaus Issler (Nashville: Broadman & Holman, 2007), 189–225.

wasn't comforted by Jesus' prayer for him; rather Peter defended his loyalty to Jesus, declaring he would go with Jesus even "to death" (Luke 22:33). Jesus then confronted Peter's pride, explaining that Peter would actually deny him three times! Later, following their last meal together and Jesus' teaching in the upper room, Jesus and the band of disciples (now without Judas) walked to the Gethsemane garden to pray, as was their custom. Perhaps it was here when Jesus' high priestly prayer was offered to the Father (recorded in John 17; John has no record of the struggling prayer in the garden).

In the garden, Jesus confided to his closest friends—Peter, James, and John—how horribly he felt, and he invited them to pray for him.

> Then Jesus went with his disciples to a place called Gethsemane, and he said to them, "Sit here while I go over there and pray." He took Peter and the two sons of Zebedee along with him, and he began to be sorrowful and troubled. Then he said to them, "My soul is overwhelmed with sorrow to the point of death. Stay here and keep watch with me." (Matt. 26:36–38)

After Jesus' struggle had been resolved with the Father, the betrayer and a multitude carrying swords and clubs arrived. The brief moment of Jesus' arrest displays a diverse array of personal challenges. Consider how Jesus responded to each. First, Jesus is betrayed by one of his own disciples, with the sign of a kiss. "Judas, are you betraying the Son of Man with a kiss?" (Luke 22:48), Jesus asked. In frustration he commanded Peter to put his sword away after Peter had lopped off Malchus's ear: "Put your sword back in its place . . . for all who draw the sword will die by the sword" (Matt. 26:52). "No more of this!" (Luke 22:51). After Jesus was seized and arrested, all the disciples abandoned him—including the three who were closest to him who couldn't keep watch for an hour (Matt. 26:56). Yet, in the midst of this sordid affair, Jesus' heart went out to Malchus, one of his "enemies." "And [Jesus] touched the man's ear and healed him" (Luke 22:51).

What was the key to Jesus' sense of security and passive reception to the arrest? At that moment, the attention of all the powers and principalities in the heavenlies was centered on the activities in the garden. And yet, despite the great temptations of distraction to sin, Jesus remained centered, centered in God's will and God's love, completely dependent on the Father. To Peter, Jesus affirmed, "Do you think I cannot call on my Father, and he will at once put at my disposal more than twelve legions of angels? But how then would the Scriptures be fulfilled that say it must happen in this way?" (Matt. 26:53–54). "Put your sword away! Shall I not drink the cup the Father has given me?" (John 18:11).[2]

---

2. Perhaps, in confronting the multitude, Jesus also experienced some anger at Satan for bringing this evil into the world: "But this is your hour—when darkness reigns" (Luke

But the "nightmare" did not end there; this was just the beginning. Jesus endured "mock trials" before Annas, father-in-law of Caiaphas the high priest (John 18:13–24), before Caiaphas (Mark 14:53–65), before the Sanhedrin (Mark 15:1), twice before Pilate (John 18:28–19:16), and before Herod (Luke 23:6–12). In the midst of false accusations, severe beatings in the face and head, being spit upon, and being scourged by professional soldiers—portrayed so abusively in the movie *The Passion of the Christ*—Jesus' capacity to remain silent (Mark 14:61; Luke 23:9; Matt. 27:14) and not respond in kind "amazed" even Pilate (Mark 15:5). Furthermore, the hatred of his own nation and its religious leadership was so spiteful that they preferred that Pilate release a murderer rather than extend any grace to Jesus (Matt. 27:20–21)!

Finally, having endured so well all the abuse to this point, including lack of sleep and food, Jesus was nailed to the cross, one of the cruelest forms of torture known to humanity. And his first recorded words were, "Father, forgive them, for they do not know what they are doing" (Luke 23:34)! Later, Jesus extended grace to the thief crucified next to him (Luke 23:42–43) and also gave his mother into the care of his disciple John (John 19:26–27).[3] The gospel writers record as the judgment for the sins of the world was being paid, Jesus cried out in anguish and desolation, "My God, my God, why have you forsaken me?" (Mark 15:34; cf. Ps. 22:1). Soon after came Jesus' cry of triumph, "It is finished" (John 19:30), followed by his words, "Father, into your hands I commit my spirit" (Luke 23:46; cf. Ps. 31:5) and his passing from death to life. Can we fathom such quality of a formed heart that endures such abuse, offers such grace, and bears the sins of the world, all while steadfastly remaining secure in the Father? As Dallas Willard notes, "A carefully cultivated heart will, assisted by the grace of God, foresee, forestall, or transform most of the painful situations before which others stand like helpless children saying 'Why?'"[4] And it is this kind of heart that God wishes to form in us, "to be conformed to the likeness of his Son" (Rom. 8:29; cf. Eph. 4:24).

Giving Sufficient Emphasis to Cultivating Our Heart

External Versus Internal Righteousness

In his parable contrasting the prayers of the Pharisee and the tax collector (Luke 18:9–14), Jesus reminds us we can't rely only on external righteousness and obedience. The external life for this Pharisee (not an adulterer, one who fasted and tithed)—good actions by themselves—sadly stemmed

---

22:53), he said. He knew that Satan had entered into Judas (Luke 22:3; John 13:2) and had requested to sift like wheat the remaining disciples (Luke 22:31).

3. It's likely that John was a cousin of Jesus; that Mary, Jesus' mother, was John's aunt. See Michael Wilkins, *Following the Master: Discipleship in the Steps of Jesus* (Grand Rapids: Zondervan, 1992), 156.

4. Dallas Willard, *Renovation of the Heart: Putting on the Character of Christ* (Colorado Springs: NavPress, 2002), 14.

from an arrogant heart. The tax collector humbly beat his chest, recognized his sin, and begged for God's mercy. Jesus concluded, "I tell you that this man [tax collector], rather than the other [Pharisee], went home justified before God. For everyone who exalts himself will be humbled, and he who humbles himself will be exalted" (Luke 18:14). This parable highlights the need to bring not only our external life into harmony with God's kingdom but our internal life as well. "Good" external actions apart from a humble heart mean nothing to God.

In his teachings, Jesus often makes a distinction between outer actions and the internal movements of the heart.

> Make a tree good and its fruit will be good, or make a tree bad and its fruit will be bad, for a tree is recognized by its fruit. . . . For out of the overflow of the heart the mouth speaks. The good man brings good things out of the good stored up in him, and the evil man brings evil things out of the evil stored up in him. (Matt. 12:33–35; cf. Matt. 6:21; 15:18–20; Mark 7:20–23)

> These people honor me with their lips, but their hearts are far from me. (Matt. 15:8)

> You [Pharisees] are the ones who justify yourselves in the eyes of men, but God knows your hearts. What is highly valued among men is detestable in God's sight. (Luke 16:15; cf. 1 Sam. 16:7)

Furthermore Jesus teaches that we must forgive from within our inner life ("from [the] heart," Matt. 18:35) and that doubt within ("in [the] heart," Mark 11:23) is a barrier to our prayer life.[5]

After years of ministry as a pastor and now seminary professor, I was clueless about the deep layer of self-righteousness that permeated my own soul, a subtle pride that limited God's work in me and through me. At age forty-six I took time away from the routines and usual demands of life for a three-week "guided" spiritual retreat. God performed open-heart surgery, uncovering dark broodings of pride. Every day on the retreat, I visited with a spiritual mentor for an hour. The rest of the time was spent alone wasting time with God: praying, reading Scripture, singing, and journaling.

During the third week, prompted to read Romans, I knelt at my bed and read chapter 1. When I read verses 30 and 31 the words jumped out at me: "arrogant," "boastful," "unloving," "unmerciful." They became living and active words of conviction. For two hours, I sobbed in God's presence

---

5. For additional passages that emphasize the importance of the inner life over external deeds, see 1 Corinthians 13:1–3 and Revelation 2:1–5. An extreme case is mentioned by Jesus of those who do great works but have no personal relationship with him and will not enter Jesus' kingdom (see Matt. 7:21–23).

as I slowly reread God's Word. Tenderly yet forcefully the God who is holy pierced my pride. He exposed me at a deep experiential level regarding my desperate need for his mercy and continuing work in my life. Even today this profound, divine encounter continues to mark me as I am in the ongoing process of becoming more transparent, more merciful, and more loving. What I've been learning is that we can't just focus on *external* obedience—an exclusive focus that my outward actions are in line with biblical directives.

Consider Psalm 19:14: "May the words of my mouth and the meditation of my heart be pleasing in your sight, O LORD, my Rock and my Redeemer." Gerald Wilson explains, "The final plea is the psalmist's attempt to achieve alignment with God's will through inner ('meditations of my *heart*') and outer ('words of my *mouth*') integrity. The psalmist is submitting all to the will and purpose of Yahweh."[6] Or, as Henry Cloud and John Townsend frame it:

> Not only does obedience deal with all of life, but it also encompasses all of us, both *inside* and *out*. Obedience is far more profound than simply refraining from external sins such as lying, stealing, and committing adultery, though it certainly includes those. Obedience has also to do with submitting our values, emotions, and hearts to Christ's lordship. . . . This external and internal nature of obedience helps us to grow up spiritually. It helps us integrate various parts of our character that are either in conflict with or alienated from one another.[7]

Spiritual formation involves attention to *both* inside ("heart work") and outside ("mouth work"). The emphasis in this chapter centers on matters of the heart—of our inner life.

Our inner life encompasses various aspects, including those of which we are conscious, such as our thoughts, our self-talk, our conversations with God, our desires, and our aspirations. Yet our internal world also includes matters of which we are often unaware, such as nervous habits (e.g., clicking a ballpoint pen off and on) and more serious compulsions and addictions that often manifest themselves in outward actions as "blind spots"—what is obvious to others but not at all on our radar screen (e.g., usually turning in projects late because they have to be done just right to the nth degree [perfectionism], biting one's fingernails, always having to be doing something and feeling guilty when you relax [workaholism]). Furthermore, in some cases, we are aware of emotional states that can range from great joy and a

---

6. Gerald Wilson, *Psalms, Vol. 1*, The NIV Application Commentary (Grand Rapids: Zondervan, 2002), 372, emphasis mine.

7. Henry Cloud and John Townsend, *How People Grow: What the Bible Reveals About Personal Growth* (Grand Rapids: Zondervan, 2001), 284, emphasis mine.

settled peace to painful grief and woundedness. At other times, we are unaware of the emotional texture of our life (e.g., "I am not angry!" said with a bit of defiance, or erupting in defensive indignation when someone raises an innocent question about your goals).

Is Our Inner Life Really That Important?

But we might wonder, how is growing deeper in our relationship with God and our spiritual formation tied up with being more aware of our inner life? Why bother? We should "bother" because honesty before God is highly valued by God, as indicated in David's psalm of confession: "Surely you desire truth in *the inner parts*; you teach me wisdom in *the inmost place*" (Ps. 51:6, emphasis mine). Gerald Wilson explains that "the instruction to assume an attitude of intimate vulnerability with God uses two unusual terms to get the idea across."[8] The first term "inner parts" (Heb. *tuhôt*) is rarely used and occurs in only one other place, Job 38:36 (NASB and NIV translate it as "mind"). The other term, translated "inmost place" (Heb. *satûm*), appears more often, yet typically in a different context, that of "'plugging up' available water sources (wells, springs, channels) to prevent their use by another party" (e.g., Gen. 26:15,18; 2 Kings 3:19, 25; 2 Chron. 32:3–4, 30). Another use occurs in Ezekiel 28:3 and Daniel 8:26, that of "hiding away." Wilson draws the connection to Psalm 51:6: "God seeks open access to those parts of our lives that we chose to keep deeply hidden within our inner world."[9] To ignore God's invitation to be open to his searching gaze would indicate a willful resistance to his loving embrace in the deep parts of our life.

According to Jesus, we are often clueless about our own foibles, blind spots, and vices. Our focus is on identifying the speck of sawdust in another's eye, but we cannot see the huge plank jutting out of our own (Matt. 7:3–5)! So it will take some effort to turn our attention toward our own limitations, weaknesses, and sins—it's not natural. And we can invite God into this inner search. David the psalmist challenges us, "Examine me, God, and know my mind; probe me and know my anxieties [*śĕrāpîm*]. See if you can find in me the way of idolatry and guide me in the age-old way" (Ps. 139:23).[10] We may want to hide within, but if we wish to continue walking with God, particularly as we immerse ourselves in God's Word, God promises his divine promptings within, "For the word of God is living and active. Sharper than any double-edged sword, it penetrates even to dividing soul and spirit, joints and marrow; it judges the thoughts and attitudes of the heart. Nothing in all creation is hidden from God's sight. Everything is uncovered and laid bare before the eyes of him to whom we must give account" (Heb. 4:12–13).

---

8. Wilson, *Psalms*, 778.
9. Ibid., 779.
10. Translation by Leslie C. Allen, *Psalms 101–150*, Word Biblical Commentary 21 (Nashville: Thomas Nelson, 2002), 318.

Knowing God and Knowing Oneself

Thus, knowing God more deeply cannot be accomplished without simultaneously being willing *to know oneself*—what is often referred to as the "double knowledge": knowledge of God and knowledge of self.[11] John Calvin (d. 1564) opened his magisterial *Institutes of the Christian Religion* within this guiding framework: "Without knowledge of self there is no knowledge of God. . . . Without knowledge of God there is no knowledge of self."[12] The concept is evident in other writers, as well. Augustine (d. 430) wrote, "God, always the same, let me know myself, let me know Thee, I have prayed."[13] And Blaise Pascal (d. 1662) said, "Knowing God without knowing our wretchedness leads to pride. Knowing our wretchedness without knowing God leads to despair."[14] Hiding and personal detachment will only prevent deeper engagement with God.

The Formation of the Heart in Our Emotional Life

When we're in a boat on a windy day, it's fairly easy to feel the rocking and rolling movement of the boat as the waves lift us up and down. For some, this rolling action sets off physical sensors, and motion sickness takes over. Yet how adept are we at noticing the various movements and turbulence within our heart? One entry point for the formation of our heart that we need to give attention to is our emotional life.

Throughout the Old Testament the term "heart" (Heb. *lēb*) represents the self, including thoughts, feelings, and the will (e.g. Ps. 22:26; 1 Kings 3:12; Exod. 36:2); the word can even be interchangeable with "soul" (Heb. *nepeš*, e.g., Josh. 22:5, 1 Sam. 2:35).[15] Normally the New Testament follows this usage for "heart" (Gk. *kardia,* e.g., Luke 21:34, Acts 14:17, 2 Cor. 5:12) and is also occasionally used in parallel with "mind" (Gk. *nous*, e.g., 2 Cor. 3:14–15).[16]

Yet on a few occasions the Greek term *kardia* ("heart) refers specifically to our emotional life (e.g., Phil. 4:7, more detail below). For example, in the upper room Jesus acknowledged the grief in the disciples' hearts (John 16:6, 22a), but he desired that they not be troubled in heart (John 14:1, 27). Jesus

---

11. James Houston outlined the development of the "double knowledge" in a lecture at Biola University: "The Recovery of the Double Knowledge: Self-Knowledge in the Light of the Knowledge of God" (Institute for Spiritual Formation Lecture, Biola University, October 11, 1999).

12. John Calvin, *Institutes of the Christian Religion*, trans. Ford Lewis Battles (Philadelphia: Westminster, 1960), 1:35, 37. In the footnote section, the editor cites others who use the notion of the double knowledge (see 36–37).

13. Augustine, "Soliloquies," II, i, 1, *Nicene and Post-Nicene Fathers*, ed. Philip Schaff, first series (1888; repr., Peabody, MA: Hendricksen, 1995), 7:547.

14. Blaise Pascal, *Pensees and Other Writings*, trans. H. Levi (Oxford: Oxford University Press, 1995), fragment 225, p. 64.

15. T. Sorg, "Heart," in *The New International Dictionary of New Testament Theology*, ed. Colin Brown (Grand Rapids: Zondervan, 1976), 2:181.

16. Ibid., 182.

predicted that when he would see them after his resurrection their hearts would be filled with joy (John 16:22b). This particular usage of "heart" is similar to how we often use this word in conversation today. For example, someone might respond to a good Bible study by saying, "The truth not only reached my 'head' (my intellect), but it also touched my 'heart' (connected at a deep affective level)."

God used Philippians 4:6–7 to open the gate for me to finally welcome feelings as an important part of my life before him. "Do not be anxious about anything, but in everything, by prayer and petition, with thanksgiving, present your requests to God. And the peace of God, which transcends all understanding, will guard your hearts and your minds in Christ Jesus." Gerald Hawthorne explains that "this expression, 'the peace of God,' is found nowhere else in the New Testament. . . . Paul seems here to be referring to the tranquility of God's own eternal being, the peace of God which God himself has, the calm serenity that characterizes his very nature . . . which grateful, trusting Christians are welcome to share."[17]

Furthermore, Hawthorne clarifies that although the term *kardia* ("heart") in characteristic Hebrew fashion usually designates the whole person, a narrower focus is intended in this passage. "But here, where Paul places *kardia* [heart] alongside *noema* [mind] grammatically in such a way as to distinguish the one from the other . . . *kardia* [heart] very likely has its meaning narrowed simply to that of designating the seat of one's emotions or deepest feelings, or simply to the emotions and feelings themselves. . . . Together these words refer to the entire inner being of the Christian, his emotions, affections, thoughts and moral choices."[18]

I may be stating the obvious, but the promise of Philippians 4:7 is based on my ability to recognize when I'm anxious or worried—an emotional feeling (Phil. 4:6). If I'm not aware that I'm anxious, I won't be prompted to share my concerns with God and then receive his deep peace—another emotional feeling.

Do We Tend to Downplay the Importance of Emotions?

Only later in life have I come to appreciate the important role of my emotions. A "train diagram" I learned many years ago communicates a helpful albeit incomplete truth. In a campus ministry I was involved with, we used this particular analogy to emphasize the importance of believing in the factual truth of what the Bible taught, yet we unknowingly *deemphasized* the value of our feelings. The train diagram connected three key concepts together: fact, faith, and feeling. The train's engine represented "fact"; the coal car represented "faith"; and the caboose represented "feeling." The main point of the illustration was that

17. Gerald Hawthorne, *Philippians*, Word Biblical Commentary (Waco, TX: Word, 1983), 43:184.

18. Ibid., 185.

the train could run with or without "feeling," but "facts" and "faith" were essential—our faith in the biblical facts is the ground of identity as believers, regardless of how we feel about our relationship with God at any particular time.

The underlying motivation of the analogy is commendable: to encourage those whose conversion experience and Christian life did not come with or evidence any particularly strong emotional responses. If you didn't feel any different *after* responding to Jesus' call for his saving grace or during your subsequent walk with Jesus than you did *before* you became a Christian, then that was acceptable. Yet the unintended effect of this teaching was to present a nonemotional model for conversion and Christian living that actually became the *norm* for how to live the Christian life! Too much emotion was considered suspect, so "it's better to tone down that side of our life" we were told since "it really isn't that important anyway." For most of my Christian life I downplayed the legitimate role of emotions, but not anymore.

Henry Cloud and John Townsend share the story of a man who was a member of a small group. He desired greater intimacy with God, and his group encouraged him in this direction, but he wasn't yet free to talk at a "heart" level. He could communicate only from his "head": he talked about his thoughts and opinions rather than his feelings, or he would just change the subject to something more comfortable to talk about.

> Then one night he confessed how lonely he was, but at the same time how afraid he was of having others know him inside. The group grew closer to him, as they could feel his heart, and they had a great empathy for him. A marvelous thing happened. He began to sense the presence of both God and others within. He was no longer blocking people out. His confession began the process of repair.[19]

Just as this man did, I'm growing more in my emotional life as I've begun to trust others to guide me into a deeper and richer emotional life.

The remaining part of this chapter focuses mainly on this aspect of the heart, the inner world of our emotional life, and offers some suggested means for nurturing this kind of heart formation to encourage inner obedience and growth in Christlikeness.

Our Emotional Life Is an Essential Feature of Being Human

By God's design, we are all *emotional* beings. The sooner we can acknowledge this basic fact of life, the sooner we can make significant headway toward growing a tender heart that can listen to God and others. In his humanity, our Lord Jesus Christ displayed a wide array of emotions: he openly wept (John

19. Cloud and Townsend, *How People Grow*, 254–55.

11:35), he felt deep compassion for people (Mark 6:34), and he even displayed righteous anger (Mark 3:5). Some aspects of his emotional life were surveyed previously in his amazing demeanor during the final hours before death.

As mentioned earlier, during an extended time of retreat God abruptly made me aware of the deep stirrings and churnings of my soul that were hidden to me. He brought a deep-felt conviction to my heart of arrogance, self-righteousness, and pride. I pondered how this could be. For many years I've studied a lot about God, having been a pastor and now a seminary professor. Shouldn't I know any better? But I was clueless nonetheless. How did God do this? How did he begin tenderizing this proud and stubborn heart so that even my wife, Beth, felt more secure that I wouldn't just look out for my own interests, reacting to her and defending myself? It doesn't happen overnight. Over the years God has been slowly transforming a stoic, stubborn, workaholic into someone whose heart is now much more receptive to God, more open to hearing truth about myself, and more ready to weep with those who weep.

This growth process can be especially difficult for us males in Western culture. It's acceptable for men to engage themselves with full emotional energy at the baseball park or in front of the television watching the football game or even while singing with gusto at church. But otherwise men are expected to contain themselves, to be strong and silent. Weeping is considered wimpy. Not only men but also women in our culture may need to learn about experiencing a more healthy and robust emotional life for mature Christian living.

I've asked Beth to pen the following paragraph to offer an idea of what happened in our marriage that began the process by which God stirred both our hearts, independently of each other, to move closer to him and each other.

> After twenty-two years of marriage we needed some help. Over the years, I (Beth) had closed my heart to Klaus and begun to protect myself. Oh, we looked all right on the outside, dutifully doing all the things that committed Christian couples do together, but there was a growing defensiveness in my heart. I had tried over the years to get at the root of our issues, but for the most part I just reacted and didn't have a clue what was going on. The Lord kept nudging me that something was wrong, but I was too busy dodging the pain to really examine root causes. That came to a halt when Klaus had a devastating eye accident and I had to supervise his life and mine for several months. I realized I was competent and could do without him and all this pain that I thought he was causing in my life. That scared me. I was committed to my marriage vows and seeing them threatened really sobered me. From that point on, it took several years for both of us to realize we had contributed to the pain and what we both needed to do to repair it.

The Hidden Layer Underneath Disagreements

The state of our inner life affects our relationships. For example, a continuing difficulty in my marriage is how Beth and I resolve conflict when we disagree, or better, how we have difficulty fully resolving our conflicts. We would often generate more heat than light, and either the strongest on a particular issue would "win," or the one who gave in first would "lose." In the last couple of years, we have begun to make greater headway toward healthier disagreements by recognizing there are at least two important layers of any discussion and disagreement.

One layer relates to the *issue* of the disagreement. It's the most obvious layer, and so it was the one I focused on exclusively with my "head." Yet another layer was hidden from me but just as important. It relates to our *feelings* and *reactions*, about *how* we approached each other in a discussion, about our feelings regarding the points of our disagreement—matters of the "heart." It's critical to identify our feelings along with attending to the issue of the disagreement. This little insight has been saving us much emotional energy—energy we were expending uselessly during our disagreements without knowing it. It's a continuing struggle for me to focus on the feelings of the matter, not just the issue of disagreement.[20]

Within every one of our relationships, our emotions always have some part to play. And this fact also applies to our relationship with God. If we desire to deepen our intimacy with God, we need to become more aware of how our emotional life affects our walk with God. How we feel can either move us closer to God or move us farther away.

Our emotions can become a window to look into the state of our soul. But if we're basically unaware of our feelings—as I was for most of my life—then our emotional life actually becomes the hidden momentum and engine behind many of our actions. We *think* we're in the pilot seat of our life. But in reality, our dark emotions drive us forward unaware, and we do stupid and sinful things. When looking back over these mistakes and disasters of life, we wonder, "Why couldn't I see how dumb that was at the time?" The word *emotion* itself includes both the word and the idea of "motion"—emotions *move* us. So the more we take notice of our emotional state and move into healthier emotional places, the more we can allow God to guide and sustain us by his grace to experience more of the abundant living Jesus promised (John 10:10).

Being Formed to Be Emotionally Healthy

Our Lord Jesus Christ, who took on humanity, showed us how to be a strong leader and yet emotionally healthy and even compassionately

20. For those of us who teach and write about God's Word, I wonder to what extent our own limited emotional growth has conveyed a rather distorted view of God to our listeners and readers? For example, believers are no longer under God's judgment and wrath (e.g., Rom. 8:1; Eph. 2:3–5), yet how often does the tone and texture of our own judgmentalism or anger in our teaching actually taint the biblical picture of God, who genuinely loves the people he has redeemed?

tender at the most challenging times. An encounter between Jesus and a "sinful" woman illustrates how sensitive Jesus could be regarding the emotional tone of a situation, while at the same time being aware of the condemning tones of some Pharisees (Luke 7:36–50). During a meal at the home of Simon, a Pharisee, another "guest" dropped in. Having learned that Jesus was nearby, a woman entered with an alabaster jar of perfume and stood right behind Jesus at his feet. Overwhelmed by feelings of love for Jesus, her Savior, and her sense of being forgiven by God, she began to weep, her tears falling on his feet. Perhaps a bit embarrassed, she quickly stooped to wipe them away with her hair and then kissed his feet. With the expensive oil she had brought, the woman anointed Jesus' feet. What remarkable courage for her, in the presence of these "holy" and austere Pharisees, to demonstrate her deep love and appreciation for her Savior. Jesus discerned her deep need for affirmation of divine forgiveness, a forgiveness she had already received from God. Compassionately, Jesus soothed her soul with these gracious words of comfort: "Your sins *have been* forgiven"; "*Your faith* has saved you; go *in peace*" (vv. 48, 50 NASB, emphasis mine). In contrast to his encouragement to the woman, Jesus rebuked Simon's lack of love for Jesus: "But whoever has been forgiven little loves little" (v. 47 TNIV).

Like Jesus, we experience a wide range of emotions, though we may not always be aware of them. Jesus' life illustrates that facing challenging situations requires significant emotional maturity and sensitivity.[21] The encouraging note is that our emotional interactions with each other can be formed like Jesus.

Learning to Talk About Our Emotions

So, once we recognize we do have feelings, another challenge many of us face is not knowing how to describe or label our various emotions in order to easily discuss our feelings. Like learning a foreign language, we need to acquire a new vocabulary that helps us describe our inner world. After discussing this problem with a psychologist friend, Bill Roth, I developed a simple five-label checklist that continues to help me become aware of how I'm feeling. I reduced the range of feelings to five broad categories, using two sets of words that sound very similar for ease of memory: "glad, sad, mad" and "dreads and dreams." When in conversation with our spouse, roommate, or close friend, we can each talk about our day by moving through the list, first one sharing and then the other.

Many fruitful times of conversation have opened up for Beth and me

21. Two studies can be recommended for further study of Jesus' emotional life. A popular treatment is by Dick and Jane Mohline, *Emotional Wholeness: Connecting with the Emotions of Jesus* (Shippensburg, PA: Treasure House, 1997). A more technical study is a Ph.D. dissertation by Gregory J. Mazak, "The Emotional Life of Jesus as a Guide for the Christian" (Bob Jones University, 1990).

by using the checklist. It's important to share something for *each* of the categories even if it's very brief because it's easy to get sidetracked and just talk about the joys and then move on to other matters. The benefit of this simple practice is moving through the *whole range* of categories, especially into arenas where we are "sad," "mad," and have "dreads."[22]

Talking About Our Emotions

1. Was I *glad* today (i.e., joyful, pleased, happy, "up")? Share one event.
2. Was I *sad* today (i.e., sorrowful, "down," disappointed)? Share one event.
3. Was I *mad* today (i.e., frustrated, annoyed, irritated, "ticked off," angry)? Share one event.
4. What do I *dread* (i.e., makes me concerned, bothered, worried, anxious, fearful)? Share one event.
5. What are my *dreams* for the future (i.e., longings, yearnings, wishes, hopes)? Share one event.

Welcoming Our Tears

Another arena to express our emotions involves welcoming our tears when they come. For example, Jesus wept at the grave of his friend Lazarus, before calling him back to life (John 11:35). As Jesus approached Jerusalem following his triumphal entry, his sadness for the situation was reflected in his tears over the city (Luke 19:41). On the Isle of Patmos, John wept greatly "because no one was found who was worthy to open the scroll or look inside" (Rev. 5:4).

The Old Testament story of Joseph is instructive on welcoming tears of grief and joy. He had been separated from his family for twenty years when his brothers came to seek food in Egypt due to the famine. At their first meeting, he wept and had to turn away (Gen. 42:24). On their second trip the brothers dined in Joseph's house. At the sight of his younger brother Benjamin, Joseph had to leave to find a private room in which to weep (Gen. 43:30–31). He then washed his face and came back for the dinner. The brothers left but when the steward caught up with them, they had to return to Joseph, since a cup was

22. For a helpful resource on emotions, see Dan Allender (Christian psychologist) and Tremper Longman (Old Testament scholar), *The Cry of the Soul: How Our Emotions Reveal Our Deepest Questions About God* (Colorado Springs: NavPress, 1994).

found in Benjamin's sack. The brothers pleaded with Joseph to let Benjamin return home, otherwise their father would die of grief. Joseph could no longer control his emotions. He commanded all the Egyptian servants to leave, while his brothers remained in his presence. "And [Joseph] wept so loudly that the Egyptians heard him, and Pharaoh's household heard about it" (Gen. 45:2). Finally, when his father, Jacob, arrived in Egypt, Joseph "threw his arms around his father and wept for a long time" (Gen. 46:29). Through his tears, Joseph was able to process both the inner turmoil over the many years of separation from his family and the joy of being reunited.

Solomon tells us in Ecclesiastes 3:4 that there is a legitimate time for weeping. And Paul commands us to weep with those who are weeping (Rom. 12:15). A healthy emotional life can welcome tears of grief and tears of joy. When was the last time we allowed tears to come to our eyes or processed our emotions by having a good cry?[23]

Discerning the Dark Side of Our Emotions

One classic framework identifies three basic emotional tendencies: an "approach" toward (participation and engagement with or toward a person, object, or event); an "avoidance" away from (moving away from, withdrawing, evading, dodging, escaping); or moving "against" (standing one's ground, defending, defeating).[24] Of course, each of these movements can be a very appropriate response within a given situation. Yet in certain situations, these tendencies may actually be a response energized by one or several of our sinful compulsions. Often these coping strategies were developed during our childhood to protect ourselves when adults wouldn't or couldn't, and they remain now as sinful compulsions that substitute for relying on God's power and grace.

How can we tell whether it's an appropriate, good movement or one that is sinful? These are complex phenomena and require mature discernment. For example, regarding my dogged "approach" when I'm writing a paper or a book, why do I keep working on a writing project as if I have all the time in the world, ignoring the looming deadline? Why can't I begin to wind down my efforts? Might it be my perfectionism kicking in? I want to chase one more rabbit trail on an issue that just "needs" to be included in the chapter. I want to tweak those phrases over and over again, so they sound just right, even though most would make good sense out of these sentences as they are. I can easily rationalize missing a deadline ("avoidance") with the claim that my reputation (or grade) is on the line. And, I reason, this additional section in the particular paper or book is necessary. People expect me to perfect my writing craft. But am I able to cease my "striving" and accept the good quality that is already there?

23. After Peter had denied the Lord, their eyes connected, and Peter wept bitterly (Luke 22:61–62). When was the last time we cried over a sin?

24. Karen Horney, *Neurosis and Human Growth: The Struggle Toward Self-Realization* (New York: Norton, 1950), 19.

Can I let it go and meet the deadline? If not, perhaps my compulsion is energizing me. Our goal is to be *drawn* by the Spirit, not *driven* by our compulsions.

Perhaps we can start noticing if there is that *added energy* that suddenly compels us into action. From down deep, something moves us from within overtaking us, an energy that seems somewhat out of line or beyond what would be appropriate in the immediate situation. I'm feverishly working on a project, and Beth calls from another part of the house asking about a task she is working on. On some occasions I get angry over that interruption. At that moment I'm not free to exude patience and grace and instead give a short answer laced with harshness or anger. I am much more energized negatively than the situation requires. Of course, in an emergency, this sudden energy can be very fitting. But at other times, it may indicate a reaction beyond what the situation calls forth. It's an *over*reaction.

Peter's prideful defense of his faithfulness to Jesus prevented him from hearing Jesus' warning about Satan and the assurance that Jesus had already prayed for Peter (Luke 22:31–32). "But [Peter] replied, 'Lord, I am ready to go with you to prison and to death'" (Luke 22:33). Later, while Peter was warming himself around the fire, he was accused of being a companion of Jesus. Peter's fears overwhelmed him, just as the waves had distracted his trust in Jesus while walking on the water (Matt. 14:28–31). His bravado evaporated, and he resorted to old sinful coping strategies of reliance on self. In moments of crises, our sinful compulsions become very obvious. Yet we need not go back to our old ways. Jesus' example of inner strength as he rested in the Father during his own trials can encourage us to do the same.

Compare Peter's overreaction with King David's response to curses aimed at him, as he and his retinue left Jerusalem during his son Absalom's rebellion. As David approached the town of Bahurim, Shimei, one of King Saul's clan, came out to curse the fleeing king and to pelt David and his officers with stones. He cried out, "Get out, get out, you murderer, you scoundrel! The LORD has repaid you for all the blood you shed in the household of Saul, in whose place you have reigned. The LORD has given the kingdom into the hands of your son Absalom. You have come to ruin because you are a murderer!" (2 Sam. 16:7–8 TNIV). Abishai, one of the officers, asked the king if he should execute the man for treason.

But David, even during this difficult crisis, while fleeing from his palace to save his life, had a heart of mercy and one open to what God might be doing: "David then said to Abishai and all his officials, 'My son [Absalom], who is of my own flesh, is trying to take my life. How much more, then, this Benjamite! Leave him alone; let him curse, for the LORD has told him to. It may be that the LORD will look upon my misery and restore to me his covenant blessing instead of his curse today'" (2 Sam. 16:11–12 TNIV). David exemplifies a heart resting in God's love and protection.

Being Alert to the Spiritual Battle

Yet there is more. This reactionary energy and our compulsions and coping strategies are not the only factors that keep us from taking on the inner life of Jesus. As believers, we also must acknowledge the active participation of the Devil and demons. For example, when Jesus announced his coming suffering and death to his disciples for the first time, Peter was not a happy camper, and he gave Jesus a piece of his mind. "Peter took him aside and began to rebuke him. 'Never, Lord!' he said. 'This shall never happen to you!'" (Matt. 16:22). Peter's sinful negative reaction to Jesus was not energized merely by his compulsions. Peter's response was stirred by Satan himself, for "Jesus turned and said to Peter, 'Get behind me, Satan! You are a stumbling block to me; you do not have in mind the things of God, but the things of men'" (Matt. 16:23). After Pentecost, when Peter was indwelt by the Spirit, he became much more sensitive to Satan's movements. As recorded in Acts 5, Peter challenged Ananias, "How is it that *Satan has so filled your heart* that you have lied to the Holy Spirit?" (Acts 5:3, emphasis mine).

We must become more aware of possible demonic involvement in our own actions. James warns, "But if you harbor bitter envy and selfish ambition in your hearts, do not boast about it or deny the truth. Such 'wisdom' does not come down from heaven but is earthly, unspiritual, *of the devil*. For where you have envy and selfish ambition, there you find disorder and every *evil* practice" (James 3:14–16, emphasis mine). Although Christians cannot be demon-possessed, we can be strongly influenced by Satan (e.g., 1 Peter 5:8).

In fact, Scripture tells us our patterns of sinful anger can become an open gate for regular demonic harassment. Paul tells us, "'In your anger do not sin': Do not let the sun go down while you are still angry, and do not give the devil a *foothold*" (Eph. 4:26–27, emphasis mine). New Testament professor Clint Arnold explains, "The most natural way to interpret the use of *topos* (foothold) in Ephesians 4:27 is the idea of inhabitable space. Paul is thus calling these believers to vigilance and moral purity so that they do not relinquish a base of operation to demonic spirits. . . . When [Paul] cautions them about surrendering space to the devil, he is warning them against allowing the devil (or a demonic spirit) to exert a domineering influence in an area of their lives. For a Christian to nurture anger, for example, may grant a demonic spirit inhabitable space."[25]

Although Christians cannot be demon-possessed (be completely in Satan's control), we can give Satan a "foothold"—a place in our lives from which he can influence us toward continuing or greater evil. When believers persist in patterns of sinfulness—whether or not we are aware of the specific area that does not reflect God's glory in our inner life—we actually may invite an opportunity for increased demonic influence in our lives!

---

25. Clint Arnold, *Three Crucial Questions About Spiritual Warfare* (Grand Rapids: Baker, 1997), 88–89.

As James reminds us, "God opposes the proud but gives grace to the humble" (4:6). If in our pride we remain imprisoned in our compulsions, God will oppose us. But if we humble ourselves before God, his grace will empower us to grow a more humble heart, ready to listen to God and to how God may be speaking to us through difficult encounters like the one King David faced.[26] This transformation will not take place overnight. But with persistent effort given to specific spiritual practices to open ourselves to the Spirit's transforming work, God will slowly release us from our compulsions and liberate us to be whole beings, in both mind and heart.

If we permit our compulsions to dominate our life, we'll miss opportunities for good and hinder our growth toward the kind of inner reality that was formed in Jesus. Therefore we need to be vigilant and seek God's help in addressing Satan's various footholds in our lives by attending to our feelings and overreactions, for God wishes to tenderize our heart to manifest more and more of the fruit of the Holy Spirit. Along with God's power and grace, we need to invite trusted others to help us notice, monitor, and begin to limit and defeat these sinful reaction patterns so that we can grow more and more into the settled rootedness of Jesus' inner life.[27]

Much More Is Possible

As believers our hearts have an increased capacity for greatness and goodness, more than we can possibly imagine. Consider how Madge Rodda responded to a repulsive evil done to her. Although she was seventy years old, Madge still played the church organ. It was her way of serving God and her church. During the week she practiced the organ—sometimes into the wee hours of the night. One late night, after finishing her practice time at the church, Madge dropped by an all-night coffee shop. But when she went to the restroom, her night of terror began. A man with a stocking pulled over his face grabbed her, sexually assaulted her, stole twenty dollars, and then slit her throat from ear to ear. In responding to some of her comments, the attacker's parting words were, "I believe in God too. But Satan has poisoned my mind."

Madge believed that God saved her life, and God's power also gave Madge the ability to forgive her twenty-three-year-old attacker. "There was never any time when I didn't forgive him. Nobody else in the world

---

26. For further information about divine guidance and hearing God, see Dallas Willard, *Hearing God: Developing a Conversational Relationship with God* (Downers Grove, IL: InterVarsity Press, 1999); and chapter 6 of my book, *Wasting Time with God: A Christian Spirituality of Friendship with God* (Downers Grove, IL: InterVarsity Press, 2001).

27. For helpful insights into the dark side of our emotions and our compulsions, see the following resources: David Seamands, *Healing Your Heart of Painful Emotions* (Nashville: W Publishing, 2005) [four previous books in one volume]; Charles Kraft, *Deep Wounds, Deep Healing: Discovering the Vital Link Between Spiritual Warfare and Inner Healing* (Ann Arbor, MI: Vine/Regal, 1993); and Gerald May, *Addiction and Grace: Love and Spirituality in the Healing of Addictions* (San Francisco: HarperSanFrancisco, 1988).

may love this man, but God loves him." At the sentencing the attacker received seventeen years in prison for attempted rape, sexual assault, and robbery. Madge was there to offer him forgiveness and a Bible. She hoped to visit with him before he was sent to prison. "He'll be there in the jail for about a month. I consider this a wonderful, rare opportunity. . . . I'll tell him that it doesn't matter what he's done." Prosecutor Jo Escobar admitted, "It's extremely unusual. Most of us are more desirous of revenge. Never in my dealings with Ms. Rodda has she expressed that. I find her attitude sincere. I admire Madge very much."[28] It's a testimony of God's powerful grace in the midst of evil. Much more is possible than we can imagine.

I have never experienced such evil as Madge, yet I have come to know the freedom of a forgiving heart in a more mundane situation—dealing with my mild road rage. I didn't realize I have an angry side until I was reading Dallas Willard's *Divine Conspiracy*.[29] Of course I was often frustrated with my computer when it wouldn't perform, but I didn't have contempt for it. Through Willard's discussion of Jesus' teaching in Matthew 5:21–22, God convicted me of my contempt for those "turkeys" and "jerks" on the freeway who couldn't wait their turn or endangered others by squeezing in front to get ahead. Jesus' words hit me hard, piercing my heart: "But I tell you that anyone who is angry with a brother or sister will be subject to judgment. Again, anyone who says to his brother or sister, 'Raca,' is answerable to the Sanhedrin. And anyone who says, 'You fool!' will be in danger of the fire of hell" (Matt. 5:22 TNIV). I became aware of my problem and was willing to admit it to God—that's the first step. And I asked him to help me develop a forgiving heart that would be gracious and not hold contempt or pour curses on these kinds of drivers.

I was surprised when God brought to my mind those powerful words of Jesus on the cross, "Father, forgive them, for they do not know what they are doing" (Luke 23:34). As I meditated on his words, I came to realize that if we really understood the devastation brought on others by our sinful words and actions, we probably would sin less and less. Yet we are often blind to that; we justify our sinful actions against others as fitting to their "crime" against us. But Jesus showed me that another way is possible.

So as I drove to work I asked God to help me become aware of my anger and contempt and to grow a forgiving heart in me. The healing process involves revisiting the first step for *each* outburst of anger and contempt that arises in a particular situation. Initially I became aware of my anger later in the day, as God would keep prompting me until I finally listened and acknowledged my wrong. Learning to listen to God will take some time if we haven't been receptive to hearing him.

---

28. Kristina Horton, "Man Gets 17 Years—and Forgiveness," *Orange County Register*, March 6, 1993, A1, A26.

29. Dallas Willard, *The Divine Conspiracy: Rediscovering Our Hidden Life in God* (San Francisco: HarperSanFrancisco, 1997).

Over the months of this intentional project, the time between the outburst of vain words and my recognition and confession to God became shorter and shorter. Soon I was becoming aware of my outburst *just after* the event prompting it; then in the *midst* of the outburst, then just *as* I was about to give the driver a piece of my mind. It required my continuing intentionality of inviting God to tenderize my heart toward these drivers, sensing his conviction in my heart, and bowing to his righteous ways. Finally, "graduation day" arrived about twelve months later when someone cut in front of me and I had no outburst at all. My heart actually remained in a state of peace throughout that event! A while ago on the way home from our Sunday morning worship and driving in the right lane of the freeway, I was so filled with God's grace that I was able to extend grace to another driver who was trying to exit the freeway from the middle lane. Of course I've had my lapses, and God is able to extend me grace for these as well. In this way I'm learning that my heart can be formed according to Jesus' way. I'm learning that it's possible to become more fully like Jesus.

Time Alone with God

Finally, spiritual formation is not a work we do alone or in isolation from God. We intentionally make space for God to do his work in us. For example, despite the demands of Jesus' public ministry (e.g., Luke 5:15), "Jesus often withdrew to lonely places and prayed" (Luke 5:16). We can't expect to deepen our inner life with God if we continue a busy pace of life. Henri Nouwen counsels, "Without solitude it is virtually impossible to live a spiritual life. . . . We do not take the spiritual life seriously if we do not set aside time to be with God and listen to him."[30] I've begun to take brief "pause button" breaks throughout my day to connect with God. Jason, one of my students, let these pause breaks with God become a part of his life as well.

Jason explained, "Once I began to purposefully do this, I started to see how important that step was to helping me engage. It took about three weeks before I started to see any effects from this spiritual discipline. In the third week it began to take on special importance. It became a sanctuary in the midst of my busy life and a place that I wanted to enter more often. . . . The greatest benefit of this practice has been to remind me that God is always there to interact with me."[31]

We may also wish to dedicate one hour a week for a special time with God, or even an overnight away.[32] It becomes a dedicated time—to just hear his

---

30. Henri Nouwen, *Making All Things New: An Invitation to the Spiritual Life* (San Francisco: Harper & Row, 1981), 69, 71. For additional ideas about taking time with God, see my *Wasting Time with God: A Christian Spirituality of Friendship with God* (Downers Grove, IL: InterVarsity Press, 2001).

31. Personal communication; used by permission.

32. For further study of taking pause breaks with God and other spiritual disciplines, see J. P. Moreland and Klaus Issler, *The Lost Virtue of Happiness: Discovering the Disciplines of the Good Life* (Colorado Springs: NavPress, 2006).

voice, to let down our defenses so that God can restore our weary and burdened souls. An extended time of retreat with God—a "vacation with God"—can test our resolve to pursue a deeper and closer relationship with him.

Conclusion

"Heart" work is an important component of spiritual formation that has not been on the radar screen for most of my life. As I attend to matters of internal obedience as well as external obedience, I am finding greater freedom and more peace. Since becoming more aware of my own troubled soul, I am sharing more of my anxious thoughts with God and, as God promises in Philippians 4:7, I am experiencing more of his peace in my life—much more peace than in the past. In addition, the psalms have become more personal to me. Of course, Psalms is mostly about our emotional life before God. Although it was the dynamic hymnbook of Israel, for me it was mostly distant historical theology. I could make sense of the words, but I hadn't developed the emotional sensitivity to enter into the wide range of emotions described in words like these: "Why are you downcast, O my soul? Why so disturbed within me? Put your hope in God" (Pss. 42:5,11, 43:5). For example, on a recent retreat, the very words of Psalm 35, a lament psalm, helped me express my own feelings to God regarding some past wounds that had come to light. As I read and reread this psalm as my prayer request to God, the Lord ministered to me. I sensed that he knew my pain and he affirmed his love for me.[33]

Although I'm not yet ready to "dance before the Lord with all my might," as David did when he welcomed the ark of the covenant into Jerusalem (2 Sam. 6:14), I am beginning to experience deeper emotions from within, as I praise our great God during our corporate worship. Moreover, the Spirit is slowly transforming my emotional life to manifest more and more of *the fruit of the Spirit*, which mostly involves significant *emotional* features that bless all of our relationships: love, joy, peace, patience, kindness, goodness, faithfulness, gentleness, and self-control (Gal. 5:22–23). So, as we grow in our emotional capacities, not only can we be more honest with God, but we are also being slowly transformed by the Spirit to experience these essential Christlike affections in the depths of our soul.

Perhaps these reflections on Scripture and my own journey may stimulate a desire to explore aspects of your own heart.

> For out of the overflow of the heart the mouth speaks. (Luke 6:45 TNIV)

> May the words of my mouth and the meditation of my heart
> be pleasing in your sight,
> O LORD, my Rock and my Redeemer. (Ps. 19:14)

---

33. For a helpful introduction to Psalms, see Tremper Longman, *How to Read the Psalms* (Dowers Grove, IL: InterVarsity Press, 1988).

CHAPTER 6

CHARACTER AND SPIRITUAL FORMATION

Reid Kisling

> We also rejoice in our sufferings, because we know that suffering produces perseverance; perseverance, character; and character, hope. And hope does not disappoint us, because God has poured out his love into our hearts by the Holy Spirit, whom he has given us.
>
> —Romans 5:3–5

Obviously, spiritual formation is much too deep to be described in just one way. It is many-sided and complex. To borrow the image presented by Kenneth Boa in his treatment of the topic, spiritual formation is a "multi-faceted gem" that must be approached with humility.[1] In this vein this chapter, like others in this work, is an attempt to present one of these facets by shedding some light on the formation process.

Most agree that character is significant to personal and spiritual growth. However, these same people may be unable to define the components of solid, mature character that develops effective personal relationships. This is especially true in popular treatments of leadership today. The common perception is that leaders who achieve good results are effective, regardless of the means used to arrive at the results. Unfortunately, we only need to glance back at the history of world leaders to find those who were despots, using people to accomplish their own purposes without regard to the effects on their followers. There is something extremely wrong with the perspective that it's all about the end and not the means.

1. Kenneth Boa, *Conformed to His Image: Biblical and Practical Approaches to Spiritual Formation* (Grand Rapids: Zondervan, 2001).

So, if there is more to life than the results of our actions, what is it? This is where character comes into play. It is through our foundational character, whether good or bad, that we develop a value system that helps us make ethical or unethical, moral or immoral, decisions about what actions to take in any given situation. Therefore, defining and understanding the components of well-developed and mature character are necessary to promote good actions and leadership as well as to further our own growth and development. This chapter will begin by investigating the theological foundations of character. It will then define character, examine in more detail how it applies to both spiritual formation and leadership, and finally consider some ways that mature character can be developed.

The Theological Foundations of Character

When we use the word *character,* we typically mean those attributes by which we identify someone or something. If we are to consider what the Bible says about the characteristics by which we should be identified, we would do well to first look at the character of God himself. Since men and women were created in the image of God, our highest aspiration should be to mirror his character as we were created to do. In fact, God has clearly identified what our primary responsibility is: "He has showed you, O man, what is good. And what does the LORD require of you? To *act justly* and to *love mercy* and to *walk humbly* with your God" (Mic. 6:8, emphasis mine). These qualities—justice, mercy, and humility—are the fundamental qualities necessary to accomplish the greatest commandments, namely, to "love the Lord your God with all your heart and with all your soul and with all your mind" and to "love your neighbor as yourself" (Matt. 22:37, 39). If these are the primary attributes to which we should aspire, how are they developed in us?

The apostle Paul considers character development when he writes, "We also rejoice in our sufferings, because we know that suffering produces perseverance; perseverance, *character*; and character, hope. And hope does not disappoint us, because God has poured out his love into our hearts by the Holy Spirit, whom he has given us" (Rom. 5:3–5, emphasis mine). Suffering provides an opportunity to develop a long-term perspective that is not rooted in our temporal surroundings. Through this change in perspective, we are able to endure that which is unpleasant or painful at the time. Continual changes in this focus develop character that lasts—character that looks to the future for the consummation of God's kingdom and his reward for our endurance. Essentially, Paul describes the spiritual formation process—the process of being transformed from our temporal perspective to an eternal one.

In addition to explicit reference to character development due to suffering, Scripture also addresses the role of discipline in the Christian life, specifically in relation to self-control. The apostle Peter tells us,

> His divine power has given us everything we need for life and godliness through our knowledge of him who called us by his own glory and goodness. Through these he has given us his very great and precious promises, so that through them you may participate in the divine nature and escape the corruption in the world caused by evil desires. For this very reason, make every effort to add to your faith goodness; and to goodness, knowledge; and to knowledge, *self-control*; and to self-control, perseverance; and to perseverance, godliness; and to godliness, brotherly kindness; and to brotherly kindness, love. For if you possess these qualities in increasing measure, they will keep you from being ineffective and unproductive in your knowledge of our Lord Jesus Christ. But if anyone does not have them, he is nearsighted and blind, and has forgotten that he has been cleansed from his past sins. (2 Peter 1:3–9, emphasis mine)

God has provided for us his power (the power that raised Christ from the dead—Eph. 1:19–20) so that we may be transformed into godly men and women. This is more than just a laundry list of attributes that we should see in our lives. Self-control is a foundation for godly behavior, including the love that we share among our brothers and sisters in Christ. This self-control is motivated by a good heart (which can only come from faith) and the knowledge of our tendency to act according to our own evil desires (2 Peter 1:4).

Like Peter, Paul too addresses the role of self-control in our formation process by describing its role in athletic training (1 Cor. 9:25). Like athletes, we "beat our bodies" to make them "our slaves" (v. 27). Otherwise, if we followed our own desires without control, we would behave in a way that would hinder our witness. Paul also makes clear when he presents "the fruit of the Spirit" (Gal. 5:22–23) that such self-control is possible only through the work of the Spirit in our lives.

Likewise, the Old Testament discusses character through the attribute of "wisdom." The theology behind Proverbs is presented in the first chapter of the book in verses 2 and 3. Solomon states that discipline, or instruction in wisdom, is his goal. In fact, the word used for "discipline" (Heb. *mûsār*) appears again and again in the book (over thirty times). Abstractly, t includes the sense of formation—of molding something from one form into another. God disciplines us for our growth and development in godliness. Unfortunately, the process of character transformation is often painful. Nonetheless, spiritual formation and character are inextricably linked.

Now that we have seen that character, specifically self-control for godly behavior, is a primary goal in the life of the Christian, how do we get there? What does it take for us to formulate this character in our lives? Better yet, what is good character, and what does it look like in our everyday lives?

What Is Character?

Our basic problem is that we don't understand what character truly is. We spoke above about character being the attributes or traits by which we identify someone or something. There are also popular definitions, such as "Character is what you do when no one is looking," but these perspectives leave us grasping for more as we attempt to better understand what is required to develop a solid character that can stand the test of time. Nevertheless, it is important to consider the popular perspectives on character as we seek to understand how we can promote good character development.

Popular Discussions of Character

Probably the most significant popular treatment of the topic of character is the book by Gail Sheehy[2] that examines the role of a leader's life story in shaping leadership decisions, specifically for those with political aspirations. She evaluated the character of the candidates in the 1988 U.S. presidential election and concluded that their character profoundly impacted the manner and propensity with which they led.

Business Literature

An entire genre of business literature has erupted in recent history examining the role of the leader's personal beliefs and spirituality in leadership behaviors. In the book *The Ascent of a Leader*, the following statement is given: "Character—the inner world of motives and values that shapes our actions—is the ultimate determiner of the nature of our leadership. It empowers our capacities while keeping them in check. It distinguishes those who steward power well from those who abuse power. Character weaves such values as integrity, honesty, and selfless service into the fabric or our lives, organizations, and cultures."[3]

The problem is we see such disparities between the public and private lives of leaders that even writers of fiction pose the question of whether character really matters to successful leadership function.[4] And yet it would appear that to discount the role character plays in precipitating action is to deceive ourselves. In fact, this deception is something to which we are all prone, even those who are our leaders. Such deception leads us all to function as if others with whom we interact are merely objects rather than real people with feelings and needs of their own.[5] Thankfully, the issue of

---

2. Gail Sheehy, *Character: America's Search* for *Leadership*, rev. ed. (New York: Bantam, 1990).

3. Bill Thrall, Bruce McNicol, and Ken McElrath, *The Ascent of a Leader: How Ordinary Relationships Develop Extraordinary Character and Influence* (San Francisco: Jossey-Bass, 1999), 1–2.

4. Suzy Wetlaufer, "A Question of Character," *Harvard Business Review* 77, no. 5 (1999): 30–34.

5. Arbinger Institute, *Leadership and Self-Deception: Getting Out of the Box* (San Francisco: Berrett-Koehler, 2002).

a leader's character is surfacing even on a popular level, in which it is considered essential to go beyond the bottom line in order to accomplish an organization's mission.[6]

If character is significant for our nation's leaders, it should also follow that it is significant for the next generation as well. It is for this reason that programs have arisen to address the anemia of virtue that seems to be present in the young people of our nation.

Character Education Programs

One of the most significant developments in the widespread popular discussion of character is the variety of character education programs in existence today. While these programs were established for a number of reasons and in a variety of contexts, most declare their purpose to be developing the character in young people that is necessary for good citizenship—locally, nationally, and internationally.

According to the Character Education Partnership, "good character involves understanding, caring about, and acting upon core ethical values."[7] In like fashion, most character education programs consider character to be the development of core ethical values in students. Although a variety of values are found on the lists of such programs, one of the best-known programs is the *Character Counts!* program established by the Josephson Institute of Ethics. This program seeks to engender the values of trustworthiness, respect, responsibility, fairness, caring, and citizenship[8] in the students who participate in the program. Speaking broadly about character development programs in general, Lickona specifies the goals of such development at the elementary school level. These goals equate to the fostering of the following qualities in students: (1) self-respect, (2) an others-focused perspective, (3) moral reasoning, (4) culturally important values, (5) teamwork skills, (6) certain character traits, and (7) openness to positive adult influence.[9]

The question, however, is whether character education programs are sufficient. Can the values that these programs attempt to foster in young people foster spiritual formation as well, or are additional factors at play in the formation process? While the popular treatments of character development and the programs in place in schools offer some guidance, perhaps the psychological community can offer insight.

---

6. Gill Robinson Hickman, "Leadership and the Social Imperative of Organizations in the 21st Century," in *Leading Organizations: Perspectives for a New Era*, ed. Gill Robinson Hickman (Thousand Oaks, CA: Sage, 1998), 559–71.

7. Character Education Partnership, "Principle 2," http://www.character. org/site/c.gwKUJhNYJrF/b.993779/k.1637/Principle_2.htm (accessed May 16, 2006).

8. Josephson Institute, "The Six Pillars of Character," http://www.charactercounts .org/defsix.htm (accessed May 16, 2006).

9. Thomas Lickona, "Character Development in the Elementary School Classroom," in *Character Development in Schools and Beyond*, ed. Kevin Ryan and George F. McLean (New York: Praeger, 1987), 180.

Psychological Definitions

Even though there is general discussion from a popular perspective on the meaning of character, the psychological community provides a definition that is more precise. Psychologically, character is an aspect of personality distinct from temperament, meaning that personality is the combination of both temperament and character.[10] Character is "consistency in behavior across time" but is "more than just a sense of self."[11] It also includes volitional and self-regulatory matters—the ability to inhibit or adjust impulsive behaviors. In addition to volitional control, personal beliefs and values are often included in the character components of personality. However, this perspective on character is not necessarily common in clinical practice, where many psychologists use the terms *personality* and *character* interchangeably. Unfortunately, many clinicians evaluate personality through standardized measures (such as personality inventories) that are later proven inadequate to predict a person's future behavior. Therefore, it seems reasonable to assume that such measures are based on conceptual models that do not adequately account for the personality components that truly influence behavior, namely, character.

If there are personality components that go beyond temperament, what are they? Psychologists have long discussed the notion of behavioral self-regulation in the process of controlling one's behavior.[12] The problem arises when one is "unable" to successfully regulate behavior in line with social or ethical norms. Baumeister and his colleagues[13] address this problem in terms of self-regulation failures. In such failure instances, it appears that an individual's resources necessary to keep one's own impulses in check are depleted.[14] These resources are essentially equivalent to the popular notion of "willpower."

One of the most significant attempts to identify and classify character is the handbook *Character Strengths and Virtues*.[15] The goal of this handbook is to provide fodder for the legitimate psychological discussion of the items identified, thereby providing significant foundation from which the cultivation of these characteristics can be promoted. The problem is that until recently no consensus has developed on the content of character upon which

---

10. American Psychiatric Association, *Diagnostic and Statistical Manual of Mental Disorders*, 4th ed. (Washington, DC: American Psychiatric Association, 2000); and Len Sperry, "Leadership Dynamics: Character and Character Structure in Executives," *Consulting Psychology Journal: Practice and Research* 49, no. 4 (1997): 268–80.

11. H. Skipton Leonard, "The Many Faces of Character," *Consulting Psychology Journal: Practice and Research* 49, no. 4 (1997): 240.

12. Charles S. Carver and Michael F. Scheier, *On the Self-Regulation of Behavior* (New York: Cambridge University Press, 1998).

13. Roy F. Baumeister and Kathleen D. Vohs, *Handbook of Self-Regulation: Research, Theory, and Applications* (New York: Guilford, 2004).

14. Roy F. Baumeister and Todd F. Heatherton, "Self-Regulation Failure: An Overview," *Psychological Inquiry* 7, no. 1 (1996): 1–15.

15. Christopher Peterson and Martin E. P. Seligman, *Character Strengths and Virtues: A Handbook and Classification* (Washington, DC: American Psychological Association, 2004).

legitimate scientific research could be based. This classification provides a significant effort toward that end.

Perhaps most interesting in the recent discussions on the topic is what is coming out of the "positive psychology" movement. Although only recently has the movement adopted this moniker, the structural components of the movement have been around for some time, though not presented in a coordinated manner. Some of the overarching constructs that are related to the overall movement are: learned resourcefulness,[16] resilience,[17] hardiness,[18] optimism,[19] sense of coherence,[20] and the psychological construct of hope.[21] Each of these components is in some way tied to an individual's ability to cope with stress. They each address the perspective from which an individual views and interprets his or her experiences—either as circumstances beyond one's control or as events that can be controlled or are under the control of a "higher power." Interestingly, a person's perspective on this matter will have dramatic consequences on the decision to abstain from or embrace immoral behavior. After all, if "life just happens," what's the point in delaying immediate gratification? Yet, the ability to delay gratification is tied to mature personality and the ability to interact effectively with other people.[22]

Interestingly, though not explicitly linked to the overall discipline of positive psychology, work has been completed on noncognitive variables essential to promote long-term academic success in college-age students. These noncognitive variables are as follows: (1) positive self-concept, (2) realistic self-appraisal, (3) ability to understand and productively deal with racism, (4) preference for long-range goals, (5) availability of strong support person(s), (6) successful leadership experience(s), (7) demonstrated community service, and (8) unusual and/or culturally acquired knowledge in a field.[23] Many of these variables are compatible with the concepts promoted in the positive psychology literature.

Relationship to Temperament

As stated above, the psychological community defines character as a

---

16. Michael Rosenbaum, ed., *Learned Resourcefulness: On Coping Skills, Self-Control, and Adaptive Behavior*, vol. 24, Springer Series on Behavior Therapy and Behavioral Medicine (New York: Springer, 1990).

17. E. Timothy Burns, *From Risk to Resilience: A Journey with Heart for Our Children, Our Future* (Dallas: Marco Polo, 1996).

18. Salvatore R. Maddi, "The Story of Hardiness: Twenty Years of Theorizing, Research, and Practice," *Consulting Psychology Journal: Practice and Research* 54, no. 3 (2002): 173–85.

19. Martin E. P. Seligman, *Learned Optimism* (New York: A. A. Knopf, 1991).

20. Aaron Antonovsky, *Health, Stress, and Coping: New Perspectives on Mental and Physical Well-Being* (San Francisco: Jossey-Bass, 1979).

21. C. R. Snyder, *The Psychology of Hope: You Can Get There from Here* (New York: Free Press, 1994).

22. Daniel Goleman, *Emotional Intelligence* (New York: Bantam Books, 1995).

23. William E. Sedlacek, *Beyond the Big Test: Noncognitive Assessment in Higher Education* (San Francisco: Jossey-Bass, 2004).

component of personality and personality is a combination of both temperament and character. Although we have discussed some of these aspects already, how do temperament and character differ? Let's look first at what temperament is and how it compares to character.

Various researchers have addressed the manner in which temperament affects how we see the world around us. Some of their work that may be familiar are the DISC profile[24] and the Jungian archetypes of the MBTI.[25] Unfortunately, none of these treatments of "personality" explicitly consider one's character when evaluating an individual's perspective of the surrounding world. Temperament is an automatic response to a specific situation, while character filters our instincts prior to taking a specific action.[26] Practically speaking, temperament is the eye through which we see the world around us. We experience different events and interpret the actions of others implicitly without thinking about how we are interpreting those events and actions. In contrast to temperament, character is the polarizing lens that filters the experiences we see with our eyes (temperament).

The Aspects of Character

While there are numerous theoretical and practical models of character, those based on experimental research have been lacking. Nonetheless, one such empirical model appears to address the conceptual ideology that has been presented thus far. The "Psychobiological Model of Temperament and Character" was developed using extensive interview data and finds its conceptual foundation in both brain research and psychotherapy.[27] Though the model also addresses temperament traits, of primary concern to us are the three primary character traits identified in the model—self-directedness, cooperativeness, and self-transcendence. These character traits comprise means of relating to oneself, other individuals, and the surrounding world, respectively.

Self-Directedness

In this model of character, each specific trait contains "bundles" of secondary traits that comprise the overall characteristic. For the character trait of self-directedness, these subtraits include responsibility, purposefulness, resourcefulness, self-acceptance, and good habits.[28] Let's examine these subtraits in more detail.

---

24. Mels Carbonell, *Discover Your Giftedness* (Blue Ridge, GA: Uniquely You Resources, 2003).

25. Isabel Briggs Myers, Linda K. Kirby, and Katharine D. Myers, *Introduction to Type: A Guide to Understanding Your Results on the Myers-Briggs Type Indicator*, 6th ed., Introduction to Type Series (Oxford: Oxford Psychologists Press, 2000).

26. Sperry, "Leadership Dynamics," 269.

27. R. Cloninger, D. Svrakic, and T. Pryzbeck, "A Psychobiological Model of Temperament and Character," *Archives of General Psychiatry* 50 (1993): 975–90.

28. C. Robert Cloninger et al., *The Temperament and Character Inventory (TCI): A Guide*

Responsible individuals generally recognize the consequences of their own choices and do not blame others or the external circumstances for their situation. This responsibility trait corresponds with the constructs of optimism[29] and hardiness,[30] in which people take charge of their own actions and believe that their actions will produce the desired results. This is also similar in concept to self-efficacy.[31]

Purposeful individuals are able to regulate their behavior by comparing behavioral choices to long-term values and goals. As such, purposeful individuals usually are able to delay immediate gratification in order to achieve their goals. Delayed gratification is a significant component of behavioral self-regulation, which was addressed above.

Resourceful individuals are able to find ways around problems. This resourcefulness trait corresponds with the constructs of learned resourcefulness[32] and hope.[33] Such individuals possess the belief that actions that they take will accomplish the results they intend, which is termed "self-efficacy." Self-acceptance includes the realistic appraisal of both one's strengths and one's limitations. Those who do not possess this trait are often distressed when presented with evidence that they are not as perfect as they wish.

Individuals with good habits have developed those habits through consistent practice and discipline. In fact, we are all familiar with self-discipline—a concept that equates well with the character trait of self-directedness. Those who discipline their own actions find that they more easily accept responsibility for their own actions and set aside short-term benefits for long-term goals. We admire people who exhibit such personal discipline because we know that it does not come easily—it always requires some cost. Yet the development of this trait is well worth the effort.

Cooperativeness

The character trait of cooperativeness includes the subtraits of tolerance, empathy, helpfulness, compassion, and ethical interaction with others.[34]

---

to Its Development and Use (St. Louis: Center for Psychobiology of Personality, Washington University, 1994), 24–25.

29. Martin E. P. Seligman and Mihaly Csikszentmihalyi, "Positive Psychology: An Introduction," *American Psychologist* 55, no. 1 (2000): 5–14.

30. Morgan McCall, "Identifying Leadership Potential in Future International Executives: Developing a Concept," *Consulting Psychology Journal: Practice and Research* 46, no. 1 (1994): 49–63.

31. Albert Bandura, *Self-Efficacy: The Exercise of Control* (New York: W. H. Freeman, 1997).

32. Gary G. Gintner, John D. West, and John J. Zarski, "Learned Resourcefulness and Situation-Specific Coping with Stress," *Journal of Psychology* 123, no. 3 (1989): 295–304.

33. C. R. Snyder, "Genesis: The Birth and Growth of Hope," in *Handbook of Hope: Theory, Measures, and Applications*, ed. C. R. Snyder (San Diego: Academic Press, 2000), 25–38.

34. Cloninger et al., *Temperament and Character Inventory*, 26–27.

Cooperativeness is one's ability to interact appropriately with others—the essence of the Golden Rule: "Do to others what you would have them do to you" (Matt. 7:12).

Tolerant individuals are able to accept even those with very different values or opinions. Practically applied, these people listen to the perspectives of others without being critical and impatient. Empathetic people can "walk in someone's shoes" and understand the feelings of others. They don't discount those feelings but rather show fundamental respect for the people who hold them. Helpful people approach others with humility, recognizing that more is accomplished through the efforts of the team than by working alone. Helpful people are often found laboring in service to others.

Compassionate individuals are willing to forgive. They do not seek revenge when wronged; rather, they try to move past the negative event. In contrast to compassionate people, those who are vengeful seek to repay others for the hurt they have caused—either through active revenge or passive-aggressive behavior.

Organizational psychologists have long agreed that leadership requires the use of power. Yet there are some leaders who use power for their own purposes, while others use it to accomplish collective goals. This orientation has been termed the "power motive,"[35] and it has been demonstrated to significantly impact leadership abilities and effectiveness.[36] The character trait of cooperativeness corresponds with this concept of power motivation since both pertain to treating others fairly and not behaving in an opportunistic manner. In addition, empathy and compassion, two additional subtraits of cooperativeness, are components of some models of emotional intelligence,[37] which itself has been shown to be significant to efforts of effective leaders.[38]

While self-directedness is paramount in the three character traits presented here, cooperativeness is also an essential component of mature character. Too often personally driven leaders "drive over" other people to accomplish their own goals. We are all aware of our own tendency to be either task- or relationship-oriented (temperament). Yet, even though we each have automatic responses in given situations, our character demands that we consider both our goals and the people around us before we initiate action. Mature character requires both personal responsibility and the humble understanding of our need for other people.

---

35. David C. McClelland, *Power: The Inner Experience* (Oxford: Irvington, 1975); idem, "The Two Faces of Power," in *Organizational Psychology: A Book of Readings*, ed. David A. Kolb, Irwin M. Rubin, and James M. McIntyre (Oxford: Prentice-Hall, 1974).

36. David C. McClelland and Richard E. Boyatzis, "Leadership Motive Pattern and Long-Term Success in Management," *Journal of Applied Psychology* 67, no. 6 (1982): 737–43.

37. Goleman, *Emotional Intelligence*.

38. John J. Sosik and Lara E. Megerian, "Understanding Leader Emotional Intelligence and Performance: The Role of Self-Other Agreement on Transformational Leadership Perceptions," *Group and Organization Management* 24, no. 3 (1999): 367–90.

Self-Transcendence

Self-transcendence refers to one's perspective on his or her relationship to the rest of creation. Such a perspective goes beyond interpersonal interaction to include the manner in which a person views his or her place in the universe. While this may seem like a purely secular orientation to spirituality, it contains some components that are a necessary part of true Christian spirituality. Self-transcendence includes the subtraits of creative self-forgetfulness, and spiritual acceptance.[39]

Creative self-forgetfulness is seen when we are involved in an activity that corresponds directly to our giftedness. At those times we may experience the feeling that "this is what I was created for" and lose track of time while we are engaged in that activity. Psychologists call this experience "flow."[40] People who possess this trait are able to transcend their own boundaries (in a healthy, not codependent manner) and become "engaged" with the activity or the person with whom they are interacting—experiencing deep meaning from the event. Self-forgetful people are able to move beyond "rugged individualism" to see the manner in which their lives connect to those around them. People with this trait are able to understand how their own actions relate to other people and what is occurring in the rest of the world—they see the "big picture."

Spiritually accepting people understand that not everything can be explained scientifically and that there is a supernatural component to life. Such people recognize that there is hope beyond that which can be seen and accept experiences beyond their control. In addition, true spiritual acceptance requires an individual to move beyond the search for personal pleasure and power and instead find meaning beyond oneself.[41] Obviously, this trait correlates strongly with a general understanding of spirituality, which has recently become a topic of evaluation and measurement.[42] In addition, spirituality has implications for effective leadership.[43]

Western society places high value on rational, objective thought. Consequently, self-transcendent individuals may appear to be weak and immature. This is true in contexts in which supernatural experiences may be discounted, which can even occur in Christian circles. But even if there is concern about overt spiritual experience, one cannot deny that there is

---

39. Cloninger et al., *Temperament and Character Inventory*, 27–28.

40. Mihaly Csikszentmihalyi, *Finding Flow: The Psychology of Engagement with Everyday Life*, Masterminds (New York: Basic Books, 1997); idem, *Flow: The Psychology of Optimal Experience* (New York: Harper & Row, 1990).

41. Viktor Frankl, "Self-Transcendence as a Human Phenomenon," *Journal of Humanistic Psychology* 6, no. 2 (1966): 97–106.

42. Will Slater, Todd W. Hall, and Keith J. Edwards, "Measuring Religion and Spirituality: Where Are We and Where Are We Going?" *Journal of Psychology and Theology* 29, no. 1 (2001): 4–21.

43. J. A. Ritscher, "Spiritual Leadership," in *Transforming Leadership*, ed. John D. Adams (Alexandria, VA: Miles River, 1998).

an element of mystery to authentic community that is misunderstood by some as irrational. After all, we are spiritual beings created in the image of God. And yet any desire to experience connection with the world around us certainly should be balanced with the need to communicate the truth of the gospel to a world that is without Christ.

Therefore, mature Christian character requires balance between appropriate self-direction and discipline, the ability to interact with others, and the ability to embrace the mystery of life that goes beyond what we can see with our eyes. The reader should recognize that this mature character—the interaction of all three traits in concert with one another—looks like humanity's primary responsibility outlined at the start of this chapter: "To act justly and to love mercy and to walk humbly with your God" (Mic. 6:8).

What Does Mature Character Look Like?

Hopefully, the discussion above regarding the character traits of self-directedness, cooperativeness, and self-transcendence implicitly addresses why mature character is necessary. But what are some of the specific implications of mature versus immature character?

At this point in the chapter, the topic of leadership has surfaced again and again. It is probably hard to escape the author's fundamental assertion that character is inextricably linked to leadership. Much more than that, leadership without mature character is not true leadership at all since leadership has as its ultimate goal the glorification of God. We were created as the crowning point of creation—God's image-bearers on this earth, created to rule over it (Gen. 1:26–28). Indeed, spiritual leadership is a worthy ambition given that a man or woman of mature character desires the role.[44] So what implications does character have for leadership practice?

Character and Leadership

Most often, a discussion of leadership includes the topic of values when discussing leadership behavior. It is true that values are essential to leadership function, both for individuals and organizations.[45] But beyond simply declaring that he or she holds certain values, the role of a leader is to integrate values with action.[46] But did you ever consider how we develop and hold the values that are so foundational to our actions? In reality, it is our character that determines the selection of some values over others and therefore defines our value system. Therefore, at its very core character is essential for effective leadership. But what exactly does effective leadership look like?

---

44. J. Oswald Sanders, *Spiritual Leadership* (Chicago: Moody Press, 1967).

45. Aubrey Malphurs, *Values-Driven Leadership: Discovering and Developing Your Core Values for Ministry* (Grand Rapids: Baker, 1996).

46. Gilbert W. Fairholm, *Perspectives on Leadership: From the Science of Management to Its Spiritual Heart* (Westport, CT: Quorum, 1998), x.

Transformational Leadership

The study of leadership has been around for centuries, with even our earliest extant writings musing about the qualities of "great men." Interestingly, before the twentieth century the general consensus was that effective leadership is the result of particular traits of the leader. However, the tide shifted following a seminal work in 1946 by Stogdill,[47] who found that no singular traits could predict effective leadership.[48] Following Stogdill's work, a shift occurred in the focus of leadership study, first to examining the role of the situation and the leader's "style" of leading and then to looking at specific leadership behaviors.[49] Amid the vast research being done on leadership effectiveness, a historian introduced the theory of leadership that has become the predominant leadership paradigm of the twenty-first century. Transformational leadership, first introduced by Burns in his classic work, *Leadership*,[50] was the first to elevate the role of values and beliefs in the leader-follower relationship.

A significant volume of research has considered the behaviors of transformational leaders[51] and the impact of their behaviors on followers,[52] the trust relationship between the leader and follower,[53] and overall measures of organizational effectiveness.[54] Unfortunately, even though there may be general consensus concerning the particular leadership behaviors that are considered transformational, there is little research concerning what motivates such behaviors.

Kanungo and Mendonça maintain that leadership is very much a moral enterprise, the determination of which depends on the underlying

---

47. Ralph M. Stogdill, "Personal Factors Associated with Leadership: A Survey of the Literature," *Journal of Psychology* 25 (1948): 35–71.

48. Stogdill, however, did propose that while no one set of characteristics was essential for leadership, there were groups of characteristics that interacted. See Shelley A. Kirkpatrick and Edwin A. Locke, "Leadership: Do Traits Matter?" *Academy of Management Executive* 5, no. 2 (1991): 48–60.

49. For an outstanding review of this historical development as well as discussion of each specific leadership theory, see Peter Guy Northouse, *Leadership: Theory and Practice*, 3rd ed. (Thousand Oaks, CA: Sage, 2003).

50. James MacGregor Burns, *Leadership* (New York: Harper & Row, 1978).

51. Bernard M. Bass, *Leadership and Performance Beyond Expectations* (New York: Free Press, 1985); Warren G. Bennis and Burt Nanus, *Leaders: The Strategies for Taking Charge* (New York: Harper & Row, 1985); James M. Kouzes and Barry Z. Posner, *The Leadership Challenge: How to Get Extraordinary Things Done in Organizations*, The Jossey-Bass Management Series (San Francisco: Jossey-Bass, 1987).

52. Shelley A. Kirkpatrick and Edwin A. Locke, "Direct and Indirect Effects of Three Core Charismatic Leadership Components on Performance and Attitudes," *Journal of Applied Psychology* 81, no. 1 (1996): 36–51.

53. Philip M. Podsakoff et al., "Transformational Leader Behaviors and Their Effects on Followers' Trust in Leader, Satisfaction, and Organizational Citizenship Behaviors," *Leadership Quarterly* 1, no. 2 (1990): 107–42.

54. Bernard M. Bass and Bruce J. Avolio, *Improving Organizational Effectiveness Through Transformational Leadership* (Thousand Oaks, CA: Sage, 1994).

motivation of the leader. They assert that "organizational leaders are truly effective only when they are motivated by a concern for others, when their actions are guided primarily by the criteria of 'the benefit to others even if it results in some cost to self.' The underlying rationale or purpose for having a leader in a group or organization is to move it toward the pursuit of objectives that, when attained, would produce benefits to both the organization and its members."[55] They then put this even more forcefully by stating that, in fact, "the altruistic motive becomes the only consistent motive for the leader role."[56] This altruistic motive is consistent with moral leadership behavior.

In contrast, immoral leadership is egotistical and benefits the leader personally rather than benefiting others or the organization. The difficulty becomes identifying other-focused versus self-focused motives of the leader. This difficulty is complicated by the fact that some personally motivated leaders may truly believe that their motives are altruistic. Bass and Steidlmeier dub these personally motivated leaders pseudotransformational—they look like they are acting transformationally (with appropriate behaviors), but their motivation is not authentic.[57]

There is a problem if the theory does not distinguish moral from immoral leaders based on their actions. But transformational leadership theory does not explicitly include character as a fundamental component of the process. If transformational leadership doesn't include character, is there a theory of leadership that does?

Visionary Leadership Theory

One theory of leadership that does include character is visionary leadership theory.[58] Visionary leadership theory is based on the same theoretical literature as transformational leadership, but it explicitly acknowledges that leadership is more than specific behaviors enacted by the leader. Visionary leadership theory declares that the leader's character is what promotes the transformational behavior of the leader. One of the primary reasons for consideration of visionary leadership theory over other existing leadership theories is the fact that visionary leadership "shows how the personal characteristics of the leader guide transformational leaders' actions."[59]

---

55. Rabindra Nath Kanungo and Manuel Mendonça, *Ethical Dimensions of Leadership*, ed. Robert A. Giacalone, Sage Series in Business Ethics (Thousand Oaks, CA: Sage Publications, 1996), 35.

56. Ibid.

57. Bernard M. Bass and Paul Steidlmeier, "Ethics, Character, and Authentic Transformational Leadership Behavior," *Leadership Quarterly* 10, no. 2 (1999): 181–217.

58. Marshall Sashkin and William E. Rosenbach, *A New Vision of Leadership* (Amherst, MA: Human Resource Development Press, 1996); Marshall Sashkin and Molly G. Sashkin, *Leadership That Matters: The Critical Factors for Making a Difference in People's Lives and Organizations' Success* (San Francisco: Berrett-Koehler, 2002).

59. Sashkin and Sashkin, *Leadership That Matters*, 184.

Visionary leadership theory does not discount the importance of leadership behaviors. Rather it attempts to include such factors that influence transformational leadership behaviors—both the leader's own personal characteristics and the characteristics of the leadership situation. Therefore, the theory appears to be more holistic than other conceptions of transformational leadership that exist.

The personal characteristics included in visionary leadership theory include the components of "confident leadership" and "follower-centered leadership." "Confident leadership" is referred to by the theory's authors as "self-efficacy"[60] and "self-control" and is also tied somehow to emotional intelligence. Leader confidence involves personal control or belief in overall unifying purpose and meaning in life's events, a concept equivalent to the self-regulatory construct "sense of coherence." All of these concepts generally correspond to the character trait of self-directedness. "Follower-centered leadership" involves the leader's motivation for leading; specifically, whether leadership actions are personally or other-motivated. Follower-centered leadership corresponds to the character trait of cooperativeness.

A third characteristic of leaders in visionary leadership theory is vision. However, within the theory it is considered an ability rather than an aspect of the leader's character. Nonetheless, the foundational components of vision are linked to leader self-regulation for they require the capacity to see long-term implications and consequences of actions before any action is undertaken, and this "big picture" perspective corresponds to the character trait of self-transcendence.

Visionary leadership theory is one theory of leadership that attempts to incorporate the leader's character into the theory to account for the motivation behind effective leadership behaviors. This theory attempts to consider how the inner life of the leader—the leader's *being*—causes the leader to act in a manner that transforms those around the leader, both people and organizations.

Having said this, if *who we are* (our character) affects the way we lead and it is also true that our very being is corrupted by sin, how can we ever expect to lead as God intended? Even our experiences of effective leadership have been tainted since all leaders, even good ones, are affected by sin. We assert that mature character is necessary to sustain effective leadership over time. Then how do we develop this mature character? As Christians, we would say that spiritual formation is the answer.

Spiritual Formation

As a leader, spiritual formation should be the primary focus of life. It is essential to effective function in a leadership capacity. This is made even more evident when the stakes are considered. Rima states, "In light of the

---

60. Ibid., 86.

reality that leadership is, at its most essential level, a spiritual activity, I would strongly contend that in the final analysis every leadership failure is, at its root, a spiritual issue. Regardless of whether the failure takes the shape of sexual immorality, unethical business practices, criminal activity, or any other impropriety that could lead to a leadership failure, at the core of all these failures is the leader's inability to recognize, diagnose, and address spiritual disease of one sort or another in his life."[61] Any such "spiritual disease" must be treated appropriately, first by recognizing that it is, at its core, a deficiency in justice, mercy, or humility—a character deficiency.

The key to understanding the leader's character lies with the first character trait presented above—self-directedness. According to research, low self-directedness lies at the root of all personality disorders.[62] The inability to regulate one's impulses and desires eclipses any attention to other people or non–self-focused perspective one possesses. Therefore, self-directedness is the pathway through which all other character traits are accessed and utilized. Practically, then, the key to unlocking the character mystery is through personal discipline. Ironically, this mystery has been understood for ages and has been cultivated throughout history in the form of spiritual disciplines.[63]

Implications for Character Development

Unfortunately, there is a great need for character development because most people haven't developed adequate character for the tasks they face. Countless stories exist of people who were unable to stand the pressure of leadership. In reality, that pressure revealed existing flaws. Left unresolved, those character flaws eventually bankrupt future leadership promise. Therefore, all who aspire to some form of leadership must commit to developing their own character.

The difficulty lies in the fact that even though it is possible to experience a transformation of character, "most people are not exposed to the types of life-changing influences that stimulate such transformations, and, further, if exposed, they tend not to change—that is, people are motivated toward consistency in character, not change or development."[64] No one enjoys suffering. Yet that is the path through which character is often developed in the life of the Christian. Additionally, we are often deceived in the

61. Samuel D. Rima, *Leading from the Inside Out: The Art of Self-Leadership* (Grand Rapids: Baker, 2000), 129.

62. Dragan M. Svrakic et al., "Differential Diagnosis of Personality Disorders by the Seven-Factor Model of Temperament and Character," *Archives of General Psychiatry* 50, no. 12 (1993).

63. See Richard J. Foster, *Celebration of Discipline: The Path to Spiritual Growth*, 25th anniversary ed. (San Francisco: HarperSanFrancisco, 1998). For more discussion on the nature and importance of the disciplines, see the chapters by Klaus Issler and Jonathan Morrow in this volume.

64. Robert Hogan and Robert Sinclair, "For Love or Money? Character Dynamics in Consultation," *Consulting Psychology Journal: Practice and Research* 49, no. 4 (1997): 257–58.

perceptions of our own virtues. What we need are courageous friends who are willing to walk through the fire with us while our mettle is refined.

Character Development Requires Community

Most psychologists would agree that "people develop character over time, primarily through socialization."[65] If this is true, we possess a desperate need for true community in which we can grow and be nurtured. This community must be one where the members practice "speaking the truth in love" (Eph. 4:15).

It is possible for a leader to be practicing authentic leadership (altruism) and be blinded by his or her own values, leading to pseudotransformational leadership in action.[66] The only safeguard against this is participation in the life of a community, which allows for the exercise of character development.

Scripture is clear that the reason the church, specifically the use of spiritual gifts, is essential in the life of each believer is "so that the body of Christ may be built up until we all reach unity in the faith and in the knowledge of the Son of God and become mature, attaining to the whole measure of the fullness of Christ" (Eph. 4:12–13). The way we are to accomplish this is by following Paul's command—"Submit to one another out of reverence for Christ" (Eph. 5:21).

We must belong to a community where each person can both know others and be known. A number of authors have attempted to call us to such expressions of true community, where we engage with each other, not try to escape from being known.[67] This ties in to the concept of self-regulation failure. It is possible for others to step in to sustain one's resources—resources that may be depleted through extreme periods of stress or significant loss. Other people can effectively come alongside the hurting person and offer their resources so that the wounded brother or sister can continue the fight and regain personal control over desires or impulses that may be raging internally. True community in such times means going the extra mile with someone, especially through those major periods of struggle and loss.

Unfortunately, my experience shows that most people rarely or never experience this kind of supportive community. Sadly, our everyday communities often do not exhibit the grace God intended his people to display.[68] Therefore, actively searching for and participating in this kind of community is paramount to the Christian's growth and development. Christians with mature character can provide the necessary leadership to create and

---

65. Ibid., 260.

66. Arbinger Institute, *Leadership and Self-Deception: Getting Out of the Box*; and Terry L. Price, "The Ethics of Authentic Transformational Leadership," *Leadership Quarterly* 14, no. 1 (2003): 67–81.

67. Lawrence J. Crabb, *The Safest Place on Earth: Where People Connect and Are Forever Changed* (Nashville: Word, 1999); and Donald Miller, *Blue Like Jazz: Nonreligious Thoughts on Christian Spirituality* (Nashville: Thomas Nelson, 2003).

68. Philip Yancey, *What's So Amazing About Grace?* (Grand Rapids: Zondervan, 1997).

sustain such communities so that others too may "become mature, attaining to the whole measure of the fullness of Christ."

Character Development Must Be Sustained

Character and value changes are not temporary. Character development is a long-term goal with setbacks along the way. It must be treated as a marathon, not a sprint. As mentioned above, lapses may occur along the journey due to self-regulation failures. These surface in a variety of ways, most readily as patterns of addiction and poor, self-centered decisions.

Paul himself exemplified the human condition when he wrote, "For what I want to do I do not do, but what I hate I do" (Rom. 7:15). The only hope is restored strength through the power of the Spirit. As Paul also encourages us, "Live by the Spirit, and you will not gratify the desires of the sinful nature" (Gal. 5:16). Again, the community takes part in this redemptive process as they collectively seek to understand how growth and development occurs through the life-giving power of worship—the heart of Christian education.[69]

Reflection Is Required to Facilitate Character Development

Considering the value of reflection in the development process, Badaracco found that the most satisfied business leaders were those who were "able to take time out from the chain of managerial tasks that consumes their time and undertake a process of probing self-inquiry."[70] For the leader, the most significant question that can be asked, according to Badaracco, is, "Who am I?" Indeed, we should make choices based on our identity. However, asking the question should also lead us to consider another one, "Who do I want to become?" which recognizes that we have not arrived and that we have much self-understanding to navigate.

Christian education is designed to function as dialectic in the formation process, examining the assumptions that form the basis for a particular belief system.[71] In fact, the educational process known as transformative learning theory[72] has much the same goal in mind—perspective transformation. This process requires an event that triggers the evaluation of one's understanding of "the way that the world works," also called one's worldview.

---

69. Craig R. Dykstra, "The Formative Power of the Congregation," in *Theological Perspectives on Christian Formation: A Reader on Theology and Christian Education*, ed. Jeff Astley, Leslie J. Francis, and Colin Crowder (Grand Rapids: Eerdmans, 1996), 252–65.

70. Joseph L. Badaracco Jr., "The Discipline of Building Character," *Harvard Business Review* 76, no. 2 (1998): 116.

71. David Tracy, "Can Virtue Be Taught? Education, Character and the Soul," in *Theological Perspectives on Christian Formation: A Reader on Theology and Christian Education*, ed. Jeff Astley, Leslie J. Francis, and Colin Crowder (Grand Rapids: Eerdmans, 1996), 374–89.

72. Jack Mezirow, *Transformative Dimensions of Adult Learning*, ed. Alan B. Knox, The Jossey-Bass Higher Education and Adult Series (San Francisco: Jossey-Bass, 1991).

At the core of the process is the consideration of what a person's actions reveal his belief system to be compared to what he says he believes. Organizational theorists call these belief systems "theories-in-use" versus "espoused theories" of action.[73] In a Christian context, Ward calls this operational versus professed theology. The goal of Christian education is to "narrow the gap" between these two belief systems through a fundamental reflection on and evaluation of our identities apart from transformed Christian character.[74]

Such theological reflection best occurs in the context of fellow ministers seeking to grow together in community. Different church traditions have seen fit to formalize this relationship between spiritual director and follower. However, it can occur in the context of internship or small group as well. Regardless of the context, the goal is "the candid application of God's truth."[75]

Conclusion

In conclusion, the development of our character is our aim, our desire being to mirror the character of God himself as just, merciful, and humble people who lead with others in mind. This development requires a long-term commitment to a loving community focused on the maturity of all its members. This process is agonizing at times and grueling at others, but there is joy that comes from loving God "with all your heart and with all your soul and with all your mind" and loving "your neighbor as yourself" (Matt. 22:37, 39). Such mature character is necessary to the creation of godly leaders who transform lives, families, communities, societies, and yes, even the world.

---

73. Chris Argyris, *Knowledge for Action: A Guide to Overcoming Barriers to Organizational Change* (San Francisco: Jossey-Bass, 1993).

74. David C. Ward, "Theological Archaeology: A Model for Theological Reflection in Field Education" (Th.M. thesis, Dallas Theological Seminary, 1998). Ward offers a process whereby one can dig through the "strata" of identity (spirituality, character, design, roles, and contexts) to determine where one's practice differs from a theologically correct praxis—the integration of theology with action.

75. Ibid., 16.

Chapter 7

Love and Spiritual Formation

Bill Miller

> Dear children, let us not love with words or tongue but with actions and in truth.
>
> —1 John 3:18

In 1995, my wife and I led a summer trip to Osh, Kyrgyzstan, with nine college students. We wanted to be a witness of God's love to Kyrgyz college students while we served them by running a cultural exchange program at the university's English department. That summer, I intentionally spent time getting to know the chairman of the English department because my wife and I had felt led to return for six months the following year to continue sowing the seed of the gospel, hoping that a Christian fellowship might eventually grow out of our witness. As we were determining what type of service we could provide to the department, I began to have doubts about the need to return the following year. After all, we were seeing great fruit. Perhaps we had done enough to serve the students and share the message of God's love with them. There was so much to be done back home as well.

In reality, I was attempting to rationalize my inherent discomfort with the location. For pampered Americans like myself, life was difficult in Osh. Water, electricity, and natural gas were scarce, and one could never tell when they might be turned off for hours or days at a time. Living conditions were very dirty and dusty. Food was prepared from scratch. There were no fast-food chains, grocery stores, or public restrooms to speak of. We were roughing it by our standards. On top of that, there were no typical American distractions to ease our discomforts. There were no movie theatres, video rental stores, relaxing vacation destinations, or health clubs.

One evening in the summer of 1995, I was standing on the small balcony of our third-floor apartment looking over the city as the Muslim call to prayer was being broadcast from the mosque. As I looked out over this city of three hundred thousand people, only a small handful of which were known to be followers of Jesus, suddenly all my doubts about returning vanished. The Lord clearly pointed out that in spite of my discomfort and discontentment with living in this place, God had called me to learn to love the people of that city and he had not released me from that calling merely by completing the first summer trip. God was pushing me to love in ways that were uncomfortable to me. I am convinced that Christian spiritual formation should always, at its core, be about learning to love, especially when loving others is uncomfortable or challenging.

Two passages dealing with the life of Peter provide particularly helpful insights into the central role that learning to love occupies in the Christian life, regardless of one's maturity level. Acts 10:1–48 and Galatians 2:11–16 describe two events in Peter's life that occur in two different locations and are separated by years of time, but both provide profound lessons for spiritual formation.

In Acts 10 while at Simon's house in Joppa, Peter receives a vision of a sheet filled with "unclean" animals prohibited for consumption by Jewish law. When the men sent by Cornelius the centurion arrive at Simon's house, we receive an indication that Peter immediately understands the meaning of the vision, for he invites the Gentile men in as guests. While the vision directs Peter to stop viewing Gentiles as unclean, the implication for Peter involves much more than merely accepting Gentiles into the new community of Christ followers. God is pushing Peter to personally love those with whom he does not naturally interact. This new directive violates everything he has been taught. Peter was not accustomed to associating with Gentiles. Of course, the vision he received makes the matter entirely clear to Peter, which is affirmed when he does not hesitate to invite Cornelius's messengers into Simon's house and proceeds to accompany them to Cornelius's house the next day. Peter understands that God is calling him to love in a way that is uncomfortable. We need to be prepared to respond in obedience when the Savior calls us to move into the lives of others in ways that make us uncomfortable, even as Peter did in this passage.

In Galatians 2:11–16, we again find Peter confronted by the issue of how to relate to Gentiles. This time Peter is in Antioch, having come up to visit the Christian community there, which included many Gentiles. Since this passage is primarily concerned with other issues that Paul is addressing, we do not get a complete picture of what occurred. However, we do know that Peter had been associating with Gentile believers during meals, but he suddenly stopped doing so when "men came from James." Paul tells us that he had to oppose Peter "to his face, because he was clearly in the wrong." This same Peter who was a primary, if not *the* primary leader of the young church, failed to apply the lessons he had learned through the dramatic vision in Joppa directing him to cease distancing himself from Gentiles.

Ask yourself these questions: "If I had as dramatic an experience as Peter had in his vision—the sheet coming down from heaven—would I ever forget? Would I ever have to relearn that lesson again?" Perhaps we should not be so hard on Peter. How many times has the Lord clearly taught us something yet we continue to struggle with living it out in our lives? It is one thing to know a principle; it is another thing altogether to apply it when trying to learn to love real people in the real world.

Five Key Principles for Learning to Love

At least five key principles emerge out of these two experiences from the life of Peter that help us in our journey of learning to love well. The first relates to our response to the opinions of those around us. The second is concerned with the prioritizing of the two Christian imperatives to resist sin and to learn to love (e.g., Gal. 5:13–14; 1 Peter 1:14, 22; 1 John 2:15–16; 4:7). The third and fourth principles deal with the dynamic nature of love in terms of both the uniquenesses of each individual and the changing life circumstances. The fifth principle relates to the sustaining power required in learning to love well.

Principle 1: Love Does Not Default to the Status Quo

The first principle is drawn from the motive behind Peter's failure in Antioch to consistently live with the vision he received in Acts 10. The text in Galatians 2 provides us with a glimpse of his heart. "But when they arrived, he began to draw back and separate himself from the Gentiles because *he was afraid of those who belonged to the circumcision group*" (Gal. 2:12, emphasis mine). The fear of others' opinions is what drives Peter to disassociate with the Gentiles. The men who came up to Antioch, sent from James, were obviously Jews who continued to live with the old "status quo approach" of the Jewish custom and law when it came to dealings with Gentiles, even those non-Jews who were now followers of Christ.

We must not deceive ourselves into thinking that we are not susceptible to this type of social pressure. If you think about it for even a few moments, you will realize your own current Christian community has developed a standard of behavior that defines what is deemed acceptable. Every community develops a status quo, usually to a greater degree of breadth the longer the community has been in existence. These status-quo standards of behavior are not always bad. The pressure to stay within accepted limits can provide powerful support against temptations. However, the principle as I have stated it is not "Love does not *follow* the status quo." Rather, it is that "love does not *default* to the status quo."

Whether or not you have given it much thought, your Christian community has a status quo when it comes to spiritual formation. In some communities emphasis is placed on personal Bible study; others emphasize participation in a fellowship group or witnessing to nonbelievers. Regardless of the subtle nuances in your community or tradition, you could probably put together a list of spiritual disciplines and practices that, if followed, give the impression to others in your community that you are a "strong Christian" or a "devoted believer."

The problem with assessing spiritual maturity according to a status-quo set of spiritual activities is that the degree to which a person is learning to love others well is often overlooked. For example, even if feeding the homeless on a regular basis is one of the valued activities of your church community, such an activity can be done in a rote, unloving manner. A person may hand out food to a homeless person without ever engaging in a process of thinking about what loving that person at that moment might involve, beyond handing the person a sandwich. Consistently following the requirements of the status quo can become the goal. Thus, emphasis is placed upon avoidance of "falling away" from such activities. Christians can begin to make avoidance of this "falling away" the primary goal. Sin is then defined as that which keeps us from living up to the standards of the status quo. Staying away from such sins becomes a primary issue.

Principle 2: Love Is Not Primarily Concerned with Sinning Less

The second principle is revealed in the sin of the men who came to Antioch from James. They were not merely influenced by the status quo; they believed in a status-quo view that was erroneous. Remember what Peter stated in the encounter with Cornelius, "You are well aware that it is against our law for a Jew to associate with a Gentile or visit him. But God has shown me that I should not call any man impure or unclean" (Acts 10:28). The "circumcision group" from James still believed that Gentiles were unclean and that associating with them would somehow make oneself unclean as well.

The circumcision group's view revealed a flawed type of thinking that still lives with Christians today. It assumes that avoiding sin is the primary objective of the Christian life. However, consider what Jesus says in Matthew 22:37–40 about the two greatest commandments. The emphasis is upon a movement from self to God and others, not a self-purification project. In Matthew 22, Jesus does not say: "Stop all of your sinning; this is the first and greatest commandment. And the second is like it, stay away from everyone who sins." Placing too much emphasis on avoiding sin can be a major distraction from the higher aim of the Christian life of learning to love others well. It becomes a distraction that blinds us from seeing and serving those whom God brings across our path.

At a New Year's Eve party recently, I experienced the subtle manner in which this exaggerated concern for sin can work. In the months leading up to the new year, I was finishing a dissertation project and preparing to complete a Ph.D. degree. My wife and I had recently learned that we had been accepted into a program that provided me with the opportunity to teach at a university in Prague, Czech Republic. Consequently, we were beginning to think through our move to Europe and our new life there. As the party approached, I was aware of two facts. (1) I did not know many people who would attend this party; thus I would be engaging in many conversations in which people would ask about my occupation. Of course, I expected to share with people that I was finishing my Ph.D. and preparing for a move to Europe to teach. (2) I tend to struggle with a lack of faith that, when interacting with others, can express itself in not exhibiting confidence about what God is doing in my life.

At the party, conversation often led to discussion of our move to Prague. I worked hard to put on a confident face about the whole endeavor, mostly with people I had never met. On my way home that night, a thought struck me like a blow from a sledgehammer. I could not recall a single question that I had asked of the people I met that night beyond, "What's your name?" or "What do you do for a living?" My attention was so centered on my own endeavor to avoid appearing to lack faith that I completely missed the opportunity to move toward others—to engage with them in a loving manner. I was attentive to self and not to others. I am convinced that my behavior is not what Jesus had in mind when he commanded me to love my neighbor as myself.

Love is not *primarily* concerned with sinning less. This is not to suggest that resisting sin is an endeavor that should be abandoned. Sinful behavior and habits are always destructive to ourselves and others. Interestingly, this points us to the reason why resisting sin, though important, is a secondary objective. Sin should be addressed precisely because sin is composed of attitudes and actions that keep us from loving well. In a sense, we can say that sin is anti-love. It does not seek the best interests of others. It does not even represent an attempt at serving oneself well. It is ultimately destructive to oneself, one's endeavor to love others well, and to the best interests of others.

In light of the above comments, one qualification must be made. While resisting sin is not the primary goal of the Christian life, there may be periods in which a person must focus his or her entire attention on dealing with a pattern of sin that is destructive to an excessive degree. I have friends who have had to take a season of life and focus their attention like a laser beam on dealing with an area of addiction, whether it be an addiction to sex, alcohol, or drugs. However, for a believer in such a season of life, the end must always be kept in sight. Overcoming the destructive behavior is not an end in itself. It should always be a means to the end of becoming capable of loving and serving others well.

Principle 3: Love Is a Dynamic Process

The third principle has to do with the nature of love. Loving another person well cannot be reduced to a formula or set of practices that can be robotically performed. Loving well requires constant thought and engagement with others. Peter learned the lesson of the equality of Jew and Gentile in a very dramatic way in a vision from the Lord, and he said, "I now realize how true it is that God does not show favoritism but accepts men from every nation who fear him and do what is right" (Acts 10:34–35). However, in Antioch he stopped thinking and learning about how to apply what God taught him. Though the principles of loving others are fairly simple and straightforward, living them out is a very complex and complicated process—as well as one that takes a great deal of energy. It requires that we develop a tenacious attentiveness to ourselves, people around us, and our circumstances.

Consider the passage concerning food sacrificed to idols in 1 Corinthians 8. Most of the sermons I have heard concerning this passage deal with the topic of liberty and a proper use of liberty. In order to gain a broader understanding of the passage, however, one has to think through the relational dynamic of what that passage requires of us. In order for the first-century Christian to know how to act when dining with a group of fellow believers, that person must know some things about the people at the table. Have you ever stopped to consider that the only way the teaching from 1 Corinthians can be personally applied is if you know the views of your brother in Christ. I would have to find out whether that brother thinks it is a sin to eat food sacrificed to idols. I would have to find out if that brother thinks the food on the table was sacrificed to idols. I have to engage with my brother. I have to ask questions and determine what he is thinking before I can determine whether I should eat certain foods or not. Figuring out what love looks like requires me to engage with each particular person in each situation.

Learning to love others is a dynamic process. One cannot assume that acting the same way with two different people expresses love to them in the same way. I have learned this many times in my family life. As a husband and father the challenge of loving my wife and two boys well is unique to each of them. If my wife is frustrated with some task she is seeking to accomplish, I have learned that the loving action is to immediately jump in and help her figure it out. If my eldest son is frustrated with some task, the loving action for him may be to simply acknowledge his difficulty with empathetic words, because he typically wants to solve the problem himself. For my youngest son, he may or may not want my help, so I have learned to first offer my help before giving it.

When my wife and I were about to be married, I heard the advice, "Be a student of your wife." That encouragement to develop attentiveness toward her has not always been heeded in our marriage, but when it has, the fruit has been abundant. Virtually every major period of growth in our marriage has started with either Lisa or me making crucial observations about the other, whether it had to do with recognizing tension in a certain communication habit or in an approach to physical intimacy. These observations led to discussion, which led to attempts to make real changes in our endeavor to learn to love one another well.

Since each individual is uniquely designed by God, with different personality traits, talents, limitations, and interests, the onus is upon us to develop a great sense of attentiveness to each person in our lives. The more time we spend with a person, the greater our responsibility becomes to love them well. The relationships I have the deepest sense of regret about are with people I spent a great deal of time with but did not exercise attentiveness. With those people, even if I wanted to express love well, I did not have the information I needed to do so. The fact that I did not exercise attentiveness with them was probably a sign that my heart was not concerned enough with their best interest from the beginning.

Principle 4: Love Must Be a Commitment in Every Season of Life

This fourth principle is certainly true in marriage but also in friendship. Life, as designed by God, will always bring us different seasons of life. It is built into the nature of human existence. We humans typically experience childhood, adolescence, young adulthood, adulthood, marriage, raising children, empty nest, and elderly stages of life. In addition to these life stages, we experience changes in geographic location (whenever we move or travel), in schools, in family dynamics (especially with the increase of broken homes), in jobs, in hobbies and interests, in friendships, and in health. All these factors result in constantly changing circumstances. I call seasons of life those periods that, generally speaking, present a person with a fairly stable set of conditions. A season of life can be short or long.

God grows us by putting us in new situations, as he did with Peter, so that we grow to trust him more and learn to love well in a variety of circumstances. To return to Peter's story, remember that he had no problem interpreting the message of the vision with regard to Cornelius and his family. Surely it was hard for him to apply since associating with Gentiles was not a regular practice of his. Nonetheless, he was able to obey God's message, and much fruit was born in his ministry in Caesarea. Peter's problem arose when he was in a different city (Antioch), in different circumstances (with Jews whom he knew did not accept association with Gentiles), and in a different time (the vision had grown cloudy). We can assume his failure involved many factors, but one was that this was a different season of life for Peter. He was in need of relearning what he knew and how to apply it in a new situation.

While I consider the nine months of my sophomore year in college to be one season of life, the seven years working on my Ph.D. was also a distinct season of life. As a sophomore in college, I lived alone and experienced a period of deep loneliness. After a fun, exciting freshman year in a social dorm, my second year found me living on the other side of campus from most of my friends, wondering how I fit in. It was a year of doubt about my ability to succeed in school and about the overwhelming time commitment of playing a varsity sport and being involved in ministry activities.

The seven years spent working on my Ph.D. was a much longer segment of time, but also a distinct season of life. It was a season of long endurance in school and raising young children. More times than I would like to remember, I had to recall that God had led me to the school I was attending and had confirmed in various ways my endeavor to finish a Ph.D. It felt like I was journeying along one of those long, winding set of switchbacks on a hike, wondering if I would ever reach the summit.

Both of those seasons of life brought new challenges to my calling to learn to love well. My sophomore year forced me to learn how to take the time to be proactive and go out of my way to sustain old friendships and make new ones. The Ph.D. years taught me how to love my wife and two boys in the midst of working full-time in ministry while a doctoral student. (A consistent prayer was that God would multiply my time, which he did on a regular basis!) I had to learn how to be present and involved in my wife and kids' lives while juggling several commitments—largely by sacrificing my sleep to early mornings. I have many memories of failure in both of those seasons of life. The point is not whether I avoided failure, or sin, or mistakes. The point is that God taught me how to love in new ways and in new circumstances. If I am wise, I will remember that he will continue to challenge me with new opportunities to learn to love in new ways in future seasons of life, and I will embrace those opportunities.

In a sense, the challenge presented by different seasons of life is simply another aspect of the dynamic nature of learning to love. One way that it warrants its own discussion, however, is that loving the same person in a different season of life can look entirely different. For example, just after our wedding day, my wife and I moved to the San Francisco Bay area, where we knew no one. In that season of life, we were newly married without any close friends nearby and were working together in ministry with college students. We were learning to be a husband and a wife to each other, but we were also each other's best and only friend, as well as coworkers. It was a great time to build a strong sense of identity as a couple. I learned over time how to draw her out with good questions. Having spent the majority of our waking hours together, including virtually all of our free time, there was an abundance of opportunities to pursue her and keep up-to-date with the state of her thoughts and her heart. It did not always come naturally; some of my questions hurt her feelings or failed to connect. Over time, however, I improved in learning not only the types of questions to ask but also how to ask them in a way that cultivated intimacy.

In the later season of life when I was a graduate student and working in ministry, she was managing our home and volunteering in our kids' school and at our church. We could go days without an hour to talk about everything that was happening in our lives. Our earlier habit of leisurely discussing, throughout the evening, our day's events was no longer a reality. After dinner, the time spent with our kids and getting them into bed left no energy for significant conversation. We had to be much more intentional and proactive in carving out time in which we could pursue each other. For example, I learned to recognize and value opportunities to have lunch dates with her, which provided us with an hour to talk about life when we were not exhausted after getting the kids to bed.

In my current season of life, as a professor in Prague with older children in a new culture, I will face new challenges and opportunities. I must remain committed to learning how to love in light of the changes. Every new season of life forces me to develop new habits and a new kind of attentiveness to my wife, my children, and others in order to keep learning to love them well. It forces me to change but also provides opportunities for growth. When I change and adjust, I communicate that I am attentive enough and committed enough to see and meet the changing needs of the people in my life.

Friendships, as well as family relationships, face the same challenges as the result of different seasons of life. One of the most common adjustments that friendships have to make comes when one of two friends either gets married first or has children before the other. During the period when I got married and started having kids, my lifetime friend and former college roommate remained single. He was a tremendous blessing during that time of my life because, while I mostly failed to uphold my side of the friendship, rarely contacting him, he sustained the friendship with frequent phone calls and trips to visit me. Now, he is married and beginning to have children and facing the pressures of that new season of life. My current schedule, while busy, is becoming more manageable. I anticipate that it is now my turn to return the favor and invest the lion's share of initiative.

The same principle operates in workplace relationships as well. My mother has experienced this dynamic in her working career. After more than twenty years in one position, she was asked to take on a position in an entirely different department. The staff she had worked with for all those years remained behind. Her relationships with those coworkers remained, but the nature of those relationships changed since she was no longer the supervisor. She has had to learn what loving them looks like as a friend but no longer as their boss. She had to be sensitive to resisting their desire to criticize their new boss in her presence, while continuing to support them as a friend.

Principle 5: Love Is Sustained When We Experience His Love

When we stop and think about all that is involved in this process of learning to love others well, it is easy to become overwhelmed. It can easily lead to a kind of stoic attempt at self-denial, in which we resist any consideration of self-interest in order to fulfill the duty to love others. Such attempts will be in vain. The reason I make this bold claim will become clear shortly. However, the reason for such extreme but erroneous approaches to love is that the task is so overwhelming.

Everything that has been discussed above is a massive challenge. How can a person sustain a commitment to invest one's mental energy, time, and even physical energy to meet the needs of other people on a consistent basis? Think of the life of a young mother. Every single moment must be tirelessly given for the sake of those little children. How does she sustain an attitude of service toward those little ones when changing hundreds of diapers, comforting them in their distresses, and keeping a constant eye out for their safety? A mother in these conditions grows tired of the infrequency with which she gets to enjoy adult conversation. She grows tired of never having enough time to care for her own needs. Exhaustion weighs her down. And if these conditions present a challenge, consider the life of a single mother of young children!

The challenge, of course, is not limited to young mothers. Consider the life of a supervisor in a typical work environment. Supervisors do not have life as easy as we might like to think. The challenge of loving subordinates well is also substantial. Managers are responsible for accomplishing certain business objectives on a monthly, weekly, and daily basis. They bear the "pressure from above" in the organization. However, a boss's calling as a follower of Christ is to love his or her subordinates well (see Eph. 6:9). With all the demands placed on supervisors to perform, and the temptation to base a sense of personal significance on the success of their working group, the task of paying attention to and serving the needs of one's subordinates is never easy. How can a boss set aside the "demands from above" and the temptation to look out for "number one" so that he or she can support and empower subordinates to succeed and find fulfillment in their jobs?

The challenge is no less difficult for the subordinate. If we take the principles in Ephesians 6 dealing with a master-slave relationship to be applicable to a subordinate-supervisor relationship, we find that subordinates are called to obey their supervisors "with respect and fear, and with sincerity of heart, just as you would obey Christ" (v. 5). Loving a boss well, then, involves nothing less than completing tasks given to you and performing them as "unto the Lord." However, loving a boss well could include such things as recognizing the boss's unique contributions, showing appreciation for his or her leadership, and working to make him or her successful. This, of course, requires you to occasionally, or perhaps often, lay aside personal concern for "climbing the ladder" and building your own reputation.

Loving others well in any setting requires a commitment to lay aside the issues in your own life in order to listen to and provide support to others in their trials and difficulties. Love does not insist that others acknowledge your problems but patiently supports them with their problems. How can this be sustained in those situations when you are struggling with a major difficulty in your own life and the problem of your friend is minor in comparison? In Matthew 14 Jesus offers a fascinating example of this kind of service toward others. Jesus was deeply grieved by the death of John the Baptist and attempted to withdraw to "a solitary place" (v. 13). However, when the crowds followed him, he did not insist that they acknowledge his difficulty; rather he spent the entire evening healing the sick and feeding the "five thousand." How is it possible to have such love, which gives itself away instead of focusing on one's own concerns and struggles? The imperative to learn to love well can feel like a hopelessly unrealistic endeavor.

The key to overcoming this great challenge is also found in the Acts 10 passage. When Peter describes the gospel to Cornelius's household, he mentions that this message is being spread "by us who ate and drank with him after he rose from the dead" (v. 41). When Peter ate and drank with the Savior after the resurrection, Jesus reinstated Peter (John 21), demonstrating his love for the apostle. The vision in Joppa of the sheet coming down three times from heaven was probably an additional reminder to Peter of Jesus' threefold questioning method for reinstatement. Just as Peter needed grace to be reinstated as an apostle and just as the lost need grace for the cleansing of sin, so followers of Christ need grace to love. The grace to love, it turns out, begins with a reception of God's love into our lives. When we experience the love of God, we are empowered to love others.

The prerequisite for loving others is receiving love from the Father. Paul's prayer in Ephesians 3 is a demonstration of that principle.

> I pray that out of his glorious riches he may strengthen you with power through his Spirit in your inner being, so that Christ may dwell in your hearts through faith. And I pray that you, being rooted and established in love, may have power, together with all the saints, to grasp how wide and long and high and deep is the love of Christ, and to know this love that surpasses knowledge—that you may be filled to the measure of all the fullness of God. (Eph. 3:16–19)

The ability to love others well is possible only when we "grasp how wide and long and high and deep is the love of Christ." It turns out that the power to love is the power of God in us. That power is manifested when we are "filled to the measure of all the fullness of God." Notice that just after the apostle Paul prays this prayer for the Ephesians, he urges them to "live a life worthy of the calling" of Christ (Eph. 4:1). That calling has as its cornerstone love. "Be completely humble and gentle; be patient, bearing with one another in love" (Eph. 4:2), Paul writes. After a discussion of the need for unity in the body and the necessity of throwing off the old life of self-gratification, Paul says, "Be imitators of God . . . and live a life of love, just as Christ loved us and gave himself up for us" (Eph. 5:1–2). This unity could only come about as a result of the body knowing and experiencing the love of Christ.

The centrality of love as an aim of the Christian life is repeated in 1 Corinthians 13 as well. This famous love chapter concludes with the statement, "And now these three remain: faith, hope and love. But the greatest of these is love" (v. 13). Faith is now critical since we trust in one who is currently invisible to us. Hope is now critical since we live in light of a better future, not for the passing pleasures of this world. Love, however, remains with us forever. The love of the incarnational Savior, who took on human form, shed his blood, and rose from the dead on our behalf, has no limitations or end. His love for us is eternal, just as he is eternal.

As we are beginning to experience "all the fullness of God," we cannot help but have that love overflow into the lives of others. We become a conduit of his love in the world. We are empty vessels or buckets into which God pours his love and out of which his love spills over. While others may wrongly conclude that the "vessel" is the source of love, a consistent expression of love in and through our lives will demonstrate to them that the source of this love exceeds the capacity of a mere human. How does a hurricane victim make sense out of the volunteer service of a computer software engineer who takes his vacation time to spend a week shoveling mud four inches thick out of her home because she has no insurance money to pay for it? How does a subordinate explain the decision of her boss to cancel an important meeting in order to go out for coffee and encourage her in light of her loss of a family member? How can anyone explain the ultimate sacrifice of an innocent one who took the capital punishment deserved by others? Such loving acts are possible only when the love of God is experienced. The software engineer shovels because he is loved. The boss empathizes because he is loved. The Savior died because he was and is loved by the Father. "And so we know and rely on the love God has for us. God is love. Whoever lives in love lives in God, and God in him.... We love because he first loved us" (1 John 4:16, 19).

Only when people are completely secure in the unchanging, unwavering, and fierce love of God are they prepared to love the way God calls them to love. Why will people risk the possibility of rejection, shame, manipulation, and pain by giving of themselves for the sake of another? The only reason people will do this is if they have a foundation so unmovable and so fulfilling that putting themselves on the line in service to another does not threaten their sense of identity. Rather, when we associate ourselves with Christ, the ultimate servant leader, we are both inspired by his example of service and secure in our identity in him.

God Will Be Glorified

Jesus' prayer in John 17 explains the relationship between the Father and the Son's love for each other, the Son's love for us, and the Father's love for us.

> My prayer is not for them alone. I pray also for those who will believe in me through their message, that all of them may be one, Father, just as you are in me and I am in you. May they also be in us so that the world may believe that you have sent me. I have given them the glory that you gave me, that they may be one as we are one: I in them and you in me. May they be brought to complete unity to let the world know that you sent me and have loved them even as you have loved me. (John 17:20–23)

The Son's love is evident in his expression of care for us. He desires good for us; he prays that we might be brought into unity with the Father. The Father loves us even as he has loved the Son. The love of Father and Son is expressed in their oneness. That oneness also is to be experienced by us. We are called to experience the love of the Father and the Son. Our experience of God's love ought to so change us that it will be evident to all. Thus, we arrive at the chief aim of our existence—to glorify him who makes us and sustains us. We are called to experience his love and be a conduit of it in the world so that "the world may believe" that the Son was sent into the world by the Father. Our experience of divine love is one of our chief evangelistic tools, if not the primary evangelistic tool.

A Call to Action

If we want to be conduits of God's love in the world, our expressions of love in the world need to be patterned after his expressions. We have not experienced God's love in an ethereal way. It is not just an abstract concept that we are redeemed through Christ. We experience God's love because we have responded to concrete and meaningful expressions of his love toward us—none more significant than the Son's physical atonement for our sins. Our love also must be a love characterized by action. Spiritual formation must never be a private experience or an entirely interior experience. It should express itself in an active love for others.

> This is how we know what love is: Jesus Christ laid down his life for us. And we ought to lay down our lives for our brothers. If anyone has material possessions and sees his brother in need but has no pity on him, how can the love of God be in him? Dear children, let us not love with words or tongue but with actions and in truth. (1 John 3:16–18)

The example given in 1 John 3 is by no means meant to be the only active expression of Christian love. Providing for the material needs of another person is a great example, but only one of an unlimited number of ways a believer can express active love in the world. The body of Christ expresses love in the world in countless ways: adoption services, feeding the poor, shelters for the abused, health care, and educational efforts, just to name a few. However, individual Christ followers have the opportunity to serve others every moment of their lives, whether simply assisting someone as they load their groceries in their car or caring for someone's children during a family tragedy.

Regardless of our track record, whether or not a person has "been in ministry" full-time or is coming out of an addictive lifestyle, every new moment we live presents an opportunity to serve others. The Spirit of God will cause us to "see" brothers and sisters in need. He will prod and guide us in the process, but each of us is responsible to act. This process, as we have discussed above, is dynamic and requires us to expend mental, emotional, and (at times) physical energy. Learning to love well is the challenge of a lifetime, and for that reason it can be the most exciting endeavor a human being can attempt. No two days are the same, and each is filled with opportunity.

"I Love You"

Nowhere in the New Testament does Jesus tell someone, "I love you." Though there is nothing wrong with this statement of affection, the gospel writers provide no evidence that Jesus ever said such a thing. Rather, he lived it. Everything he did was an expression of love for his enemies—since we were all slaves to sin, in need of redemption.

I know someone who had a childhood experience that was the exact opposite of my own. This person's father consistently told his children that he loved them with a persuasive sense of emotion. Unfortunately, the children were not left with childhood memories of being deeply loved. The father's verbal commitments were not effectively expressed in action. He was not abusive or overbearing, but neither did he engage with and communicate with his children in a way in which his words were lived out. My own father, to my memory, rarely told me he loved me as a child. However, this fact in no way hindered his ability to effectively express love. I have never in my life questioned that fact. His actions have communicated care, concern, and support to me at every point along the way.

My greatest fear for the body of Christ is that we might consistently say that we are committed to loving others—we might give cognitive assent to the primacy of the Great Commandment—and yet never effectively express love in action. If spiritual formation does not result in a people who are learning to love well in every season of life and in every community, then we are engaged in a spiritual formation that is missing the mark. All of our efforts to develop intimacy with the Savior—Bible study, prayer disciplines, journaling, meditation, and so on—ought to deepen our experience of his love in such a way that we are moved to love with action. May we, like Paul, be so compelled by the love of God that we cannot help but act in service of others.

CHAPTER 8

LEADERSHIP AND SPIRITUAL FORMATION

Andrew Seidel

> Leadership is one of the most observed and least understood phenomena on earth.
>
> —James MacGregor Burns, *Leadership*, 158

> Now that I, your Lord and Teacher, have washed your feet, you also should wash one another's feet. I have set you an example that you should do as I have done for you.
>
> —John 13:14–15

Leadership and spiritual formation have a symbiotic relationship. Both, by their very nature, require the production and experience of continuous change. From one perspective, spiritual formation involves individual change while leadership involves group or organizational change, which also requires individual change. Certainly spiritual transformation in a group or ministry setting requires effective spiritual leadership. But the most critical element of the symbiotic relationship is that effective transformational leadership[1] in any environment, religious or secular, requires the spiritual transformation of the leader. As leadership studies have progressed over the

1. *Transformational leadership* is a term first made popular by James MacGregor Burns. In *Leadership* (New York: Harper & Row, 1978), he contrasts "transactional leadership" and "transformational leadership." Transactional leadership is founded on a transactional agreement between leader and follower that each will provide what the other desires: for example, the leader will provide pay and benefits; the follower will provide forty hours of work per week to accomplish the leader's goals. On the other hand, transformational leadership "looks for potential motives in followers, seeks to satisfy higher needs, and engages the full person of the follower. The result of transforming leadership is a relationship of mutual stimulation and elevation that converts followers into leaders and may convert leaders into moral agents" (p. 4).

last few years, the role of the inner life of the leader is becoming more commonly recognized.

Even with the avalanche of new books on leadership, there is still no common agreement on the meaning of leadership. A surprising number of these new books claim to provide the "secret" to effective leadership, as though there is some previously undiscovered simple key to leadership success. Definitions of leadership seem to multiply at an alarming rate, with each mutation focusing on the particular writer's own perspective or reflecting the values of the current culture. The frustration with so much detail but so little definition is expressed by one of the leading researchers in the area of leadership: "Four decades of research on leadership have produced a bewildering mass of findings. . . . It is difficult to know what, if anything, has been convincingly demonstrated by replicated research. The endless accumulation of empirical data has not produced an integrated understanding of leadership."[2]

While the lack of resolution is frustrating, what is encouraging is the fact that more and more writers in the area of leadership are recognizing the importance of the inner life of the leader. Leading "from the inside out" has become a recurring theme, even in the secular arena. The inner motivations of the leader are not hermetically sealed in a secure place within the leader. Rather, they stretch far beyond the leader and have a powerful impact on the followers as well as on the organization as a whole.

Jim Collins, in his excellent book, *Good to Great*, notes that one of the key factors that enable good companies to make the transition to become great companies is the presence of what he calls "Level 5 Leadership." His researchers noted a striking similarity in the great companies studied: all the CEOs of these companies possessed two traits in common. They were not charismatic personalities; none were favorites of the media, and their names were not commonly recognized. But they were characterized by the two qualities of "extreme personal humility and intense professional will."[3] Together, these qualities describe the inner motivation of a leader who focuses his strong passion on the good of the company he leads, not on his own personal ego needs. In contrast, for self-centered leaders "work will always be first and foremost about what they *get*—fame, fortune, adulation, power, whatever—not about what they *build*, create, and contribute."[4]

Collins might have called this type of leadership "servant leadership"; in fact, some of his researchers suggested that he do so. But the title was rejected because of the current common use of the term. In fact, "servant

---

2. Ralph Stogdill, as quoted in Harris W. Lee, *Effective Church Leadership: A Practical Sourcebook* (Minneapolis: Augsburg, 1989), 12.

3. Jim Collins, *Good to Great* (New York: HarperCollins, 2001), 21.

4. Ibid., 36.

leadership" has enjoyed a resurgence in the secular leadership literature. Robert Greenleaf's *Servant Leadership*, published in 1977, began the current interest in the connection between leadership and servanthood. Writers, both secular and Christian, now focus on servant leadership. The connection between leadership and servanthood moves the leadership discussion into the inner life of the leader. No longer can the leader's inner life be crowded out by the pragmatic emphasis on the skills of leadership.

The Meaning of Servant Leadership

Servant leadership is a biblical concept that Jesus worked diligently to impress on his disciples. They, like us, had a difficult time with it. Jesus' last and clearest statement of servant leadership occurred on the way to the garden of Gethsemane shortly after the Last Supper. By this time the disciples had been with him almost three years. They had seen him heal the sick, raise the dead, and cast out demons from afflicted people. They had heard his teaching, experienced close community with him, and, only a few moments before, reluctantly allowed him to wash their feet.

But as they walked toward the garden that night, they went back to a common issue among them: they got into a heated argument about which one of them was regarded to be the greatest! If it were not also so true of us, we might chide them, wondering how they could possibly be so blind and self-centered.

> And there arose also a dispute among them *as to* which one of them was regarded to be greatest. And He said to them, "The kings of the Gentiles lord it over them; and those who have authority over them are called 'Benefactors.' But *it is* not this way with you, but the one who is the greatest among you must become like the youngest, and the leader like the servant. For who is greater, the one who reclines *at the table* or the one who serves? Is it not the one who reclines *at the table*? But I am among you as the one who serves." (Luke 22:24–27 NASB)

With great patience Jesus draws their attention to the self-centered leadership of the Gentile political leaders of their day, leaders who had the audacity to require their subjects to call them "benefactors," while these same leaders selfishly used their subjects and lorded it over them. This kind of leadership is better described as self-serving leadership. Jesus challenged his disciples to be different; in his view the leader is to be like a servant. While there is much talk about servant leadership today, there is also much confusion. Some suggest that servant leadership is simply a passive style of leadership in which the leader has no agenda. But Jesus himself was anything but passive, and he certainly had an agenda.

Servant leadership is not a style of leadership at all; it is much more foundational. Servant leadership is primarily expressed in the inner motivation of the leader. Stated simply, a servant leader is not motivated by personalized power or benefit. A servant leader is primarily motivated by two things: (1) the fulfillment of God's mission for his or her ministry or organization and (2) the fulfillment of God's purpose in the lives of the people who are part of the ministry or organization. This means that the passion of this leader is not focused on his or her power, benefits, reputation, perks, or privileges; it is on the fulfillment of a godly purpose and on the good of the people being led. This is a high and unselfish focus. No wonder we, like the disciples, have such difficulty living it.

How God Develops His Servant Leaders

Servant leadership is so critical to God's purpose in the world that God will go to great lengths to develop it in his followers. The missionary statesman J. Oswald Sanders comments, "It has been said that in achieving His world-purpose, God's method has always been a man. Not necessarily a noble man, or a brilliant man, but always a man with capacity for a growing faith. Granted this, there appears to be no limit to the pains God is willing to take in his training. He is limited by neither heredity nor environment."[5]

In the past several years, leadership training has concentrated on knowledge and skills. But from a Christian perspective, there is more to leadership development than knowledge and skills, as important as both are. God is more concerned with the development of the person of the leader. Through the course of life, God works in our lives to mold and strengthen us, to prepare us to be his leaders. God either brings or allows experiences into our lives; some are pleasant and enjoyable, and others are excruciatingly painful and anything but enjoyable. Either way, God uses our experiences to work on our heart. He orchestrates our experiences as challenges to mold our heart, to jar us out of our comfort zones, to shake up our complacency, to make us look inward, deep into our heart, until some crisis shows who we have become. God focuses his effort on our heart, because, at its core, leadership is more a matter of heart than it is of knowledge or skills.

God will involve each of us in something that is more of a pilgrimage than a process. "Process" is much too mechanical; "pilgrimage" is much more personal. Pilgrimages are powerful experiences. A pilgrimage is "a transformative journey to a sacred center full of hardships, darkness, and peril."[6] People make pilgrimages in order to be transformed by the experience. Sometimes they are religious pilgrimages; most of the time they are personal pilgrimages. Either way, there must be an element of difficulty and hardship, even danger, something that challenges us to the depths of our souls. Without the hardship there would be no extending of ourselves past the boundaries of our comfort zone, no true transformation.

---

5. J. Oswald Sanders, *Robust in Faith* (Chicago: Moody Press, 1965), 9.
6. Phil Cosineau, *The Art of Pilgrimage* (Berkley, CA: Conari Press, 1998).

God will see to it that you are stretched far enough that the effect of your pilgrimage will be to get you to examine your heart, your inner life.

This is why your willingness to enter deeply into your own "life story" is so critical (see chapter 10 for a discussion of life story). We are so immersed in the pressured flow of life that we move from one crisis to the next activity to the following event, seldom if ever pausing to reflect on what those experiences are teaching us. Unless we stop and reflect on the formative experiences and relationships of our life, we will miss the transformative purpose that God intended. But there is indeed "no limit to the pains God is willing to take in our training."[7] In all our experiences, his goal will be to teach us to depend upon Christ . . . for everything, including a secure sense of personal identity.

Personal Identity: The Enabling Element in Servant Leadership

Through our pilgrimage, one of the primary elements God wants to deal with is our sense of personal identity. He has good reason for doing this. Leadership is primarily an expression of who we are. No matter what leadership style we use, or what leadership skills we employ, our actions as leaders always come through the grid of who we are. One might expect Christian writers to focus on the inner life of the leader, but even secular writers are recognizing that, first and foremost, leaders lead out of who they are. Bennis observes that "no leader sets out to be a leader per se, but rather to express himself freely and fully. That is, leaders have no interest in proving themselves, but an abiding interest in expressing themselves. The difference is crucial, for it's the difference between being driven, as too many people are today, and leading, as too few people do."[8]

Leadership is about self-expression. In its best form, leadership is about the outward expression of the reality that is within the heart of the leader. The reality in the heart of the leader is related to the leader's sense of personal identity. The importance of this for leadership is that we will either lead out of our sense of personal identity, or we will lead in order to establish our sense of personal identity. The difference is critical, for those who lead in order to build an identity for themselves will end up selfishly using those they lead to gain from their followers what they themselves desperately desire. At this point, servant leadership crosses that dim line in the sand into self-serving leadership.

On that same night in which the disciples got into the argument about which one of them was regarded to be the greatest, Jesus had given them an experience that was a visible model of servant leadership. As the disciples entered the borrowed room that had been arranged for the supper, most of them seemed primarily concerned about getting the prime positions at the table. One of them was preoccupied with the betrayal he had already

---

7. Sanders, *Robust in Faith*, 9.

8. Warren Bennis, *On Becoming a Leader* (Reading, MA: Addison-Wesley, 1989), 5.

committed himself to accomplish. All of them passed by the basin and the towel set near the door to enable them to wash the dust of the road off their feet. Because it was a rented room, there was no servant at the door to wash their feet; and none of the disciples was willing to take on the role of a servant, not even temporarily.

The gospel of John describes in vivid terms what happened during the supper. Jesus got up from supper, took the basin and towel, and performed the role of a servant by washing the disciples' feet, one at a time. Some were embarrassed, Peter so much so that he resisted. It was inconceivable to Peter that one in Jesus' position, "the Christ, the Son of the living God" (Matt.16:16), would be willing to act as a servant. Even today, two thousand years later, it is still astounding. But John gives us insight into Jesus' thinking, which gives perspective on what enables the greatest leader to act as the humblest servant. If we diagram John 13:1–5, the insight becomes evident:

John 13:1–5

1 Now before the Feast of the Passover,
Jesus
knowing that His hour had come
that He would depart out of this world to the Father,
having loved His own who were in the world,
He loved them to the end.
2 . . . .
3 knowing that the Father had given all things into His hands,
and
that He had come forth from God
and
was going back to God,
4 got up from supper, and
laid aside His garments; and taking a towel, He
girded Himself.
5 poured water into the basin, and
began to wash the disciples' feet. (NASB)

John indicates that it was what Jesus knew about himself that was a precursor to his washing the disciples' feet. Jesus had a secure sense of his personal identity. He had a thorough understanding of his divine origin, his eternal purpose, his authority as the Son of God, and his destiny to be seated again at the right hand of the Father. With this secure sense of his own personal identity, taking the role of a servant was not the threat to him that it was to the disciples. For any of us, the ability to be a leader who acts as a servant will depend on the presence of a personal identity that is secure enough that we do not need to focus our attention on protecting an insecure identity that is threatened by unselfishly focusing our attention and efforts on the good of others. A secure sense of personal identity is what sets us free to focus on the good of others.

The Meaning of Identity

A sense of personal identity is a complicated concept to describe. It has many elements, some visible, some invisible. Parker Palmer describes the complexity this way: "By identity I mean an evolving nexus where all the forces that constitute my life converge in the mystery of self. . . . identity is a moving intersection of the inner and outer forces that make me who I am, converging in the irreducible mystery of being human."[9]

Starting with the most concrete and visible elements, personal identity includes a person's gender and ethnicity. These are outward marks of who we are. Identity also includes our temperament and our gifts, our strengths, weaknesses, and character flaws. Identity includes who we have become as a result of the life experiences God has taken us through. These experiences, and especially our responses to them, have shaped and molded us.

But identity is still more than that. Residing deep within us is a powerful need to feel secure and significant.[10] Each of us desperately longs to feel warmly and securely loved and accepted and to sense that we are persons of substance, that our life makes a meaningful difference. Thus our sense of identity at a deeper level includes feelings of competence and a sense of significance, that our life has value and worth. Because of the strength of these normal human longings, our early experiences play a dominant role in the formation of our sense of identity. Our experience of relationship with our parents, siblings, and other family members leave a powerful imprint on our sense of identity, an imprint that we carry into later life. Feelings of rejection, criticism, shame, or abuse make us feel deeply devalued and expendable. Because our very survival seems to be at stake, and we do not have the maturity to know how to get the help we so desperately need, we develop coping strategies to dull the pain and create the illusion of being loved and valued. These strategies become such a part of us that we no longer recognize them, even while they control our search for identity.

All of these elements, both positive and negative, are blended together in a powerful mix that strongly impacts the way each of us lives our life. One way of picturing our personal identity is to view it as a personal inner map, a map that is part of a larger map. In this view, our identity becomes a boundary that marks us off as different from others. The borders on our part of the larger map distinguish us from the rest of the map and show us how and where we fit into the larger scheme of things. Our identity, filled out by our gifts and abilities, indicates what we uniquely contribute. In this

---

9. Parker J. Palmer, *The Courage to Teach: Exploring the Inner Landscape of a Teacher's Life* (San Francisco: Jossey-Bass, 1998), 13.

10. Larry Crabb, *Understanding People* (Grand Rapids: Zondervan, 1987), 109–15.

sense the boundary is one that frees us to focus on doing well those things that are unique to us. We can concentrate on the things God has gifted and developed us to do. We do not have to spend energy trying to focus on other parts of the larger map. This kind of boundary is an expanding boundary. The more we work and lead from the center of our giftedness, the greater our fulfillment.

However, if we do not have a positive and secure sense of our personal identity, the boundary can be one that limits us to self-centered attempts to fill up that painful sense of emptiness we feel because we are insecure about who we are and what significance and value we have. In this case we begin to feel a sense of compulsion and drivenness to demonstrate to the world that we are persons of value and substance, worthy to be loved and respected.

It is from within this boundary of identity that we exercise leadership. As Warren Bennis suggested, there is a difference between being driven and leading. A driven person feels a powerful sense of being compelled to gain a desired response from others in order to fill up an empty pit of internal need. He needs their approval, or applause, or acquiescence, or adoration. So he will relate to them in whatever ways he feels will get them to give the desired response. This is not real leadership; it is actually manipulation of others so that the person in a leadership position can gain whatever he thinks will meet his identity needs. His concern is for himself, not for the good of those he is responsible to lead.

In contrast, true leading is enabled by the internal security that gives a joyous sense of freedom to use one's gifts and developed skills to express oneself for a godly purpose and for the good of those led. This secure personal identity allows a leader to turn his or her attention away from personal needs to focus on the needs of the ministry or organization and the people in it. There is no servant leadership without it.

How Identity Impacts Our Leadership

Our sense of personal identity becomes a boundary that determines how we see reality. This is one primary reason why people see things differently. For example, a church was split into two opposing sides in a controversy over the form the church would take in the future. Would it become more contemporary and "seeker" focused, or would it continue in its more traditional and "blended" form? As the argument gained power, the opposing camps became more antagonistic toward each other. After an especially heated congregational meeting, a church member who had been out of town and missed the meeting asked friends from both sides of the conflict about what happened at the meeting. The two descriptions he heard were so different that he wondered whether they had been at the same meeting! The different accounts were the result of selective perception. People tend to see what they expect to see. Even more, we tend to see what we need to see. If our sense of identity is connected to a need to be right or to be on the winning side, we tend to see things in harmony with that, and other information is screened out. And, of course, people on the other side do the same thing. Our ability to lead well is in this way severely restricted.

Second, our identity tends to strongly impact what we do. If we are attempting to construct our identity from our work or ministry, we will feel a strong compulsion to be successful, or to be needed, or to be in control of things, or to be in a position of recognized power. Or we will feel an inner need to always be "right," or always have the last word, or to be recognized and applauded. A leader in this situation will be strongly self-focused as he tries to make sure that he gets what he feels he cannot do without.

Third, it follows that our sense of personal identity will strongly influence how we relate to others. If our sense of identity is not satisfying and secure, we will sense a painful inner deficit. That personal deficit will become a powerful motivator to fill up our sense of emptiness, and we will begin to manipulate others to get from them that which we think will give us a satisfying sense of personal identity. In this way, an inadequate sense of personal identity leads directly to self-serving leadership.

Saul, the Example of a Driven Leader

Saul of Tarsus was clearly a driven man. He was driven to extremes of cruelty and oppression that would certainly qualify him as a terrorist in today's terminology. The first time we encounter him in Scripture is in Acts 7:58, where he is cheering on the angry crowd in its stoning of Stephen. Putting several descriptions of Saul together, we get this picture of him.

- He was in hearty agreement with stoning Stephen to death (Acts 8:1).
- He was ravaging the church, entering house after house, and dragging off men and women, and putting them in prison (Acts 8:3).
- He was breathing threats and murder against the followers of Christ (Acts 9:1).
- He asked for and received letters from the high priest authorizing him to search the synagogues in Damascus for followers of Jesus so that he might bring them bound to Jerusalem (Acts 9:2).
- He persecuted the church beyond measure and tried to destroy it (Gal. 1:13).
- He was a blasphemer (1 Tim. 1:13).
- He was a persecutor (1 Tim. 1:13).
- He was a violent aggressor (1 Tim. 1:13).

The natural question is, "Why was he so extreme; why did he lead such intense and brutal opposition to the followers of Christ?" Surely he thought that his own religion was threatened by the growth of the followers of Jesus. But there was more to his violent opposition. Paul, in his own words, indicates that there was a deeper, more personal motivation in his heart. The first indication of this comes in Galatians 1:10, where Paul hints that earlier in his life he was "seeking the favor of men" and "striving to please men" (NASB). But, now, having become a bond servant of God, he would do no such thing, especially regarding the truth of the gospel. Three verses later (Gal. 1:13), he specifically states that in his former life in Judaism he went to extremes in persecuting the church. It was through his extreme zealousness that the Pharisees over him recognized him as a young man of promise. As Paul describes it, "I was advancing in Judaism beyond many of my contemporaries among my countrymen, being more extremely zealous for my ancestral traditions" (Gal. 1:14 NASB). He is here pulling back the cover over his heart to expose the fact that the motivations for his extreme zealousness in persecuting Christians included competition with his contemporaries and a desire for personal recognition and advancement. His identity needs drove him to extremes in his search for significance and value through his persecution of Christians.

Paul is a good example of the power of identity needs because they drove him to such extremes in an attempt to fill the gaping hole within his heart. Most of the time in our lives the extremes will not be so clearly visible. Nevertheless, the identity needs show up in the pastor who is all about numbers, who is only too happy to announce to anyone who will listen that his church has passed the three-thousand mark. They show up in the elder who always has to have the last word, no matter what the discussion is, or in the leader who must always be in control of everything and is not willing to truly delegate responsibilities to others. What Paul did, and what each of these contemporary examples do, is allow their own identity needs to impact their leadership in such a way that they do not lead others; rather they manipulate others and use them for the leader's own benefit. For such leaders, identity is a zero sum game: If I let you do things that strengthen your sense of identity, that takes away from my sense of identity. So in order to protect my identity, I take away yours. Parker Palmer put it this way: "When leaders operate with a deep, unexamined insecurity about their own identity, they create institutional settings that deprive other people of their identity as a way of dealing with the unexamined fears in the leaders themselves."[11]

Palmer's description is seen very clearly in Saul, whose bondage to his own identity needs drove him to extremes in denying other people their identity. It may be difficult to admit, but the same is true in varying degrees of all of us. In contrast, a leader with a secure sense of personal identity is free

---

11. Parker J. Palmer, "Leading from Within," in *Insights on Leadership: Service, Stewardship, Spirit, and Servant-Leadership*, ed. Larry C. Spears (New York: John Wiley & Sons, 1998), 204.

to create organizational culture that allows everyone to express their giftedness, take responsibility, and enjoy the blessing that comes from making a significant contribution. Such a leader can take pleasure in the success of others and has no hesitancy in celebrating that success for them.

Identity or Image?

Each of us must deal with two competing characteristics in our own life, and the competition between them spills over into every area of our life. Each of us has some sense of personal identity. It may be healthy and satisfying, or it may be deficient and demanding, clamoring for us to do something to sustain it and increase it. We also have an outward image that we project to others in our interactions with them. We inflate an image of ourselves much like the huge, inflatable gorillas car dealers put on the top of their buildings to attract the attention of drivers on the freeway as they speed by the dealership.

When our sense of identity is strong and satisfying, our need to project an image to others tends to decrease. This situation could be pictured like this:

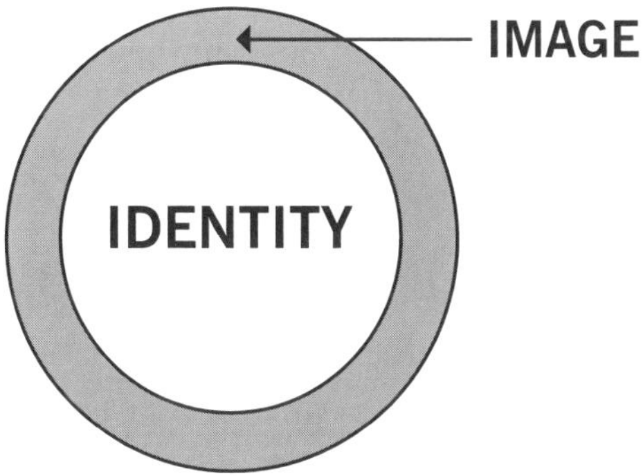

However, if our identity is weak and unsatisfying, we will feel the need to project an image to others. We develop an image of what we want others to think about us, an image that seems to satisfy the emptiness within our own hearts. Then we relate to others through the medium of this image, which now looks like the one at the top of the next page.

We project an image in our interactions with others because we feel we must. We long for others to view us in the way the image suggests. We project images of competence, importance, superiority, knowledge, or value, hoping that people will think of us in these ways. The problem, however, is that others are not really relating to us, only to the image of ourselves that we are setting up and pointing in their direction. In normal relationships, this is empty and unsatisfying. In leadership situations, it is not only empty and unsatisfying; it is also painfully destructive.

The difference between leading out of a secure identity and leading from image, or insecure identity, is the difference between light and darkness. If I lead from a secure identity, I can be who I am. I can use my gifts

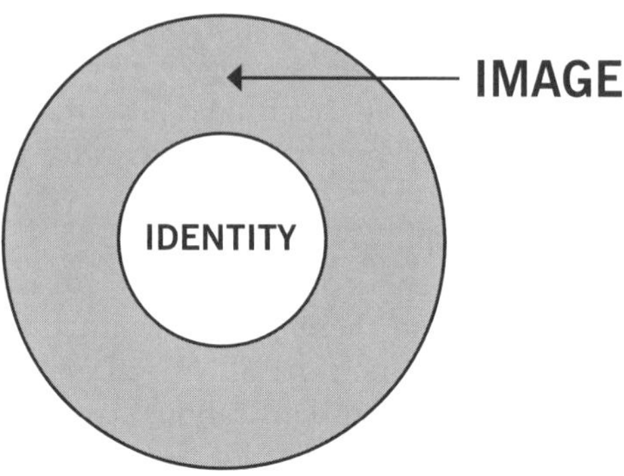

and abilities to the maximum. I do not have to hide my weaknesses; I can allow others, whose gifts and abilities are different from mine, to use them fully. There is a high level of authenticity in this. On the other hand, if I lead out of an image that I have constructed, I relate to those I lead out of who I think I have to be. In other words, I have to act a part, play a role. Of course, I have chosen the role myself; I have designed the part I play because I think that by playing that part people will think of me and relate to me in ways that I think will provide the sense of identity I am desperately seeking. The trap is that I have to continually play the part, because if they really knew me, they would not think of me in the way I desperately need.

LEADING FROM IDENTITY and LEADING FROM IMAGE	
IDENTITY	**IMAGE**
Who I am	Who I think I have to be
Authenticity	Acting
Freedom that enables me to: • Be concerned for others • Serve others • Trust others	Bondage that requires me to: • Be concerned for myself • Use others • Fear others
Openness	Control
Courage	Avoidance
Relaxed	Uptight

The difference between these two ways of leading is the difference between freedom and bondage. When I lead out of a secure sense of identity, I am free to be concerned about others. I can serve them by giving their needs priority over my own. Because they know I am concerned for them, they do not have to be in competition with me, so I can also trust them. But if I am leading out of image, I am in bondage, because I have to constantly make sure that the image I have blown up is not leaking. In fact, I have to use others to get what I think I need to fill up the emptiness within me. And, simultaneously, I have to fear them, because if I am not careful, they might withhold from me the very thing I desperately need from them. So, I have to always be in control and very careful to avoid anything that might expose the emptiness of the image or cause others to act in ways that are contrary to what I want.

If I am leading out of a secure identity, I am much more free to lead with openness and to invite the real participation of others in the process. I can also lead with greater courage, because if someone does not like one of my decisions and pulls back from agreeing with my position or even from following me, it is not a threat to my survival.

We might be tempted to think that we can control the expression of these identity issues so that they will not impact our leadership relationships. As appealing as this may sound, it is not true. The leader's inner struggles always work their way into his or her leadership relationships. No matter how hard we try to hide them or cover them up, they come out in unexpected ways. "Leaders not only embed in their organizations what they intend consciously to get across, but they also convey their own inner conflicts and the inconsistencies in their own personal makeup."[12]

This was the problem with the disciples; they continually argued about which one of them was the greatest. Their inadequate identities required it. The problem with the Gentile leaders was not only self-serving leadership, but also self-deceived, self-serving leadership. Rather than deal with their own hearts as leaders, they projected blame on others and elevated themselves by glorifying their own motives, congratulating themselves for being "benefactors" of the people (Luke 22:24–27)! Leaders struggling with their own identity rob those they lead of theirs! A modern-day version of this might look like the following examples.

Identity Issues: The Pastor Who Always Has to Be the Authority

The congregation of a church on the East Coast had been without a pastor for almost two years, so it was an exciting day when the new pastor arrived and began his ministry. The search process had been very thorough, and the congregation was sure they had called the candidate with the best credentials. Things started out well; Pastor Jim preached with compelling authority. Much to their delight, the church began to grow again. But it was not long before people began to notice an annoying habit in their new pastor. Whenever someone made a comment about a passage in the Bible or a concept in theology, Pastor Jim always had to have the last word. It did not matter whether it was a casual conversation or a discussion in one of their community groups, the resulting comment by Pastor Jim was inevitable. Sometimes the comment was overtly corrective; the original statement was

12. Edgar H. Schein, *Organizational Culture and Leadership* (San Francisco: Jossey-Bass, 1987), 319.

not biblically accurate and needed Pastor Jim's correction. The rest of the time there was still a hint of correction. At first, people were impressed with the breadth of their pastor's biblical and theological knowledge. But, after a while, the inevitable comments and corrections became annoying. After a couple of corrections, people began to feel like they did not have much to offer; they just became quiet and did not volunteer any comments. After a while, they began to drift away.

Identity Issues: The Elder Who Always Has to Be in Control

After recently graduating from seminary and going through a long search process, Bill and Mary were excited to begin their ministry at Grace Evangelical Church. It was a small but growing group of people, excited about being a place in their community where people could find Christ and begin to grow in their relationship with him. One of the core values of the church was teaching the Bible, so Bill felt that the church was a great fit for him. As he became more and more active in the ministry of the church, he was gratified to see the church grow and was impressed with the responsiveness of the people. As the church grew, Pastor Bill and the other six elders had to make significant decisions about organizing the church to handle the growth. The elder meetings were congenial, and most everyone participated in the discussions, though one of the elders, Bob Driner, who had helped start the church, did not say as much as the others. After lengthy discussion, a decision would be made, and Pastor Bill would begin planning the steps to implement the decision. But more times than he liked to think about, Pastor Bill would get a call from one of the elders a day or so after the decision saying that three or four elders had gotten together to discuss the decision and had concluded that the original decision was a mistake. Usually they had an alternative that was "backed by a majority of the elders." After this same scenario was repeated a few times, Pastor Bill pursued the details of the process only to discover that the same three elders would regularly meet at Bob's house and discuss the recent decision made at the elder meeting. They would reject the decision for a "better" one and then lobby the other two elders to accept their new proposal. As time progressed, Bob's three colleagues became more and more vocal in the elder meetings, and the other two elders became quieter. When Pastor Bill finally tried to confront Bob's role in these maneuvers, he was accused of trying to get his way by criticizing Bob and trying to undermine his authority as an elder. The meeting got heated, but neither Bob nor the other two elders said very much, just Pastor Bill and Bob's three allies. After a while, the two quiet elders dropped off the board. And most of the people in the church were surprised when, after only two years, Pastor Bill accepted a call to be the associate pastor of a church in the next state.[13]

---

13. Both the pastor story and the elder story are constructed from similar real situations, though no actual names of people or churches are used.

A Secure Sense of Identity Enables a Leader to Be a Servant Leader

A secure sense of personal identity is so essential to servant leadership that God will work on our hearts to develop that identity. He will use the experiences of life to get us to do something that is counterintuitive to us, something we would normally avoid unless forced to deal with it. He will get us to look deep into our hearts to examine the motives and strategies that reside there, strategies that control the way we live life and the way we lead others. But most of us resist this process until we have no choice.

The reality is that in ministry our daily decisions will be determined by inner dynamics that we rarely reflect upon unless we have the courage to do so or we are forced by circumstances to do so. The problem, of course, is that sin has introduced a complication. Sin has corrupted elements of our inner being to such an extent that when we catch a glimpse of them, we instantly want to avert our eyes and go somewhere else. The pain and embarrassment is such that we would far rather deny the reality than deal with it. At that point we are extremely vulnerable to the attractive temptation to shift the blame outside and away from ourselves, and, if we are in leadership, onto other people!

This is why leadership development is much more like a pilgrimage than a pleasure cruise. Even though the transformative purpose of a pilgrimage is appealing, the hardship, darkness, and peril scare most of us into signing up for the pleasure cruise. "Why would anybody want to take such a difficult and dangerous journey? Everything in us cries out against it. That is why we externalize everything—it is far easier to deal with the external world. It is easier to spend your life manipulating an institution than dealing with your own soul."[14] It is so much easier to stay focused on the externals. So we try desperately to

- be successful;
- be in control;
- be in positions of power;
- be right;
- be needed;
- be recognized;
- be an authority;
- be known as a "water walker," a "rainmaker," a "key player."

---

14. Palmer, "Leading from Within," 202.

And the world cooperates with us. Most leaders are chosen to positions of leadership because they demonstrate competency in the external world, not because their internal world is in order. Our culture, in fact, separates the external and internal, saying that you can be whatever you want in your internal world, just so you produce results in the external world. It is not surprising, therefore, that our focus is so overwhelmingly on the externals. Nor is it surprising that we feel so much more comfortable staying on the surface, dealing only with the externals; and all the while we avoid dealing with our inner life, with our hearts.

> Human beings have always employed an enormous variety of clever devices for running away from themselves. . . . We can keep ourselves so busy, fill our lives with so many diversions, stuff our heads with so much knowledge, involve ourselves with so many people and cover so much ground that we never have time to probe the fearful and wonderful world within. . . . By middle life most of us are accomplished fugitives from ourselves.[15]

But God will not allow us to remain fugitives from ourselves. He will orchestrate the experiences of our lives to make us deal with our internal identity and heart issues. For someone as extreme as Saul, the experience was dramatic. In the midst of his persecution of the Christians, Christ himself appeared to him unexpectedly on the Damascus road in such overpowering glory that Saul was blinded for days and was dependent upon a Christian named Ananias to recover his sight (Acts 9:1–19). Saul was converted, but his development was not complete. God took him through experiences of failure, disappointment, and rejection (Acts 9:20–30) before he began his ministry as Paul the apostle. Nor were the ministry years without painful learning experiences. The result of this process was a drastic change in Paul's thinking. In his letter to the Philippian believers, he exposes his previous source of identity and then reveals that he had exchanged it for something infinitely better (Phil. 3:3–11).

His confidence before had been in the flesh, in his Hebrew background and in the zeal with which he persecuted the church. He was creating an identity for himself through his own efforts, and he worked hard at it. But now, at this point in his development, Paul recognizes the foolishness and emptiness of his previous strategies. Earlier Paul had written to the Corinthians about a painful experience God gave him to keep him from exalting himself (2 Cor. 12:1–10).

What is illuminating in this passage is that at this point in his life Paul is boasting in his weaknesses rather that parading his strengths as he had done before. In verse 10 he is now content to experience the very things he used to

---

15. John W. Gardner, *Self-Renewal: The Individual and the Innovative Society* (New York: Norton, 1995), 13.

inflict on the Christians as he persecuted them in a vain desire to advance his own reputation in Judaism. To say this, and to live this way as he did, required a different sense of identity than he had before. No longer is he trying to inflate his own value by his abuse of others. Rather there is a peace and contentment and security that enables him to give himself in serving others.

Not all of us will have a Damascus road experience. But that does not mean that God is not strongly at work in us, moving us to begin to look into our own hearts, to those places we don't really want to go, to examine our motives and honestly see what we are trying to use to establish an identity for ourselves. Because of the depth of his love for us, God guides each of us through a pilgrimage process. He will not leave us where we are, hiding behind a self-constructed image, so he brings into our lives experiences that make us ask questions of ourselves, questions we would rather avoid. As our false attempts at identity construction are demolished and cleared away, the opportunity for true inner spiritual transformation is created.

The Source of a Secure Sense of Identity

After trying a multitude of ineffective and disappointing ways to establish an identity for ourselves, we, like Paul, will be brought to a point of emptiness. And there we will find waiting for us the one who has loved us through it all, even when we had not the slightest desire to look his way. If our identity has to do with our gender and ethnicity, abilities and limitations, gifts and strengths, he is the Designer who made us this way. If it has to do with our sense of being deeply and securely loved, he is the only one who loves us with such a love. If it has to do with a sense of significance that comes from accomplishing something that lasts forever, he is the one who has gifted us and called us and empowered us to make just such a contribution in his eternal kingdom.

Scripture from beginning to end is full of messages to us related to those things that make up our identity. The following are a representative sample:

- Psalm 139:1 — I am known by God.
- Psalm 139:13 — I am personally made/created by God.
- Psalm 139:14 — I am fearfully and wonderfully made by him.
- Psalm 139:16 — I am the object of his planning and will.
- Romans 5:1 — I am justified, at peace with God.
- Romans 5:8 — I am so greatly loved that, even while I was a sinner, Christ died in my place.
- Romans 6:6 — I am freed from sin's power.

• Romans 8:1	I am forgiven, not condemned!
• Romans 8:15	I am personally loved as God's dear child.
• Romans 8:38-39	I am absolutely secure in the love of God through. Christ; nothing will ever separate me from his love.
• Ephesians 1:3	I am blessed with every spiritual blessing.
• Ephesians 1:11	I am an heir of God according to his will.
• Ephesians 2:10	I am his workmanship, and he has equipped me to make a significant contribution to his kingdom.

Of course there are many, many other passages that could be added to the list. These are simply representative. All of them say, in one way or another, that God is our true source of a secure and satisfying sense of personal identity. Only God loves us perfectly; only God loves us with a love that we can never lose. After all, he loved us enough for the Son of God to leave heaven, come to earth, be born as a man, and ultimately die for us even while we were still his enemies (Rom. 5:8–10)! Only God loves us with a love that is not connected to our performance. Only God equips us and empowers us to make an eternal difference.

Set Free: A Secure Sense of Identity

The ultimate effect of what God has done is that we are set free. In addition to being set free from the guilt and penalty of sin, we also are set free from many other forms of bondage. We are set free to become the people God designed us to be, not what others think we should be or what we think we should be in order to be accepted by others. And we are free to be true servant leaders, free from that bondage of trying to get from others what we think we need in order to have a secure identity, free from being dependent upon others to define us. The only way we, as God's men and women, can provide the leadership needed in the days ahead is if our sense of personal identity is firmly grounded in our relationship to Jesus Christ. Only that will set us free to be servant leaders.

> The great spiritual gift that comes as one takes the inward journey is to know for certain that who I am does not depend on what I do. Identity does not depend upon titles, or degrees, or function. It depends only on the simple fact that I am a child of God, valued and treasured for what I am.[16]

16. Palmer, "Leading from Within," 205.

Chapter 9

Calling and Spiritual Formation

George Hillman

> Therefore do not be ashamed of the testimony about our Lord, nor of me his prisoner, but share in suffering for the gospel by the power of God, who saved us and called us to a holy calling, not because of our works but because of his own purpose and grace, which he gave us in Christ Jesus before the ages began.
>
> —2 Timothy 1:8–9 ESV

I was the king of changing majors in college. In my academic career, I think I had four different majors. I started out wanting to be a medical doctor—it sounded like a noble pursuit. I had good grades in high school and I liked science, so I thought that it was a fit.

My first semester, I made the best grades of my entire academic career in college. Granted, my classes were things like Biology 101 and Racquetball, but I was off to a great start. In my second semester, things definitely took a turn for the worse. The culprit was biology lab.

Now, I had loved my biology classes in high school and my first semester in college. I had even enjoyed some of the "lab stuff" that I had done in high school biology lab. I can remember dissecting a worm and a frog. But the biology class I was in this time around was a completely different animal (literally).

Our big project for the semester was dissecting a fetal pig. (OK, so it's a little larger than the earthworm and frog that I dissected in high school, but how bad can a pig be?) Well, the lab teaching assistant gave us worksheets, and we had to fill in the blanks with the various discoveries we were making: How big is the heart? Where is the liver? And so on. I soon discovered that I was finishing my worksheets long before everyone else. I just wanted to finish my worksheet on the pig and move on. But I would look around at everybody else and see that they were being meticulous in their pig examination.

Then came the time for the final. After working on our pigs for a couple of weeks, our teaching assistant announced that we could take our pigs home to study before the exam. *Excuse me? Who is going to take their pig home!* Well, I was the *only* person who did not take a pig home that day.

You see, the other members of that lab had a passion for science. Don't get me wrong. I enjoyed the class. I loved learning the facts about this animal or that. Why, even today I find myself glued to the Discovery Channel, watching some show about the hunting habits of an obscure breed of penguins. However, I did not have the same passion as the other students. I could do the work, but it was a chore. These other students would make wonderful surgeons, with painstaking accuracy in their work. I probably would have ended up being the doctor with all of the liability cases because of my shoddy work. I probably changed my major the next week.

After a brief swim as a wildlife and fisheries major, I left my pursuit of science. For some unknown reason, I became a history major. Again, it was one of those subjects I liked, so I thought I would test out the water. The problem I ran into with being a history major was that I had to have two years of a foreign language. I had taken a year of Spanish in high school, but I was never particularly good at grasping languages.

So I finally ended up a sociology major. Why sociology? It was one of the only majors in the School of Liberal Arts that did not have a language requirement. Now that's the kind of logic that makes your parents proud. "Hey, Dad, I picked this really great major with no real career options because I discovered that I am not a science, math, or language guy."

Some of you can really relate because you have been down that exact same path. Some of you have a very similar experience in life. Some of you graduated college and discovered that the career you trained for was not that great a fit. Some of you have really wrestled with your "call to ministry." Some of you have shown up at school with no clear idea of why God has brought you here. Some of you are at a crossroads in life and have no clue what the next step is. And some of you are going to end up in future settings where you will begin to question all of this stuff all over again.

A Call for Calling

In the opening paragraph of his fantastic book *The Call*, Os Guinness lays out the following challenge:

> Are you looking for purpose in life? For a purpose big enough to absorb every ounce of your attention, deep enough to plumb

> every mystery of your passions, and lasting enough to inspire you to your last breath?[1]

Guinness goes on to vividly describe the inward longing to find purpose in life, a purpose "bigger than ourselves." Concluding that only the call of God can ever fulfill this longing, he describes calling as "the truth that God calls us to himself so decisively that everything we are, everything we do, and everything we have is invested with a special devotion, dynamism, and direction lived out as a response to his summons and service."[2]

All of us come to a point in our lives where there is a serious examination of our gifts, our personality, and our passions. We come to a point in life where we really examine our "uniqueness" and how God has "wired" us. We come to a point in life where we really contemplate how to engage people and contexts around us, loving people as God would have them loved. We join the saints of old in looking at how God has called us.

For most of the last two thousand years, thoughtful Christians have struggled with the idea of "calling" and "vocation." William Placher, in his recent compilation, *Callings: Twenty Centuries of Christian Wisdom on Vocation*, reflects,

> Down the centuries, Christians have looked for definitions of "vocation" somewhere between the trivial sense of "just a job" and the hard-to-believe image of a miraculous voice from heaven. *Central to the many Christian interpretations of vocation is the idea that there is something—my vocation or calling—God has called me to do with my life, and my life has meaning and purpose at least in part because I am fulfilling my calling.* . . . Amid all the controversies Christianity has preserved the fundamental idea that our lives count for something because God has a direction in mind for them. . . . If the God who made us has figured out something we are supposed to do, however—something that fits how we were made, so that doing it will enable us to glorify God, serve others, and be most richly ourselves—then life stops seeming so empty: my story has meaning as part of a larger story, ultimately shaped by God.[3]

The concept of "calling" or "vocation" (from the Latin *vocare*, meaning "to call") has been a central theme in Christian writers throughout the centuries. Unfortunately we live in what some people have called a "postvocational" or "callingless" world. In the postvocational or callingless world, jobs

1. Os Guinness, *The Call: Finding and Fulfilling the Central Purpose of Your Life* (Nashville: W Publishing Group, 1998), vii.

2. Ibid., 3–4, 29.

3. William C. Placher, ed., *Callings: Twenty Centuries of Christian Wisdom on Vocation* (Grand Rapids: Eerdmans, 2005), 2–3.

are just paychecks, relationships are random and unconnected, and deeper meaning in life is missing. With this outlook, it is very easy to slip into seeing life as boring drudgery, an aimless wandering. But when we recover a biblical sense of vocation or calling, when we live our lives with an understanding that our lives have purpose and meaning, then the everyday becomes holy.

Primary and Functional Calling

When I applied for seminary, one of the questions on the application asked about my call to ministry. Now, as far as I knew, I had not heard a voice from heaven telling me to apply to seminary. I had not seen any bright lights giving me signals as to what my career path should be. So how should I understand "calling"?

When someone throws out the terms *calling* or *vocation*, there must be an understanding of both our primary and our functional calling. While these terms are not found in Scripture, it is a helpful way of categorizing a sometimes confusing theological concept. The Puritans of American history actually coined these phrases, distinguishing these two aspects of calling.

Primary Calling

Our primary calling is to a living and dynamic relationship with God. Throughout Scripture, the chief concern is always God calling his children to himself and calling his children to a life of holiness. Our primary calling is the umbrella under which we function as believers. We are called first and foremost to God, not to just a role, a career, or a location. Our call to salvation and sanctification is paramount to any talk about the specifics of our life. The primary call for all believers is to God. The functional call (which follows) is how we live out our primary calling.

Below are just samplings of the Scripture references that discuss this idea of the primary call to God and to a life of holiness:

> For the promise is for you and for your children and for all who are far off, everyone whom the Lord our God calls to himself. (Acts 2:39 ESV)

> . . . through whom we have received grace and apostleship to bring about the obedience of faith for the sake of his name among all the nations, including you who are called to belong to Jesus Christ, to all those in Rome who are loved by God and called to be saints: Grace to you and peace from God our Father and the Lord Jesus Christ. (Rom. 1:5–7 ESV)

> And we know that for those who love God all things work together for good, for those who are called according to his purpose. For those whom he foreknew he also predestined to be conformed to the image of his Son, in order that he might be the

firstborn among many brothers. And those whom he predestined he also called, and those whom he called he also justified, and those whom he justified he also glorified. (Rom. 8:28–30 ESV)

To the church of God that is in Corinth, to those sanctified in Christ Jesus, called to be saints together with all those who in every place call upon the name of our Lord Jesus Christ, both their Lord and ours. . . . God is faithful, by whom you were called into the fellowship of his Son, Jesus Christ our Lord. (1 Cor. 1:2, 9 ESV)

But we preach Christ crucified, a stumbling block to Jews and folly to Gentiles, but to those who are called, both Jews and Greeks, Christ the power of God and the wisdom of God. (1 Cor. 1:23–24 ESV)

. . . having the eyes of your hearts enlightened, that you may know what is the hope to which he has called you, what are the riches of his glorious inheritance in the saints. (Eph. 1:18 ESV)

I therefore, a prisoner for the Lord, urge you to walk in a manner worthy of the calling to which you have been called . . . There is one body and one Spirit—just as you were called to the one hope that belongs to your call. (Eph. 4:1, 4 ESV)

I press on toward the goal for the prize of the upward call of God in Christ Jesus. (Phil. 3:14 ESV)

We exhorted each one of you and encouraged you and charged you to walk in a manner worthy of God, who calls you into his own kingdom and glory. (1 Thess. 2:12 ESV)

For God has not called us for impurity, but in holiness. (1 Thess. 4:7 ESV)

To this end we always pray for you, that our God may make you worthy of his calling and may fulfill every resolve for good and every work of faith by his power. (2 Thess. 1:11 ESV)

To this he called you through our gospel, so that you may obtain the glory of our Lord Jesus Christ. (2 Thess. 2:14 ESV)

Fight the good fight of the faith. Take hold of the eternal life to which you were called and about which you made the good confession in the presence of many witnesses. (1 Tim. 6:12 ESV)

> Therefore do not be ashamed of the testimony about our Lord, nor of me his prisoner, but share in suffering for the gospel by the power of God, who saved us and called us to a holy calling, not because of our works but because of his own purpose and grace, which he gave us in Christ Jesus before the ages began. (2 Tim. 1:8–9 ESV)

> But you are a chosen race, a royal priesthood, a holy nation, a people for his own possession, that you may proclaim the excellencies of him who called you out of darkness into his marvelous light. (1 Peter 2:9 ESV)

This quick swim through Scripture should show that God's primary interest in your life is who you are, not what you do. Unfortunately for most of us, we naturally gravitate to "doing" versus "being." Especially in an American context, we usually jump to thinking about employment or marriage when we speak of the call of God or the will of God. But God is not merely an employment agent or a matchmaker. The concept of calling in the New Testament is always focused on salvation and sanctification, not on occupation or location or marriage. God wants you to seek him, not just his services. God wants your heart.

Functional Calling

The functional call is how you live out the primary calling in daily life. The purpose of this functional call is always to serve the primary calling, not to find you a career or a spouse. You are called first to God, not to a particular job or location. Your primary call to God is so vast that how your functional call plays out is a comparatively minor issue.

But the truth is that you are called to be a Christian in concrete social locations. So the dimensions of your functional calling include the following:

- How do you relate being a Christian to your immediate and extended family?
- How do you serve your neighbor in Christian love?
- How do you function in the local body of Christ?
- How do you serve the greater society in stewardship and mission?
- How do you spend your time in work and rest?

Everything that brings you into relationship with other people is a part of your functional call. In fact, living out your primary calling in the various avenues of your life actually has the power to transform all the spheres of your life into functional callings.

More Than a Paycheck

Your primary identity is that of a "living sacrifice." It is not, "I am a youth minister" or "I am a doctor." What I have labeled a *functional calling*, Os Guinness labels a *secondary calling*. He notes that secondary callings "are our personal answer to God's address, our response to God's summons. Secondary callings matter, but only because the primary calling matters most."[4] Too many of us, though, put the cart before the horse.

Never confuse your career choice (how you pay the bills) with your functional calling. Scripture never limits or equates calling with a paycheck. And there is a great danger to thinking only in terms of your identity being completely wrapped up in your career. In fact, the most important things in life are usually the things that we do not get paid for. Every rightful human task is some aspect of God's own work: making, designing, doing chores, beautifying, organizing, helping, bringing dignity, and leading. Our work, then, is to reflect God's work. As the apostle Paul proclaims, "Whatever you do, work heartily, as for the Lord and not for men" (Col. 3:23 ESV).

Some of you will have the wonderful opportunity to receive a paycheck for living out your functional calling in the body of Christ. For the vast majority of the body of Christ, their functional calling lies outside of a ministry paycheck. But the city employee, the pastor, the construction worker, the missionary, the farmer, the professor, the artist, the schoolteacher, the salesperson, the stay-at-home mom, the utility worker, and the retired person all have functions in the body of Christ.

Stations of Life

Unlike our primary calling, which does not change, our functional calling changes as we move through the many "stations of life." As you change roles in life and as you go through the normal seasons of life, how you live out your primary calling in the many contexts of life will change.

For example, my first paying job was as a newspaper carrier in my neighborhood for my hometown newspaper. Since that day, I have received a paycheck from a wide variety of jobs through the years: retail sales in a toy store, day camp counselor, resident advisor in a dormitory, after-school day-care supervisor, nonprofit youth organization worker, college pastor, education pastor, and now a seminary professor. But while my resume for the past twenty plus years reflects a wide variety of paycheck sources, my primary calling from God has not changed.

Now consider my relationships. Before I was married, I had relationships with my parents and my two sisters, plus relationships with friends at

4. Guinness, *The Call*, 31.

school and church. Once I got married, my relationships changed for now I had parents-in-law, brothers-in-law, sisters-in-law, and nephews and nieces. Now as a parent, I have a relationship with my daughter as well. Just as my career roles have changed, my relational roles have changed too. But my primary calling from God has not changed.

So even with these changes in life, we must never lose focus on our daily call to love the Lord and love our neighbor, no matter what the context. As Jesus tells us,

> You shall love the Lord your God with all your heart and with all your soul and with all your mind. This is the great and first commandment. And a second is like it: You shall love your neighbor as yourself. On these two commandments depend all the Law and the Prophets. (Matt. 22:37–40 ESV)

So whether you find yourself washing dishes, changing diapers, carpooling kids to activities, driving to work, buying groceries, or any other "humdrum" activity, your calling is to love God and love your neighbor in the circumstance God has placed you. The relationships, duties, and daily work that God has you in are where you live out your calling. The tasks are not sacred in and of themselves, but they become sacred because they come from God.

Gene Veith, in his book *God at Work*, reminds us, "Christians need to realize that the present is the moment in which we are called to be faithful. We can do nothing about the past. The future is wholly in God's hands. Now is what we have. . . . The life of vocation is comprehensive and day-by-day, involving almost every facet of our lives, the whole texture of relationships, responsibilities, and focuses of attention that take up nearly every moment of our lives."[5]

Most of the leaders of the Reformation saw this command to love God and love one's neighbor as being very freeing. The main concern of the Reformers was not whether they had missed God's will for their life but whether their decisions were made out of gratitude to God, trust in God's word of grace, and desire to serve God and neighbors. If one was loving God and loving others, the choice of career or spouse was flexible. For example, the Reformation leader Martin Luther stressed that "so long as they seek God's kingdom and its righteousness, it matters little whether they marry this person or that one or choose this profession or that one."[6] So as long as we love God and love our neighbor, the Reformers said that there is a great deal of freedom in our choices.

---

5. Gene Edward Veith Jr., *God at Work: Your Christian Vocation in All of Life* (Wheaton, IL: Crossway, 2002), 59, 133.

6. Douglas J. Schuurman, *Vocation: Discerning Our Callings in Life* (Grand Rapids: Eerdmans, 2004), 127.

The primary calling to salvation and sanctification is the same for all believers in Jesus Christ. The functional calling in how you live out this primary calling in the contexts of life is unique to each believer. So the natural question is, How do you discover how to live out your primary calling in a functional way? Much of this is revealed in your divine design.

True to Your Uniqueness

A proper view of God and his works reveals that our very lives reflect God's intentions for our lives.

> For you formed my inward parts;
> you knitted me together in my mother's womb.
> I praise you, for I am fearfully and wonderfully made.
> Wonderful are your works;
> my soul knows it very well.
> My frame was not hidden from you,
> when I was being made in secret,
> intricately woven in the depths of the earth.
> Your eyes saw my unformed substance;
> in your book were written, every one of them,
> the days that were formed for me,
> when as yet there were none of them. (Ps. 139:13–16 ESV)

> Your hands fashioned and made me,
> and now you have destroyed me altogether.
> Remember that you have made me like clay;
> and will you return me to the dust?
> Did you not pour me out like milk
> and curdle me like cheese?
> You clothed me with skin and flesh,
> and knit me together with bones and sinews.
> You have granted me life and steadfast love,
> and your care has preserved my spirit. (Job 10:8–12 ESV)

There are no accidents or surprises in God's plan. If you believe in a sovereign God, then you must believe that there is a fit between who you are and what God desires for you to do. Our heritage, our geography, our personality, our learning styles, our natural talents, our spiritual gifts, our life experiences, our opportunities, our values, and our passions all come ultimately from the hand of God. Even our limitations and our concerns are under God's watchful eye. It is not fate or chance that rules our lives but the sovereignty of God. If you are able to discover this fit, then you are able to discover your functional calling.

Arthur Miller, in the very insightful book *The Power of Uniqueness*, stresses, "In truth, we cannot become anything other than who we already are, if we wish to be fulfilled in our lives and vocation. We must stop trying to 'become' something else, or to 'develop' or 'cultivate' some trait that we fundamentally lack, and instead start being who we already are by identifying our giftedness and living it out."[7]

Assessing Who You Are

It is true that some people have served effectively in an area where they had no apparent capability for the required tasks. But those examples are very rare. God's normal mode of operation (if I can be so bold as to say that) is to gift people for their service. Moreover, when the alignment of giftedness (based on God's grace and not your efforts) and environment occurs, God-honoring and God-empowered ministry takes place. When this ministry calibration has taken place in your life, you have known it, and the people benefiting from your grace gifts have known it too. However, the reverse is true as well. When you have tried to force yourself into a role that was never meant for you, you have felt the frustration and, guess what, the people receiving your ill-fitting efforts have known it too.

This is exactly what the apostle Paul is saying to the believers in Rome.

> For by the grace given to me I say to everyone among you not to think of himself more highly than he ought to think, but to think with sober judgment, each according to the measure of faith that God has assigned. (Rom. 12:3 ESV)

This verse comes immediately after one of the crescendos in Paul's letter to the Romans, where he writes, "I appeal to you therefore, brothers, by the mercies of God, to present your bodies as a living sacrifice, holy and acceptable to God, which is your spiritual worship. Do not be conformed to this world, but be transformed by the renewal of your mind, that by testing you may discern what is the will of God, what is good and acceptable and perfect" (Rom. 12:1–2 ESV). Romans 12:1–2 is an example of our primary calling of salvation and sanctification.

Our renewed mind (Rom. 12:2) must be active in evaluating our identity, our gifts, and ourselves. The original language in Romans 12:3 repeats the idea of "think" four times, emphasizing this role of the renewed mind. This is the idea of spiritual discernment. As a believer in Jesus Christ who is in the process of the transformation process of the renewed mind, you are capable of evaluating yourself properly through the Holy Spirit. Paul speaks of a balance of honest reflection on who we are, not overselling our strengths or selling ourselves short.

Paul's emphasis is on the humble acceptance of the grace that we have

---

7. Arthur F. Miller Jr. and William D. Hendricks, *The Power of Uniqueness: How to Become Who You Really Are* (Grand Rapids: Zondervan, 1999), 98.

received and of how we have been gifted. As Gordon Smith, in his book *Listening to God in Times of Choice*, reminds us,

> Humility means recognizing both our limitations and our potential, recognizing where we need others and where we can make a contribution to meeting the needs of others. Humility graciously accepts both dimensions—our limitations and need for others and our potential, our ability to contribute to the well-being of others. The former does not diminish us; the latter does not inflate us. With sober judgment we simply accept who we are. And this humility is essential for effective discernment.[8]

Understanding our calling must force us to assess our uniqueness, talents, and personality. Your divine design reveals God's call on your life. Ministering out of who you are is the only real key to Spirit-empowered effectiveness and joy. Miller poetically states, "[Giftedness is] the lifeblood of a person, the song that his heart longs to sing, the race that his legs long to run. It's the fire in his belly. It's his reason for being. So any time you tap into giftedness, you hit a nerve that runs right to the core of the individual."[9]

Natural and Spiritual Gifts

As we continue on in Romans 12, Paul fleshes out how our primary calling is lived out in the body of Christ.

> For as in one body we have many members, and the members do not all have the same function, so we, though many, are one body in Christ, and individually members one of another. Having gifts that differ according to the grace given to us, let us use them: if prophecy, in proportion to our faith; if service, in our serving; the one who teaches, in his teaching; the one who exhorts, in his exhortation; the one who contributes, in generosity; the one who leads, with zeal; the one who does acts of mercy, with cheerfulness. (Rom. 12:4–8 ESV)

And this is not the only place where Paul talks about ministering our giftedness. For example, Paul says a very similar thing to the believers in Corinth.

> Now there are varieties of gifts, but the same Spirit; and there are varieties of service, but the same Lord; and there are varieties of activities, but it is the same God who empowers them all in

8. Gordon T. Smith, *Listening to God in Times of Choice: The Art of Discerning God's Will* (Downers Grove, IL: InterVarsity Press, 1997), 90–91.
9. Miller and Hendricks, *The Power of Uniqueness*, 39.

> everyone. To each is given the manifestation of the Spirit for the common good. To one is given through the Spirit the utterance of wisdom, and to another the utterance of knowledge according to the same Spirit, to another faith by the same Spirit, to another gifts of healing by the one Spirit, to another the working of miracles, to another prophecy, to another the ability to distinguish between spirits, to another various kinds of tongues, to another the interpretation of tongues. All these are empowered by one and the same Spirit, who apportions to each one individually as he wills. (1 Cor. 12:4–11 ESV)

While in this brief chapter I am not able to go into an in-depth analysis of the various theological arguments concerning spiritual gifts and natural talents, suffice it to say that all believers in Jesus Christ are blessed by God with certain abilities to minister to others in love. One of the first steps in understanding your functional call is to understand your giftings. Through taking one of the many spiritual gifts inventories or (more importantly) as you serve others in biblical community, you can come to a better understanding of your natural and spiritual gifts.

Passions

Along with our giftings, God also has developed within each of us certain passions. Some have called this internal oughtness or compulsion. Passion is that thing that we cannot not do. God shapes each of us to have certain subjects, objects, or concerns that motivate us. The idea behind the concept of passions is that a person will naturally become more energized and work better in an area that he or she is passionate about.

Can passions be bad? Of course they can because we are still "of flesh." But when we center our lives on the mandates of God's Word and the empowerment of the Holy Spirit, God is able to align our passions with his desires. As we walk close to God in our daily lives, God is able to shape our character and our passions. As King David noted, "Delight yourself in the LORD, and he will give you the desires of your heart" (Ps. 37:4 ESV).

The discovery of passions can come from asking the following questions:

- What topics or activities excite you?
- What topics or activities keep you up at night?
- What topics or activities cause you to jump out of bed in the morning?
- What are the themes of the greatest accomplishments in your life?
- What activities or discussions cause you to lose track of time because you are so focused?

- Where do you feel like you are making a difference?[10]

So how do we get to the point that his desires become our desires? That is where the dance of discernment begins.

The Dance of Discernment

I think that sometimes we long for the days of the exodus. We read that during the Israelites' desert travels,

> the LORD went before them by day in a pillar of cloud to lead them along the way, and by night in a pillar of fire to give them light, that they might travel by day and by night. The pillar of cloud by day and the pillar of fire by night did not depart from before the people. (Exod. 13:21–22 ESV)

In certain moments of life and at certain crossroads, we probably think how much easier life would be if we could just follow the trail of cloud and fire. We are sure life would be great if only every major decision of life could be accompanied by a supernatural trail marker like these pillars.

Does God speak to us today? Absolutely! For us, God's leadings are no less spiritual but maybe less dramatic. However, we have two things that the children of Israel did not have. First, we have God's complete Word in written form to offer guidance in our lives. Second, we have the indwelling Holy Spirit. Douglas Schuurman reminds us, "Though some Christians have encounters of a miraculous nature, God's callings and leading are for the most part quietly and gently received, mediated by prayerful individual and communal discernment of gifts and needs. Though miracles can attend these processes, they usually do not."[11]

Learning to Dance

Instead of living in the age of the dramatic, we as believers in Jesus Christ live in the age of the dance. What do I mean? Smith paints this beautiful word picture:

> Discernment, indeed the whole Christian experience, is like a dance with God. God in his love and holiness invites us into a dialogue, a conversation, a relationship that includes not only submission but also the engagement of our will and our freedom with God.[12]

While we might long for the days of the pillar of cloud and fire, it is

---

10. Bruce Bugbee, *What You Do Best in the Body of Christ: Discover Your Spiritual Gifts, Personal Style, and God-Given Passion*, rev. ed. (Grand Rapids: Zondervan, 2005), 82–86.

11. Schuurman, *Vocation*, 127.

12. Smith, *Listening to God in Times of Choice*, 22.

very hard to dance with a cloud or a flame. Instead of distance, God desires intimacy with his children. In his preparations for the next generation of Israelites to enter the Promised Land at the end of the desert wanderings, Moses reminded the people, "You have seen how the LORD your God carried you, as a man carries his son, all the way that you went until you came to this place" (Deut. 1:31 ESV).

One Christmas, my daughter got *The Barbie Nutcracker* on DVD. Yes, you read right, *The Barbie Nutcracker*. It is a computer-animated cartoon in which Barbie and Ken reenact *The Nutcracker* in an hour-long movie. Before our purchase of this DVD, I probably could not have told you a single thing about *The Nutcracker* (of the Barbie variety or otherwise). But as any good dad would do, I watched the movie with my daughter too many times to count. After a while I could even whistle the tunes and quote most of the lines.

But my daughter wanted to do more than just watch *The Barbie Nutcracker*. She wanted to experience *The Barbie Nutcracker*. So at the big climax at the end of the movie, she would get up and dance as the role of Barbie in the grand finale. And as any toy aficionado will tell you, you cannot have a dancing Barbie without a dancing Ken. Since I am the only male in a house full of females, you can guess who got the part of the dancing Ken.

As I am writing this, I am smiling because my days of being the "dancing Ken" with my daughter are some of the most special memories of my life. Now my daughter has moved past Barbies, but I still get to steal a dance with my daughter now and then. My daughter dances with zeal to the music, but she will dance only when her dance partner dances with her.

God desires to dance with us as well. As we have said all along in this chapter, our primary calling to God is paramount. God desires us to draw close to him in relationship so that he can mold us into the likeness of his Son. God does not just want to give us answers to our questions. God wants to dance with us. There are no shortcuts to the dance of discernment. The dance of discernment is a slow dance. Discernment is the spiritual exercise of drawing near to the heartbeat of God so that he can lead us in the dance of life.

Charles Swindoll, in his book *The Mystery of God's Will*, confesses,

> I now believe that God's will for us in this life is not some black-and-white objective equation designed to take us to an appointed destination here on earth as much as it is about the journey itself. It is not so much about our own well-thought-through "mission" for our lives as it is about what matters to Him in our lives. Our human tendency is to focus solely on our calling—on where we should go, how we should get there, and what exactly we should do about it. God's concern is the process that He is taking us through to mature us and ready us, making us more

> like His Son. In other words, all of us—including you—are works in process.[13]

Slowing Down to Hear God

The problem is that we move too fast in life doing our own thing to slow down to dance the slow dance of discernment with God. We are able to hear the heartbeat of God in our lives only when we slow down, quiet ourselves, and invite him to dance with us. Ronald Wilson, in his book *Call Waiting*, paints the following word image.

> The discord and harshness of our culture is so overwhelming that it takes a special effort on our part to hear the voice of God. The bright lights of the carousel distract us, and the music drowns out any message God might whisper. It takes a special effort on our part and time set aside especially for the task to hear what God is saying to us and to read the obvious signs he has left for us.[14]

Unfortunately some people think that a "call" from God can only come through some type of "cataclysmic emotional experience." In reality, most people come to realizations about certain aspects of God's leadings in a more gradual nature through the experience of life. In fact, we are many times less likely to stick with commitments driven by emotional impulses alone.

Along with sound biblical study, the key to learning the dance steps of discernment is prayer. You discern the leadings of God in the context of the dancing relationship. You must remain in close communication with God if you have any chance of discerning well. Instead of the focus of your prayer being for God to "reveal his will," your prayers should be for him to create his character and his wisdom in you. When your actions, thoughts, and desires reflect God's priorities, then you are in a better place to discern well.

Called in Community

Community is essential in spiritual discernment of our functional calling. We are called to faith in community. We live out our transformed life in community. The purpose of our functional calling is for the service of the community. Sober judgment of our functional calling can take place only in community. And trust me, community keeps you humble. With very few exceptions, God's functional calling comes through other people speaking truth into our lives.

---

13. Charles R. Swindoll, *The Mystery of God's Will: What Does He Want for Me?* (Nashville: Word, 1999), ix.

14. Ronald Wilson, *Call Waiting: Hearing and Answering God's Call on Your Life* (Nashville: Broadman & Holman, 2005), 3.

Smith reminds us,

> We never discern in isolation; we discern in community. Every significant choice we make reflects the fact that we are profoundly interconnected with the lives of others. Our decisions inevitably affect others but are also affected by the choices that others make. It is only appropriate that we are accountable to others in our choices; others need to be able to challenge us and confirm whether what we believe to be God's will is truly of God. We need the wisdom and counsel of others.[15]

Serving Others in Love

Two brief things about the role of community should be noted. First, your functional calling is to serve the community of faith. Somehow in Western Christianity, we have forgotten this. Remember that you are not called to live on some island of self-existence. Self-sufficiency is just an illusion of pride. In the body of Christ each member belongs to each other, just like pieces of a finely crafted puzzle. Spiritual gifts are not to be hoarded and kept only for our own benefit. They are to be used for the benefit of the body.

As we already have seen earlier, Paul stresses this unity in diversity in several places.

> For as in one body we have many members, and the members do not all have the same function. (Rom. 12:4 ESV)

> For just as the body is one and has many members, and all the members of the body, though many, are one body, so it is with Christ. (1 Cor. 12:12 ESV)

There is a unity of the church, a plurality of the members, and a variety of gifts. Spiritual gifts mean that you are both weak and strong. You are strong in the area of your gift. You are weak in areas where others have been gifted. Thus, you must minister to the body of Christ and others out of your strength, and you are dependent upon the ministry of the rest of the body in your areas of weakness.

Under the umbrella of your primary calling to salvation and sanctification, your functional calling is how you love and serve others. With this proper understanding, loving others as God would love them becomes the benchmark of whether you are fulfilling your functional calling. As Reformation leader Martin Luther believed, "Reflect on your condition, and you will find enough good works to do if you would lead a godly life. Every calling has its own duties, so that we need not inquire for others

15. Smith, *Listening to God in Times of Choice*, 128.

outside of our station."[16] For Luther, serving one's neighbor was the greatest physical manifestation of our love of God.

Confirmation of Calling

Second, the community usually affirms your functional calling. This is the idea of corporate calling. Theologians discuss the idea of both personal/ inward calling and corporate/outward calling. I believe strongly that when God calls a person into a functional ministry, the body of Christ confirms that calling. I want to say that God's normal mode of operation is the public confirmation of one's functional calling, as the community of faith sees you function.

Seeking wise counsel is a strong biblical theme. Because of the potential for self-deception, it is vital for us to seek an outside perspective from others. Consider the following sample verses from Proverbs.

> Let the wise hear and increase in learning, and the one who understands obtain guidance. (Prov. 1:5 ESV)
>
> Where there is no guidance, a people falls, but in an abundance of counselors there is safety. (Prov. 11:14 ESV)
>
> The way of a fool is right in his own eyes, but a wise man listens to advice. (Prov. 12:15 ESV)
>
> By insolence comes nothing but strife, but with those who take advice is wisdom. (Prov. 13:10 ESV)
>
> Without counsel plans fail, but with many advisers they succeed. (Prov. 15:22 ESV)
>
> Listen to advice and accept instruction, that you may gain wisdom in the future. (Prov. 19:20 ESV)
>
> Plans are established by counsel; by wise guidance wage war. (Prov. 20:18 ESV)
>
> Oil and perfume make the heart glad, and the sweetness of a friend comes from his earnest counsel. (Prov. 27:9 ESV)

Testing One's Functional Calling

Many of you reading this chapter are in college or seminary. In school,

---

16. Martin Luther, "Luther's Church Postil: Gospels, Advent, Christmas and Epiphany Sermons," in *The Precious and Sacred Writings of Martin Luther*, ed. John Nicholas Lenker (Minneapolis: Lutherans in All Lands, 1905), 282.

you are in the process of confirming or nullifying different aspects of "vocational understanding." Testing your functional call is what you are supposed to be doing during this time in your life. A great internship can help confirm or nullify different aspects of "vocational understanding." As I constantly tell students who come into my office, it is much better to discover now what God is calling you to do than to spend thousands of dollars in tuition, move your family to the middle of nowhere, and discover that you hate what you have been trained to do.

For example, it is one thing for a ministry student to have grand visions of the "glorious adventure" of being a foreign missionary. It is quite another thing to actually live on the mission field for a semester and discover the reality of missions work once the honeymoon is over. My personal belief is that the student who is truly called to the mission field will find such an experience challenging, but confirming and fulfilling. The student who is not called to the mission field will only feel frustrated.

For some students with significant ministry experience background and clear vocational vision, an internship will help to confirm their known call and vocational direction. Their internship experience is just a verification of what they already know. For example, a veteran missionary returning to seminary and switching from a church planting focus to a Bible college teaching/administration focus could complete an internship in a formal classroom teaching setting and discover very quickly whether he enjoys developing syllabi and lesson plans for pupils.

For other students with less ministry experience, an internship will help to clarify their call and vocational direction. At most schools, this is probably the vast majority of the student population. In these cases, an internship serves as a "trial run" to see if there is a fit without a long-term commitment. For instance, a counseling student completing an internship with a women's shelter will discover quickly if she enjoys the demands of seeing clients and facilitating support groups on a daily basis. If this student decides that she does not enjoy intensive counseling because of her internship, it is better to discover that realization now than to graduate with a counseling degree and take a job she dreads and finds frustrating.

Finally, for some students an internship will serve as a catalyst for discerning their call and focusing their vocational development. Some students show up on campus with no idea of vocational direction. The internship process and the wise words of a site supervisor might be just what is needed.

It is one thing to realize and accept that God desires the involvement of all Christians in ministry. It is another to understand what that involvement entails. Developing your ministry vision can give you that understanding. Ministry vision is where you fit in the body of Christ. Ministry vision articulates what your ministry will look like in a clear "word picture." In other words, when you describe to other people your future ministry, what type of "word picture" do you paint?

Unlike a one-sentence mission statement, which expresses purpose, a ministry vision captures the essence of what it will look like when that purpose is met. Here is an example.

> I see myself working with college students on a major state university through a parachurch ministry, such as Campus Crusade for Christ. I am passionate about evangelism, so I see myself on campus engaging students in spiritual conversations and introducing them to a life-changing relationship with Jesus Christ. I would love meeting with new believers and discipling them in a one-on-one context, teaching them how to read the Bible for themselves. I would also love to be involved in a true multiplication ministry, where the students that I discipled would be able to share your faith with others and disciple others in the basics of the faith as well. Finally, I would love to introduce college students to a passion for world missions.

Joy in Our Callings in Life

One of the tests of your functional calling is the experience of joy in your life. The author of Ecclesiastes joyfully proclaims,

> There is nothing better for a person than that he should eat and drink and find enjoyment in his toil. This also, I saw, is from the hand of God, for apart from him who can eat or who can have enjoyment? For to the one who pleases him God has given wisdom and knowledge and joy, but to the sinner he has given the business of gathering and collecting, only to give to one who pleases God. This also is vanity and a striving after wind. (Eccl. 2:24–26 ESV)

Scripture teaches us that it is not wrong to have joy in serving. The apostle Paul even writes, "But the fruit of the Spirit is love, joy, peace, patience, kindness, goodness, faithfulness, gentleness, self-control; against such things there is no law" (Gal. 5:22–23 ESV). But biblical joy is very different from what the world calls joy. Joy is not just an emotional response. Joy is grounded upon God and derived from God.

Some of the greatest times of joy in my life have been when I have been serving "in my element," allowing God to use me as his instrument in the lives of other people. Joy is one of the payoffs when you love others with your Spirit-enabled giftedness. True biblical joy is not merely self-seeking pleasure. True biblical joy is experienced as you live your life with a clear understanding of the sovereignty of God and the purposefulness that knowledge brings to your life. A true understanding of calling makes every task potentially sacred and joyful.

Actually the opposite of joy is not sadness but burnout. When you are forced to serve in an area where you are not gifted or where you violate your functional calling, burnout very easily sets in. Parker Palmer, in his revealing book *Let Your Life Speak*, reflects, "Though usually regarded as the result of trying to give too much, burnout in my experience results from trying to give what I do not possess—the ultimate in giving too little! Burnout is a state of emptiness, to be sure, but it does not result from giving all I have: it merely reveals the nothingness from which I was trying to give in the first place."[17]

Of course there is a balance here. Joy is a by-product of serving, but pleasure or even self-fulfillment should never be the intended purpose of serving. Most of Christian history has taught that pleasure and comfort should never be the intended focuses of your life. Our Christian heritage is lined with the blood of martyrs. Sometimes in your calling to love God and love your neighbor, you will be led to do things that are not pleasurable or enjoyable.

I doubt that Jeremiah or Hosea, for example, experienced pleasure in their God-given tasks. Sometimes we will serve others where there will be little visible rewards for our tasks. But ultimately you are called to love God and love others. As Paul reminds us, "Whatever you do, work heartily, as for the Lord and not for men, knowing that from the Lord you will receive the inheritance as your reward. You are serving the Lord Christ" (Col. 3:23–24 ESV).

Gordon MacDonald, in an article in *Leadership*, states,

> When one lives obediently in the center of a call, one feels God's pleasure; one knows joy. Let us be frank: Men and women have obeyed God's call and become martyrs. Others have undertaken unspeakably difficult and discouraging tasks and barely survived. Some have lived obscure lives in far off corners of the world and have finished the course never feeling that they accomplished anything of measurable value. There have been others, of course, whose lives have sparkled with spectacular results—who in their preaching, their writing, their organization-building, their ability to envision and empower people have left their mark on church history. What did they all have in common? They felt God's pleasure; they had joy.[18]

Remember that the goal of serving is never joy, but we can be thankful when joy is experienced.

Being Comfortable with the Mystery of God's Will

We must acknowledge that while we can strive to discern well, there are times when the work God is doing in our lives will be a mystery to our finite minds. Life is very rarely wide boulevards. Instead there are "detours, unmarked intersections, forced exits, blind alleys, and cul-de-sacs."[19]

---

17. Parker J. Palmer, *Let Your Life Speak: Listening for the Voice of Vocation* (San Francisco: Jossey-Bass, 2000), 49.

18. Gordon MacDonald, "God's Calling Plan," *Leadership* 24 (2003): 42.

19. Lee Hardy, *The Fabric of This World: Inquiries into Calling, Career Choice, and the Design of Human Work* (Grand Rapids: Eerdmans, 1990), 87.

It always seems like just when we get things figured out, something happens in our lives that leaves us scratching our heads, wondering what God is up to.

Scripture very boldly pronounces that there are some things of God that we just do not understand.

> How great are your works, O LORD! Your thoughts are very deep! (Ps. 92:5 ESV)

> Great is the LORD, and greatly to be praised, and his greatness is unsearchable. (Ps. 145:3 ESV)

> He has made everything beautiful in its time. Also, he has put eternity into man's heart, yet so that he cannot find out what God has done from the beginning to the end. (Eccl. 3:11 ESV)

> Have you not known? Have you not heard? The LORD is the everlasting God, the Creator of the ends of the earth. He does not faint or grow weary; his understanding is unsearchable. (Isa. 40:28 ESV)

> For my thoughts are not your thoughts, neither are your ways my ways, declares the LORD. For as the heavens are higher than the earth, so are my ways higher than your ways and my thoughts than your thoughts. (Isa. 55:8–9 ESV)

> Oh, the depth of the riches and wisdom and knowledge of God! How unsearchable are his judgments and how inscrutable his ways! "For who has known the mind of the Lord, or who has been his counselor?" (Rom. 11:33–34 ESV)

God's work in your life is bigger than you. This mystery of God is one of the things that keep humility active in your life. Charles Swindoll humbly admits,

> When we do a serious study of the will of God, we go from an unconscious to a conscious awareness of how mysteriously He leads us along. . . . No matter how educated we are, no matter how much power and influence we may think we have, no matter how long we have walked with Him, no matter how significant we may imagine ourselves to be in His plans (if any of us could even claim significance), none of that qualifies us to grasp the first particle of why He does what He does when He does it and how He chooses to do it.[20]

---

20. Swindoll, *The Mystery of God's Will*, 4, 10–11.

This humble admission should keep us from ever arrogantly proclaiming that we have all of the details of God's plan figured out. It is dangerous ground when we boldly state, "God told me this morning . . ." Even with our best efforts in biblical study, theological reasoning, and Spirit-enabled discernment, we are still human, and God is still beyond our thoughts.[21]

Conclusion

So by this point, you are probably asking, "When is this guy going to tell me which job I should take?" While I wish there was a simple formula or easy process, spiritual discernment is more art than science. But more importantly, I am not sure that is the right question to be asking in the first place. Questions about God's specific plans for your life's work or finding your future spouse are not the crucial questions. The most important question is, Where is God in the circumstances of life in which you find yourself? When you are loving God and loving others in the various contexts of life, then you have your calling in life.

I want to return to the metaphor of dancing with God in drawing my thoughts together because I have never found a more appropriate image of the Christian walk. As I look at the path that God has taken me down, it has been a journey of incredible emotional highs and some dark times as well.

Bruce Waltke, in his provocatively titled book *Finding the Will of God: A Pagan Notion?* states,

> We ought to stamp out of our vocabulary the non-biblical and misleading expression "finding God's will." Rather than talk about "seeking the will of God," we ought to speak of following the guidance of God. This is not just semantically different, since He is calling us to draw close to Himself and to live holy lives. God's will for us is that we be holy; there is no mystery to His will. As for those questions about changing jobs, getting married, going to school, and the like, finding answers will require growing close to God.[22]

Throughout Christian history, the words *calling* and *vocation* have meant different things. Some read the word *calling* and think of professional ministry. But the call of God is so much bigger than that. In the simplest terms, calling is the place in life where God has brought you, and where in your uniqueness you can love God and love others.

---

21. Smith, *Listening to God in Times of Choice*, 66.

22. Bruce K. Waltke, *Finding the Will of God: A Pagan Notion?* (Grand Rapids: Eerdmans, 1995), 169.

Chapter 10

Life Story and Spiritual Formation

Gail Seidel

> You intended to harm me, but God intended it for good to accomplish what is now being done, the saving of many lives.
>
> —Genesis 50:20

A Story Before the Story: In a Lawn Chair by the River

The gnawing disruption I felt that summer afternoon, sitting in a lawn chair at our campsite by the Guadalupe River in the hill country of Texas was real. My husband and our two junior-high-age children were canoeing on the river. It should have been a pleasant, relaxing afternoon reading the book my husband had given me, *The Sensation of Being Somebody*. But on every page my values of where "life" was found were being challenged, and I felt exposed.

Now deep into vocational ministry, I learned early in life the concept of "image management" as a strategy to make life work, to compensate and cover the oddness I felt in being the only one in my church youth group whose parents were divorced and the only one in my school group who lived in an apartment. The longing to "look normal," be accepted, and fit in like the rest was powerfully creative, morphing into all forms of compensating behaviors—looking good in appearance, seeking academic achievement, being liked by everyone, responding appropriately to adults, being a "good Christian"—idols useful to make my life work apart from God. These may seem minor compared to the harsh, addictive, protective strategies of our postmodern day. But even "mild, appropriate-looking idols" are steel-trapped snares

> keeping prisoner the one whose heart longs to seek God and preventing the very work of formation the Spirit of God desires to perform.
>
> This legitimate unsettling was an exhausting, fraudulent feeling. If only I had had the needed vehicle or group in which to gain insight and give meaning to the disruption. The freeing power of seeing my story as charted by the hand of God had not been unleashed.

My life story is God's story, authored by him. He has uniquely orchestrated and providentially created me to bring him glory through my story. As I chart his hand in my life, I gain insight into his purpose. I am the only one who can reflect his glory through my story. Understanding and accepting my story becomes a tool of personal spiritual formation. As my story intersects with your story as a part of his story, we become story keepers of God's story and offer, in community, his story to the world. Story is a catalyst tool of God, growing the individual and building community so that they bring him glory and offer the visible presence of Christ to a watching, needy world. My story has a beginning, middle, and end. The last chapter of my story will end in eternal worship of the Father, the Son, and the Holy Spirit.

Reflecting on Story

Story as Genre: The Power of Story

From ancient times story has been a primary genre in the history of communication. The very first words in Genesis confirm that a story is about to be told: "In the beginning God . . ." Over two thousand years ago, Aristotle used the classic beginning-middle-end story structure, seeming to reflect how the human mind seeks organization.[1] A story is the unfolding of events, circumstances, and relationships that have a beginning, middle, and end. Multiple civilizations used stories to pass on information, heritage, and truth from generation to generation long before technological multimedia capabilities. Some of the Eastern civilizations up to the present day use only story to communicate to their people, speaking to them in hidden metaphor. There are oral cultures that learn only by the spoken word, heightening the inherent value of story.[2]

Storytelling is the oldest tool of influence in human history. It is no wonder the master teacher Jesus' most powerful teaching device was a story. You can grab the attention of most children by saying quietly, "Once upon

1. Herminia Ibarra and Kent Lineback, "Key Elements of a Classic Story," Harvard Business Review Online, http://harvardbusinessonline.hbsp.harvard.edu/hbrsa/en/issue/0501/article/R0501F_A.jhtml (accessed August 20, 2005).

2. Avery Willis and Steve Evans, comps., *Making Disciples of Oral Learners* (Lima, NY: Elim Publishing, 2007), 6.

a time there was. . . ." Since our postmodern culture values relationships and sharing life stories help build relationships, stories are essential. Telling your story for the purpose of being known is a bridge builder today. Oral learning is on the rise.[3]

Each of us has a story, our own individual story. From the beginning God has been writing each of our stories. God created each one of us in his image. He created us for his glory. God is the one who did the creating. Man did not create himself (Gen. 1:27; Ps. 100:3). God created his chosen people Israel and the Gentiles by adoption for his glory. God is all about story, as we discover from the Bible, a book about God's story woven through the lives of real people with real problems and real temptations. No detail is spared. The truth is not hidden.

Stories have the power to influence in a way bare facts do not. The story the Lord sent Nathan to tell King David convicted David's heart in a way that confrontational facts would not (2 Sam. 12:1–15). Stories touch the heart and are remembered, while facts are often forgotten. God told his people to tell their stories to the next generation so that generation would remember the works and care of God.

Each of these individual stories fit into the larger story. Each of our stories—my story, your story—is a part of a bigger story, the metanarrative, the overarching, all-embracing story of humankind. For the Christian, this metanarrative is the biblical narrative of salvation history—creation, fall, redemption, and finally, the new creation.[4]

You are the only one who can live out the story God intended for you. No one else can live your story. Understanding your individual story as a vehicle of spiritual formation energizes and frees you personally. You are the only one who can bring God glory through your story because it is your unique story. But you don't live your story in isolation. Understanding your story in light of this larger story, the "metanarrative," encourages and gives relevance to corporate spiritual formation.

The fact that God has purposed human history and works all things together for good provides courage to investigate our own personal stories in order to better fulfill the protocols of building unity—the New Testament "one anothers."[5] This unity can serve as an apologetic for the deity of Christ, becoming the magnet of attraction for others to observe community and investigate his story.

Story as Vehicle: What Does It Matter?

Looking at my life in the context of a story gives meaning and helps me accept more readily the ambiguities and disruptions in life. A story

---

3. Ibid., 57.

4. Stanley J. Grenz, David Guretzki, and Cherith Fee Nordling, *Pocket Dictionary of Theological Terms* (Downers Grove, IL: InterVarsity Press, 1999), 77.

5. See end of this chapter for complete list.

is simply the unfolding of events, circumstances, and relationships that have a beginning, middle, and end. The process of charting the hand of God in my life through my story is first undertaken individually and then corporately. It is an important tool in individual and corporate spiritual formation.

A spiritual formation leader who worked through this process noted, "Seeing my life in the form of a story is powerful. I see my life in ways I never considered as a part of a bigger picture of what God is doing. It can be a painful process but one that can act as a bridge from just 'coping with life experiences' to living purposely in what God is doing through them."[6]

Author Annette Simmons writes, "In a land of complex reality story makes sense of chaos and gives people a plot. Story gives definition to the experiences of the past. A story can reframe frustration, suffering, or extra effort as meaningful."[7] Story is a way to recognize God's process in my life and how he is developing me. I see his grace, his goodness, and times of blessing, challenge, and protection woven into the mundane details.

The "theme" or "themes" of a story helps make sense of the parts, offering cohesion to the whole and reducing the frustration and questioning. The theme provides clarifying connecting threads that pull together disjointed parts. "Meaningful frustration is much easier to bear than meaningless frustration."[8]

Often, in the same story, paradoxes exist simultaneously—awful/exciting; fearful/courageous; cautious/risk taking; sovereign/free will. As the Dallas Seminary Spiritual Formation curriculum states, "You can submit intellectually to the compatibility between human responsibility and God's sovereignty, but that doesn't always ease the emotions of grappling with the hard parts of your story."[9] As the author, God takes the paradoxes and the hard times and uses them for his purpose and glory. This gives hope. He takes the pieces of my story and puts them together in a new offering for new beginnings. My story is a letter written for the world to read (2 Cor. 2:14–15).

Author Eugene Peterson writes, "Story is the most natural way of enlarging and deepening our sense of reality, and then enlisting us as participants in it. Stories open doors to areas or aspects of life that we didn't know were there, or had quit noticing out of over-familiarity, or supposed were out-of-bounds to us. They then welcome us in. Stories are verbal acts of hospitality."[10]

---

6. Myndi Lawrence, private e-mail, May 4, 2006.

7. Annette Simmons, *The Story Factor: Inspiration, Influence, and Persuasion Through the Art of Storytelling* (New York: Perseus Books Group, 2002), 37.

8. Ibid.

9. Center for Christian Leadership, Dallas Theological Seminary, *Community: Discovering Who We Are Together* (Colorado Springs: NavPress, 2004), 23.

10. Eugene Peterson, *Christ Plays in Ten Thousand Places: A Conversation in Spiritual Theology* (Grand Rapids: Eerdmans, 2005), 13.

Story gives perspective to the overall focus of one's future. God, the author of my story, uses the power of Christ to transform my weaknesses. His healing often is the agent that propels me into future ministry. God never wastes any painful experience, especially when surrendered to him.

One of our spiritual formation leaders states, "Experience teaches me that the most significant connections between people are established through story. Life Story establishes a safe forum where such stories can be crafted and presented in a way that helps a new group understand one another more fully, and quite quickly too. Everything to which the group attains is built on this foundation."[11]

Story is the potential glue for community since my story is a part of the bigger story. Dieter Zander writes, "We value individualism in our tradition, but individualistic Christianity is an oxymoron. The fact is we need other human beings and meaningful relationships to grow."[12]

A Story About a Beginning

Seven strangers entered the room about the same time. Being quite an eclectic group from all over the United States, their only common thread was that they each were 1986 Ph.D. applicants to the Fielding Institute, a fully accredited graduate program in Santa Barbara, California. Their mentor advisor for the entirety of the program, Dr. Barbara Mink, told them that many people begin but do not finish the program and they needed to encourage one another through the process. She handed each of them a 24 x 36-inch piece of paper with the instructions to use any creative idea they wanted to draw something that represented each of their lives from start to finish. She gave each of them a set of colored pens and thirty minutes to complete the assignment. When they returned, each person was given twenty minutes to tell their life story and then the rest of the group had time to ask questions. Pete Deison recalled that it was one of the most profound experiences of his life. Inside of a few hours, he saw this group bond with a depth he had not experienced before and felt he knew each person as well as he knew his best friend.

When he left that weekend, he knew telling one's life story was a valuable tool, having learned several things in the process. First, he observed the amazing creativity people had in the way they chose to depict their lives. There were mountains, spirals, rivers, graphs, trees, and so on. Each one served as a perfect metaphor for that particular person.

---

11. From private e-mails March–June 2006 from the following Dallas Theological Seminary Spiritual Formation staff, fellows, leaders, or Dallas Theological Seminary students: Joye Baker, Nick Berquist, Terry Boyle, Liz Burley, Rebecca Duff, Karen Fountain, Nikkol Harper, Dipa Hart, Terry Hebert, Sherry Klein, Myndi Lawrence, Carolina Mena, Alicia Mc Nairy, Carrie Morgan, Mandi Morrow, Laura Murray, Terry Nettleton, Paul Pettit, Jonathan Phipps, Tom Pussel, Joycelyn Seybold, Monty Waldron.

12. Dieter Zander, "The Apprentices," *Leadership* 26 no. 3 (Summer 2005): 25.

Second, everybody had something in their story with which everyone else could identify, whether it was a hardship, a family issue, a trip, a club, athletics, moving, or schools. They were all drawn into each other's stories in ways that connected them to the storyteller. Twenty years later Pete can still remember stories from that day about people he has now not seen in over twelve years. Thirdly, he learned that painful events were just as valuable if not more so than positive events.

When Pete Deison was asked to join the Leadership Center at Dallas Theological Seminary he began using this tool as Life Mapping. Viewing one's life as a whole provided a new way to determine personalized vision for a person and perform assessment based upon abilities. It also helped identify pain patterns that gave insight into God's shaping work of providence. Pete's concept of Life Mapping—combined with the 4 H's, heritage, heroes, hard times, and high times, developed by Brad Smith—helped launch the tool Life Story. All students in the Spiritual Formation program at Dallas Seminary currently work through in the second semester Spiritual Formation curriculum book called "Community."[13]

Life Story: A Catalyst for Individual Formation in Preparation for Community

What's Your Story?

Author Frederick Buechner affirms the value of life story in listening and reflecting on your life. "What quickens my pulse now is the . . . search through where I have been, for some hint as to who I am becoming or failing to become that I delve into what used to be . . . I think of my life and of the lives of everyone who has ever lived, or will live, as not just journeys through time but as sacred journeys. . . . What I propose to do now is to try listening to my life as a whole . . . for whatever of meaning, of holiness, of God, there may be in it to hear."[14]

The format for how to write out the story of your life is clarified in "Community, Discovering Who We Are Together," the second semester curriculum of the Spiritual Formation program at Dallas Theological Seminary. This four-part series proposes "knowing your identity in Christ *so that* you can make yourself known to others in a Christian community *so that* you can pursue a lifetime of growth in the context of community *so that* you are best equipped to glorify God by serving others."[15] This life story tool is used in the context of a small group. Some of the comments inserted in this chapter are made by the

13. Pete Deison, pastor of disciple making and adult communities, Park Cities Presbyterian Church, Dallas, Texas, private e-mail, April 9, 2006.

14. Frederick Buechner, *The Sacred Journey: A Memoir of Early Days* (New York: HarperOne, 1991), 6.

15. Center for Christian Leadership, *Community*, 13.

leaders of these small spiritual formation groups at Dallas Theological Seminary to show the benefit and tested value of this tool.

Should I Do This?

A female student comments, "I had never taken the time to step back and intentionally look at my entire life seeking to identify an overarching theme or identify lessons that God had continually been trying to teach me. The experience of Life Story presented this opportunity for me. In processing through my life story I was able to gain a greater awareness [and] certainty of God's ongoing work in my life. I have a unique story of my individual and personal walk with him. Having come to terms with it, I now can share it."[16]

A spiritual formation leader offered, "Processing through the Life Story tool showed me personally that God has intricately authored my life and allowed me to approach the difficulties in my past logically but with emotion as well—it made my life less overwhelming especially understanding one theme that the first year of anything I do is always harder because I want to perform more than be myself."[17]

The key is to discover who God intended you to be and then camp there, embrace it, engage in it, and live out of his authentic creation, serving him and others. You are unique. No one else can live your story! Don't try to live someone else's story. You need not feel guilty about your uniqueness, then, when you are misunderstood. The body of Christ is missing something if you don't offer your story and you.

One spiritual formation leader offers, "Keep in mind your life story is your story and God's story. Your life story is your story of your life as you remember it from birth to now. Your life story is also God's story of your life as he has providentially created you, cared for you, and walked with you. It is your story and God's story that you have to tell."[18]

Beginning to Uncover Your Story

To start the process of uncovering the details of your story, you need a legal pad and a pen or a computer, time, a willingness to reflect, and prayer for God's guidance and illumination, and you are ready to begin.

The basic structure is to group the facts of your life in chronological order in categories under the topics of heritage, heroes, high times, and hard times. These provide insight into God's working and when reflected upon help surface themes, patterns of reacting to circumstances, and areas of God's sovereignty to embrace, rejoice in, and minister from. Always keep in mind the process can be messy and may require writing on multiple sheets of paper until some of the events begin to gel into patterns or themes. It

16. From private e-mails March–June 2006.
17. Ibid.
18. Ibid.

takes time to uncover and reflect on the hand of God in your life, sometimes weeks or even months, as you allow the memories and information to surface the common threads and themes.

While gathering insights about your life, think about the effects of past experiences and relationships in order to identify the formative experiences. Consider the various stages of life: early childhood, elementary school years, junior high, high school, college, postcollege, marriage, parenting, later years, and so on. As you reflect on the following questions, you may want to record your thoughts under each of the following categories with each category on a separate sheet of the legal pad.

One woman writes, "Recording and reflecting on the events of my life to write out my life story is a challenging process, and one in which there are painful moments. When I put my life story together, I am reliving and reflecting on all of my life decisions, both the obedient ones as well as the sinful ones."[19]

The Categories

Heritage

Heritage is "that which comes or belongs to one by reason of birth; an inherited lot or portion."[20]

- How have my parents or primary caregivers influenced me?
- Whom did my nuclear family consist of? Describe the relationship with my mother, my father, my siblings.
- What was the general atmosphere in my home as I grew up?
- How have my ethnicity and culture played an important role in my life?
- What have my peer relationships been like over the years? Why have they been this way?
- How have geographical factors influenced me?[21]

Heroes

A hero is "a person who, in the opinion of others, has heroic qualities or has performed a heroic act and is regarded as a model or ideal."[22]

---

19. Ibid.

20. *Webster's Encyclopedic Unabridged Dictionary of the English Language* (New York: Gramercy Books, 1996), s.v. "heritage."

21. Center for Christian Leadership, *Community*, 74.

22. *Webster's*, s.v. "hero."

- Who has influenced me for good? How did they specifically do so?
- After whom would I like to model my life? Why?
- Who shaped my character or directions in life? How? Why?[23]

High Times

High times are those periods or events that have a distinctly positive meaning in your life.

- What accomplishments have brought me fulfillment or special recognition? How? Why?
- What events or people have brought me great joy?
- At what points in my life did I feel particularly good about life? Why?
- When have I made my greatest contributions to life or others? How?[24]

Hard Times

Hard times are those seasons of life or relationships that have been particularly difficult or painful.

- What incidents in my life are hard to talk about with others? Why?
- Who or what has been a source of pain in my life? When? Why?
- Toward whom do I harbor anger or bitterness? Whom do I struggle to forgive? Why?
- What has brought me great disappointment? Why?
- Through what injustices have I had to suffer?
- To what addictions or abuse have I been exposed, either in my own life or in the lives of others?[25]

---

23. Center for Christian Leadership, *Community*, 75.
24. Ibid.
25. Ibid., 76.

General Questions

- Who are the memorable people from my past?
- What have been the most influential experiences in my life?
- What life dreams have I had in my past?
- When I think of my parents, what memories come to mind?
- What do I remember about where I grew up?
- What are the significant questions with which I have wrestled in my lifetime? What experiences triggered the questions?[26]

After answering and reflecting on all these questions (and whatever else comes to your mind), connect these together into a story, one most likely with a theme that has come to the surface.

"Aha" Moments

One student writes, "In preparing and sharing my life story, God has revealed to me themes—of both ways he has worked in and through me, as well as ditches and areas I seek to control, rather than trust him with. I saw in amazement that God's grace has created me with gifts and a heart to love people in unique ways. I also saw themes and patterns of people pleasing and performance, and a desire to protect myself from rejection. Confessing these to the group and receiving his grace and acceptance through them has been key to moving forward in renewing my mind, repenting, and growing in these areas."[27]

Another student comments, "Due to the individual process of writing one's life story over many weeks, each participant brings an examined authenticity and openness to the group/community, as well as a keener awareness of themselves, and God's utter faithfulness."[28]

A small group leader shares, "As you systematically reflect on his sovereign hand working in your life, it enriches your walk with the Lord. It causes you to glorify God as you see him working in others' lives too. Sometimes, as you listen to another's story, you can see ways that God has worked that he or she may have not even realized. Then, you have the privilege to share this observation with them."[29]

Deciphering the meaning of my personal story cannot be done

---

26. Ibid.
27. From private e-mails March–June 2006.
28. Ibid.
29. Ibid.

without consideration of how my individual story fits into the larger story. My story, one piece of the puzzle, fits into the rest of the puzzle—the community or the body of Christ. One cannot understand the individual part in isolation from the whole because we are intricately connected with others. As my life intersects with others in the body of Christ, with my family, or with colleagues, I am impacted and influenced by them and they by me. Our lives are intertwined in our God-given design and in our depravity. We share a commonality in our humanness. We are created in the image of God. We are fallen and in need of a Savior. When I am excited and happy, my mood spills over and impacts those I live and interact with. Similarly, when I am discouraged or suffering, my response has a huge impact on those around me. Author Frederick Buechner writes, "My assumption is the story of any one of us in some measure is the story of us all."[30]

Presentations

Annette Simmons in her book on story says, "Authenticity is so very important for a storyteller. Your body, voice, or posture will betray your true feelings and intentions. You may as well get your true feelings and intentions straight first before you try to influence others with your stories."[31]

Once I process my story, the presentation becomes a tool to be used however it seems appropriate. The idea is to share my life through my personal story in an inviting and influential manner, considering that the way I tell my story affects the process of building community. The following are examples of presentations of stories that have been used in the spiritual formation small groups at Dallas Theological Seminary and subsequently in private conversations and in larger audiences for the purpose of training.

Energy Channeled Under Pressure: Disruption into Focus and Offering

My story begins before my conception. God was writing my story even before I knew what charting the hand of God in my life would mean to me through the Life Story tool. God created me for his glory and purposes for me to reflect his glory to the world through my story and corporately in the community story.

> For you created my inmost being; you knit me together in my mother's womb. I praise you because I am fearfully and wonderfully made; your works are wonderful, I know that full well. My frame was not hidden from you when I was made in the secret place. When I was woven together in the depths of the earth, your eyes saw my unformed body. All the days ordained for me

30. Buechner, *Sacred Journey*, 6.
31. Simmons, *The Story Factor*, 103.

> were written in your book before one of them came to be. (Ps. 139:13–16)
>
> For he has rescued us from the dominion of darkness and brought us into the kingdom of the Son he loves, in whom we have redemption, the forgiveness of sins. (Col. 1:13–14)

From my earliest memory I stirred several pots at once. My mother always said of me that I was in high gear.

From 1716 to 1721 Johann Sebastian Bach composed six concertos and sent them to Margrave Christian Ludwig of Brandenburg. The Brandenburg Concertos are six uniquely diverse concertos, each a masterpiece in its own right, performed with six instruments. The music is contrapuntal, marked by counterpoint, a combination of two or more independent melodies occurring at once, back and forth, bumping into each other and woven together into a single harmonic texture with much energy. The tempo is fast with lots going on at once.[32]

When I listen to Bach's Brandenburg Concertos, I feel like I have come home. The theme of my life story, "Energy Channeled Under Pressure—*Disruption into Focus and Offering*," is so reflected in this music. I feel like Bach wrote these scores just for me, about me. Intense energy directed toward purpose and conclusion forged under the pressure of initial disruption became a pattern of my life. The energy comes from God. The initial disruption comes from the impact of circumstances over which I had no control early on but to which I responded by trying to get control. The melodies come from decisions to make choices to pursue excellence, to seek security and normalcy through perseverance and hard work modeled by my parents, and to welcome people into relationship and into hospitality. The discordant notes and minor melodies play out in several well-forged beliefs about where life is found: "I have to hold it together"; "I have to be the one to make it happen or it won't happen"; "I have to compensate to appear normal"; "my value is measured by affirmation and recognition." These were just a few of the inaccurate mantras I found myself repeating.

I live with tension of motive held in tandem between legitimate pursuit of excellence in living out my gifting and being driven to pursue excellence for identity. This energy works for both. From my story emerge caution questions that I must ask to guard my heart. Can I really relax in God's care, or am I compelled to live in constant vigilance to ensure that my life "holds together"? Can I pursue excellence in what I commit to without it having to be in a bad strategy category? Will God be my anchor of support if all my earthly constants disappear? Do I really believe God loves me for who I am and not for what I do for him? Is God enough?

---

32. Benjamin Chee, *The Brandenburg Concertos*, The Flying Inkpot, http://inkpot.com/classical/brandenburg.htm (accessed June 4, 2006)

The chart form of my story (see page 230) is understood more fully with the Brandenburg Concertos playing in the background.[33]

Another Story: "In the Dance"

> Since I was a little girl, music and dance were always a huge part of my life so when it came time to choose a vehicle for my life story presentation, Broadway musicals seemed a fitting choice. I made a Broadway musical billboard for each musical. Each one I chose represented an overall "feel" or theme of that period of life. The imaginative, creative fun of the musical *CATS* well represented my happy, creative, and relatively carefree childhood. The theme of my teenage years was summed up in *Fiddler on the Roof*, a story in which Tevya, the father, struggles to keep his family together despite constant radical changes. Family issues during that time in my life left me feeling like it was my responsibility to be the peacemaker and hold everything together. An unhealthy relationship during my college years led me to choose *Phantom of the Opera* for that period. Its dark, haunting nature mirrored a difficult time in my life. For the years that have followed, *Les Miserables'* tale of a man seeking to clarify his identity and to honor God with his life seemed fitting. My hope and prayer for my life is that the Lord will continue to show me who he wants me to be for his glory.[34]

Another Story: "Lost and Found"

"The title of my story, 'Lost & Found,' captures what most of my life has felt like spiritually, relationally, vocationally. The Lord has graciously found me in many dark, lifeless, self-centered places only to lead me to light, vibrant, Christ-centered places that are so because of his good presence, thus the cover verse (Ps. 73:28)."[35]

The basic layout of this presentation includes:

- Chapter title
- Thematic illustration
- Chapter time frame
- Scripture that captures a life lesson from that chapter

---

33. Life story of Gail Seidel, mentor advisor, used with permission, Department of Spiritual Formation and Leadership, Dallas Theological Seminary.

34. Life story of Myndi Lawrence, used with permission, private e-mail, May 31, 2006.

35. Monty Waldron, teaching pastor, Fellowship Bible Church, Murfreesboro, TN, used with permission.

ENERGY CHANNELED UNDER PRESSURE

Disruption into Focus and Offering

Life Story—Gail Seidel

A Beginning Composition with Brand-New Notes	Discovering the Melodies	Practicing the Score	Combining Melodies for Life	Increasing the Harmony Balancing the Volume
1 — 4	5 — 18	19 — 23	24 — 49	50 — 62
PARENTS DIVORCE **Mother**: Church Beauty Persevering **Father**: Self-made Hardworking Alcoholic	★Grandmother: Renna Kate Hearns Hinkle Aunts, Uncles—"Normal" †SALVATION 4th grade—"teacher in training" 9th grade—discovering comfort and delight in leading and speaking up front †16 yrs: My all to Christ	★Andy: steady anchor, passion University of Texas Campus Crusade staff • vehicle for training • passion ignited for mentoring younger women	†MARRIAGE ★Hospitality Students at U of Illinois Children Cadets: West Point Students: Texas A & M †Leaving pastorate for pastors in Eastern Europe and Russia Marriage of our children	Vienna Eastern Europe Russia DTS: Spiritual Formation DTS Students DTS Graduation Grandchildren
		Circle of Friends		

Melodies

- Searching for security and what is normal
- Determination and striving toward excellence

(Ages 19–62:)

- Influencing through hospitality, networking, welcoming in
- Passion ignited for leading, teaching, mentoring ever-present students
- Longing for "home"—creating one in 22 places

Countermelodies, minor, discordant notes

- "I have to hold it all together"—Super-responsible
- "I have to compensate to appear normal"
- Contribution and value measured by affirmation and recognition

LOST & FOUND

But for me it is good to be near God; I have made the Lord God my refuge, that I may tell of all your works. Psalm 73:28 ESV

1

Roller Coaster

Preschool Through Junior High (birth–13)

There is a way that seems right to a man, but its end is the way to death. Proverbs 14:12 ESV

2

Mountains & Valleys

High School (14–17)
Stillwater, OK

Foolishness is bound up in the heart of a child. Proverbs 22:15a NASB

3

Tug-of-War

Oklahoma University (18–22)
Norman, OK

For God is opposed to the proud, but gives grace to the humble. 1 Peter 5:5b NASB

4

Doulos

Family Life (23–28)

The greatest among you should be like the youngest, and the one who rules like the one who serves. Luke 22:26

5

Immersion

Dallas Theological Seminary (29–32)

Be diligent to present yourself approved to God as a workman who does not need to be ashamed, accurately handling the word of truth. 2 Timothy 2:15 NASB

6

Broad Spaces

Fellowship Bible Church (33+)

But thanks be to God, who always leads us in triumph in Christ, and manifests through us the sweet aroma of the knowledge of Him in every place. 2 Corinthians 2:14 NASB

The two prominent themes revealed in this story are grace and anger. "My parents' divorce ignited rage in me that was perpetuated by my own failed efforts to 'make life work' on my own, by my own strength. Throughout my journey God has lavished his grace on me (sometimes very painfully) to draw me away from self-reliance to greater dependence upon his all-sufficient care."[36]

And Another: "Looking for a Father"

> I chose as the overall theme of my story "Looking for a Father who loves me" because it captured the influence of my father in my life and also my journey of understanding the grace of God's love for me. In each stage of my life story, I related how my father's inability to express love when I was a child affected me and how I handled it. In each part of my life I showed how God's presence and work in my life gradually healed and filled my need for a father's love, so that God's grace overpowered the negative effects and revealed that my heavenly Father was the one who loved me all along.
>
> Because I had long ago forgiven my father and come to understand his background and difficulties, I did not feel it was dishonoring to him to be honest about our family struggles. He was a hardworking man who provided a home for us, and in his last years he softened considerably. Life story is about seeing life as it really is, but recognizing the providential power of God to work all things for good.
>
> In the divisions of the chart of my life story, I have three themes running concurrently. At the top the titles represent seasons of my life—Early Days, Foolish Days, Blessed Days, Growing Days, and Good Days, each with a verse from Psalm 139, my theme Scripture. Along the bottom the theme of the Father's love is shown: my Father knows me, my Father sees me, my Father seeks me, my Father comforts me, and my Father loves me. I spelled out G R A C E—a letter in background in each column—showing how I can see that God's grace covered my life.[37]

Stories Intersecting Stories

Now, It's Your Turn . . . to Tell Your Story

As you write and share your life story, keep in mind the goal of this process—to gain insight into God's purpose for you so that you will be

36. Ibid.
37. Alicia McNairy, private e-mail, used with permission, May 31, 2006.

better able to live out of who he intended for you to be. Understanding and accepting your story is a valuable tool of personal spiritual formation. Telling your story can be a catalyst for building community, which contributes to corporate formation—my story intersecting your story for his story.

One leader comments, "It is intimidating to share your past with others. Will they reject me? Will they understand? What's so important about what I have to share? I am able to begin to see myself through God's eyes, as well as admit to sin cycles of self-defense stemming from legitimate past hurts and abuse. I can also see more of my passions and dreams that God has given me and am now free to pursue them more fully in my walk with Christ."[38]

Invite People in by Telling Your Story

Telling my story is the closest thing to allowing others to walk in my shoes. It delivers context, viewpoint, and understanding of who I am and why I do what I do. I share my story so I can be known, which matches the longing of my heart to be known and accepted for who I am, a redeemed child of God and fellow traveler in community.

As others notice God's redemptive work in me, they have the opportunity to respond in a redemptive manner by loving, forgiving, encouraging, and rejoicing in God's redemptive work. One spiritual formation leader says, "One's life story must redeem the community by moving the listeners to their own need for redemption, to deeper faith in the knowledge of the Son of God. Some listeners need to repent and confess their own sins as discovered in another's story. If the speaker and listeners respond by means of the Spirit in a Christlike manner to the story, then the Spirit has built community. We call this Spiritual Formation."[39]

Telling the story of one's past can create vision, awareness, and desire in both the teller and the listener for a new story, a refurbished, renovated story. New stories demand courage and extra effort, and can invalidate past choices, giving hope for future good choices. Using a metaphor that captures your essence enhances your story, as in "Energy Channeled Under Pressure: Disruption into Focus and Offering" told to Bach's Brandenburg Concertos; "Lost & Found" done with graphic art; or "Looking for a Father Who Loves Me."

In whatever form you choose, creatively present your story and God's story. Whether shared in a formal setting, in an informal small group, or even in a one-on-one encounter, telling your story demonstrates your willingness to be vulnerable. It is a gift to offer your story. It involves the risk of being misunderstood and the uncertainty of response, but it may be sweetly encouraged and embraced. The response cannot be predetermined, but you can determine to leave the responses to God. More than likely your

38. From private e-mails March–June 2006.
39. Ibid.

vulnerability in telling will be a catalyst for community between you and the listeners.

A student comments, "Most of the time we tell people our stories because we like to talk about ourselves, which is why Life Story is vital. I can see you and your experiences, whether positive or negative, in light of who God has made you to be."[40]

Another student comments, "As a result of sharing myself (good and bad) with the group, I experienced a lot of emotional and spiritual healing. It was very freeing."[41]

Sweet Release

One leader writes, "Many of us keep certain things hidden from others out of fear—fear of rejection or disapproval. These secrets keep me chained to shame. I hear a whisper, 'Don't tell. If people know, they will turn away from you.' The day comes. I tell my story. As I share the secrets, his light shines in. The secret lies bare, unshackled. My group responds in love. They reflect Christ to me. Together, we listen to each member's life story. We see God's workmanship—his unique design for each one of us. We celebrate his power. We draw near to him in worship. The power of Christ within community causes us to worship our God."[42]

From What Are You Hiding? From Whom Are You Hiding?

Paul Pettit stated, "The Devil wants you to keep your secrets to yourself, to live in shame and condemnation. In Christ there is NO condemnation (Rom. 8:1). Being willing to share your heart exposes the shame and gives opportunity to see it for what it is—an imprisoning weight. When forgiveness and acceptance are offered by the community, freedom replaces the shame and the community is fully functioning. The process of accepting and loving one another is a powerfully releasing tool."[43]

Another leader said, "The final woman who shared found courage to talk about the abortion she had had for the first time with others. She shared that she felt she could share because we had been willing to be honest with our hurt and sin. Rather than being something hidden behind a secret door in our lives, sharing a life story presented an opportunity for all of us to be honest about our lives, rather than live on the surface. With honesty, the process of true healing can come in receiving the forgiveness and grace of God through Christ."[44]

Ask yourself these questions: If I do not make myself known, what will the community miss? If I do not make myself known, what will I miss?

---

40. Ibid.
41. Ibid.
42. Ibid.
43. Paul Pettit, director of spiritual formation, Dallas Theological Seminary, verbal comments in Spiritual Formation Lead Lab, April 18, 2006
44. From private e-mails March–June 2006.

The Telling and Listening: Catalysts for Community, Corporate Formation

> She seemed distant from the very start of their small group. Even her leader tired to draw her out and make connection, inviting her to meet for coffee or lunch or even a study break. She was the one who acted disinterested when the group wanted to set a date for a dinner together. Her ministry job required a lot of time. At one point she even said she really didn't need the group. She had her own friends. Evaluating her body language during the group meetings and her seeming disinterest in engaging in any way other than being present in body made it difficult for her leader, and gradually some of the group members, not to make certain evaluations of her. Then, one day, deep into the second semester, as she shared her life story an amazing thing happened. Slowly as she laid out the pieces of her life, her vulnerability and self-disclosure became a magnet that drew the group members closer in to her and to each other. Understanding the difficult circumstances that she had come through opened the group's eyes as to how to love her more effectively, motivating them to continue their persistence to draw her into the relationship of the group. From "sitting on the sidelines" to risking to offer her story, her action became a catalyst for a deeper level of intimacy within the group. She risked telling, and they embraced. Community happened.

It takes time for some individuals to feel safe enough to share their life story. Confidentiality is key. Learning how to build trust is crucial. Feeling safe in a group invites being known, and being known creates a safe place—the mysterious reciprocity of community that only God's Spirit can achieve. In small groups deep community is inhibited when even one of the members is unwilling to share his or her story. Life story's effectiveness is dependent on each group member owning the process.

When telling the highlights of their year in their groups, the spiritual formation leaders responded: ". . . definitely Life Story. It helped us gain insights into others' personalities." "Best definitely was Life Story." "Yes, Life Story." "Yes, Life Story gave connection between divine authorship and my choices and ended in worship." One man shared, "You guys know things I have never told anyone, not even my wife . . . I have a feeling that this is going to be part of my ministry."[45]

What the Leaders Find: A Window into Impact

"Sharing Life Story helped to break down 'walls of separation' that were between us as we are all from different backgrounds. It helped us to

45. Pettit, Spiritual Formation Lead Lab, Dallas Theological Seminary, April 18, 2006.

understand each other better. After Life Story, we began to develop friendships outside of the group that weren't there before."[46]

"I don't think true community can happen until people are familiar with the details of one another's lives. Life Story allows for this to happen and becomes a catalyst for relational intimacy and true biblical community."[47]

"Life Story helped us to appreciate each other more, and gave glory to God as we witnessed how he has authored each diverse life path. You can only understand someone (and yourself for that matter) when you know where they have been and what they have been through—this tool facilitates this. Life Story was a very essential strategic community-building exercise that broke down barriers, gave respect and insight for each other and awe in a sovereign God."[48]

"Since doing Life Story together, I have heard my group members offering advice that is informed specifically by something they'd shared about their past in Life Story. Having someone do this 'joining of the dots' of the past objectively can help another person understand a present situation better."[49]

"I have seen several group members realize their true calling and ministry focus because of the process of going through their life story. And, it has helped many of us see that the pains of life ARE there for a reason, and that they are there to fulfill God's calling in our own lives."[50]

"Sharing our life stories within a small group allows us to get to the heart of who we really are, where we are coming from, and why we act and think the way we do. We are able to focus in on the driving forces, which are the goals and passions that God has designed us with. He has allowed these motivations to be molded through life's circumstances. When these themes and desires are realized, we can then share, clearly and purposefully, what God is doing in our lives. We make a greater impact as a body of Christ when we know ourselves and others better."[51]

"I believe that sharing and entrusting one's story to one another is helping build community in the group of men I lead. Community in our postmodern culture means little to Christianity. The greatest expression of community in our postmodern culture is Starbucks. By contrast, the Christian community shares a common faith in the knowledge of the Son of God (Eph. 4). Thus, the Christian community is built on Christ and the Spirit. Moreover, Christianity strives for more than mere community; Christians seek communion through Christ and by the Spirit with the almighty God our Father. Anything less than the community's communion together through Christ and the Spirit with the Father denies the mission of the incarnation."[52]

---

46. From private e-mails March–June 2006.
47. Ibid.
48. Ibid.
49. Ibid.
50. Ibid.
51. Ibid.
52. Ibid.

"One of my group members made some wrong choices in her life because she felt trapped by always having to look perfect. Eventually, she was able to look back to the self-defensive patterns in her life story and acknowledge them before God within the group."[53]

Knowing Leads to Loving Rather Than Judging

A group leader shares, "There was a particular woman who was harder for me to get to know. It was an effort for me to pursue her and want to spend time with her. The opportunity to share our life stories as part of the group curriculum was a turning point for me. This woman shared honestly of an extremely hard childhood and family situation, which included much pain and rejection. She explained how this had been so painful and that she had resolved to live life to protect her heart from more pain. This opened my eyes to see her in a new way beyond the surface of someone who seemed guarded and hard. My love for her grew. I wanted to be someone she could trust as a safe person who would embrace and love her. In this situation, and in others, God has used the process of sharing stories as a way to knit me together to people in my community, ministry teams, and life."[54]

"Life Story" and Church

"The church is the church only when it exists for others."[55]

The Substitute

> The unexpected rain preempted the traditional afternoon football game at the men's retreat that weekend. What a disappointment, especially for the former high school players in the group; there would be no chance to relive the state championship that day. Suddenly the out-of-town speaker had to come up with something fast. With no preparation for the men and with brief instructions, the speaker grouped the seventy-five men together. He asked them to jump into an activity they had not prepared for and most had never done. Later that afternoon when the small groups finished telling their "stories," none of them expected the dynamic that occurred. No one would have realized what telling their life stories would do for them or for the cohesion of their group. Even the brief time they had together that afternoon was worth it. Some of the men told parts of their lives they had never shared before. Football had never bonded them like this.

---

53. Ibid.
54. Ibid.
55. Dietrich Bonhoeffer, *Letters and Papers from Prison*, ed. Eberhard Bethge (New York: Macmillan, 1975), 382.

A Cohesion Barometer

In January of 2002, Northwest Bible Church, Dallas, Texas, featured for their January evening four-week event, "Personal Profile Series," the process of modeling and doing life story using the "Life Story" tool developed by the Spiritual Formation program at Dallas Theological Seminary. Approximately 400 of the 1,200 people in the church were in attendance for the event led by Dianne Miller, women's minister and Jeff Lawrence (at that time men's minister). Several from Dallas Theological Seminary's Spiritual Formation staff presented their stories modeling "Charting the Hand of God in Your Life," using the categories of heritage, heroes, high points, and hard times. During this four-week event, those in attendance wrote and presented their stories. Because Neil Tomba, the senior pastor, was specifically vulnerable in sharing his story, permission was given to his church body to be vulnerable in telling their stories. Learning each other's stories tightened and developed the ongoing sense of community in their church by providing a catalyst to go deeper in relationships. The effectiveness of this tool led to Life Story being a component of each small group in a church of small groups.

Prior to this event, anticipating their church body going through the Life Story process, the staff of the church went through the Life Story tool as a staff group. After processing through each of their stories and sharing them with their colleagues, greater bonding in community occurred among the staff. Doing "Life Story" has become a part of the small group leader training beginning with the mock small group they are a part of on the training day. They move into sharing some of their life story before going into other curricula. Condensed versions of the process have been written by their staff and used in small groups, and portions of life story questions have been used as small group icebreakers. It is used as a cohesion barometer determined by whether or not a group has incorporated sharing life story into their group.[56]

One writer states, "The leaders of the future, whether they are executives, politicians, or educators, are going to have to do two things really, really well. They are going to have to learn to talk in pictures, and they are going to have to be storytellers."[57]

Offering God's Story: A Gift from Community Reflecting His Glory

Protocol for Community

One of our spiritual formation leaders comments, "The idea of the lone, rugged individualist is foreign to New Testament Christianity. The church is by nature a community of people who are on mission to make disciples for the glory of God. In the context of that mission, we are also called to

---

56. Summary of telephone conversation between Dianne Miller and Gail Seidel, April 3, 2005.

57. Jim Crupi, "Executive 2000," *American Way*, August 1, 1998, 56–57.

'bear one another's burdens, and thereby fulfill the law of Christ' (Gal. 6:2 NASB). What does it look like to 'bear someone else's burdens'? This is a big responsibility, but at the very least it involves knowing that brother or sister in Christ."[58]

Author Henri Nouwen says, "Community is the fruit of our capacity to make the interests of others more important than our own (see Phil. 2:4). The question, therefore, is not 'How can we make community?' but 'How can we develop and nurture giving hearts?'"[59]

Because the unity of believers in community is one of the greatest apologetics for the deity of Christ, efforts to accomplish this are critically urgent (John 17:21, 23). The enormity of the assignment to care for one another, to love one another, and to bear one another's burdens in community is balanced by the power of God's Spirit in us to make it possible. Knowing someone else's story facilitates this process as a beginning point. Life Story should never be understood as a self-centric, self-analysis tool, but only that which helps inform us of God's sovereign loving pursuit of us, drawing us into community with himself and others in the body of Christ.

The New Testament protocols for community preclude any justification of the self-focused life our narcissistic culture touts. Being other-focused in community often runs against the grain of our own fallenness, however, making unity seem like an unreachable option. How in the world can we do these "one anothers" of the New Testament,[60] especially when some of us are so hard to get along with and have certain task-oriented bents where "finishing our lists" precludes availability to a brother in need? It is hard to relate to and accept someone who is our opposite. It is hard to bear others' burdens if they have their completely sufficient wardrobe wrapped so tight that no offer of help can penetrate.

Jesus anticipated our need for help and our resistance. Knowing human nature he asked the Father, on our behalf, for our sanctification, the process Jesus provides for believers to be spiritually formed (John 17:17, 19). It involves the sanctifying work of his Spirit in each person in their own story intersecting with others in their stories. Jesus prayed for the unity of believers. He knew how hard it would be for us to get along with other believers, for in our flesh we are difficult people who want our own way. He also knew that seeing unity among believers attracts nonbelievers to Jesus and God. Only God by his Spirit has the power to sanctify any of us. What he began in us he will finish. He uses the community to do it.

One pastor writes, "This is spiritual formation—allowing the gospel to transform us internally so we live differently externally."[61]

---

58. From private e-mails March–June 2006.
59. Henri J. M. Nouwen, *Bread for the Journey* (New York: HarperCollins, 1997), 24.
60. See end of this chapter for complete list.
61. Zander, "The Apprentices," 25.

I Got Me Some Jesus Friends: A Reason She Would Look Closer

> She was larger than life in every way, an intelligent feminist who left her professional career to accompany her corporate husband to his new assignment in the emerging international business scene of Eastern Europe. Her competence was punctuated by the words interesting, fun, and responsive to friendship. A mother of two, her antics with them made you wish you were a part of her family. She became our friend. As she led an instructional small group for us out of her professional training, she was surprised our issues were not with men, but with being able to say no in a healthy manner to the many pulls in our lives of ministry. We fell in love with her. Upon leaving our international city after the farewell gathering we hosted for her, she told me candidly that experiencing our "community" was the reason she might take a closer look at who Jesus really is.

The power of story is real. People are looking for authenticity, not perfection. Listen, offer, engage, and be present. We may be the visible presence of Christ joining others in the middle of their stories. Jesus does this. He enters ours right where we are, redeems us, and offers us the privilege of offering him as he did with the woman at the well in John 4, the woman caught in adultery in John 8, Zaccheus in Luke 19, and many others. A campus ministry staff in the east looking at Jesus' life and the way he did evangelism has been motivated to rethink the way they minister. Finding ways to enter students' lives in the middle of their stories seems natural and viable in their passion to make the gospel known.

Like Ben the baker in the children's video series about the first-century Christians, *The Story Keepers*,[62] we live out of our stories as a part of keeping his story alive. Using the delivery of fresh bread to the citizens of Jerusalem as an opportunity to keep Jesus' story alive, Ben's family absorbed into their family children whose parents were impacted by Roman persecution of the early church. Within our stories are many opportunities to reflect and offer perspective about the Master Storyteller. My story intersects your story for his story, keeping his story alive for the glory of God. In each of our stories lived out, we are the visible presence of Christ.

Author Phillip Yancey writes, "We would in fact know nothing about him except for the traces he left in human beings. That was his design. The law and the prophets had focused like a beam of light on the One who was to come and now that light, as if hitting a prism, would fracture and shoot out in a human spectrum of waves and colors."[63]

---

62. *The Story Keepers* DVD series (Grand Rapids: Zondervan Publishing House Children's Video in association with Focus on the Family).

63. Phillip Yancey, *The Jesus I Never Knew* (Grand Rapids: Zondervan, 1995), 228.

Embracing Your Story: Honoring the Story Maker

The Young Girl in 2 Kings 5:1–3, 15

You need to see yourself in the middle of your story as truly set apart for the sole purpose of bringing God glory.

You may not like your story. No one would voluntarily choose pain, or difficulty, or the particular parts that have been hurtful and damaging. But because of redemption we have the choice to embrace our story as difficult as it may be or to resist it. God authors our stories, the good and the bad, to bring him the most glory. The young girl in another story highlights this well.

She embraced her story, and God used her as he intended—to bring great glory to himself. She is unnamed. We know little about her except that she was a slave girl captured from Israel by the marauding bands of Arameans during one of their raids on Israel. She is mentioned only briefly in three verses in 2 Kings 5. She is seemingly insignificant, but here I am today writing about her and the principles her life visualizes. She served the wife of Naaman, the highly respected head of the army of the king of Aram, whom God had used to give his nation victory in battle. Naaman was a valiant warrior but also a leper.

In the midst of her captivity in a foreign land, foreign language, and foreign culture, away from her family and all that was familiar—we're not even sure if she was literate—this young girl, maybe a teenager, spoke to her mistress, simply saying that she wished her master was with the prophet in Samaria because he would cure General Naaman of his leprosy.

In this story, a young, unnamed Jewish girl was the instrument by which a pagan general of Israel's greatest found God. Amazingly Naaman and his wife listened to her (maybe because the leprosy had made them willing to try anything). Naaman traveled to Israel and was healed. Afterward by his own words, he said, "Behold now, I know that there is no God in all the earth, but in Israel" (2 Kings 5:15 NASB). Her story intersected his story for the purpose of God's ongoing story.

This young girl had several choices or options within her story—to keep quiet and cower in fear of her captors, to rebel, or to let God use her however he would choose. My husband and I have been blessed with five granddaughters and one grandson. I can't imagine how terrifying it would be if any one of them were captured from an airplane in a hijacking and taken hostage into a totally pagan environment. What would it be like for them? How would they respond? I have lived in another country and know how intimidating it is not to know the language or the "rules" of the culture; never mind how it would be if one were a slave or a captive. The simple faith of this young girl in her captivity jumps out of the pages of Scripture, capturing our attention. She *was* captive, but God was not. He is never captive. He will write his story in and through his instruments regardless of the circumstances. He had a purpose for her, and she fulfilled it even in the most desperate of circumstances. She was the visible presence of God, reflecting his glory in the story he had carefully written for her. You don't have to be an important person (even a free person) in an important story to have an eternal impact through your story.

What parts of your story have you not embraced? How does the Lord want you to respond to the insight he has given you through processing your life story? What is he calling you to be and do? How has he used your story to draw you closer to him? What brings you the most delight in how God has created you?

Carole's Story: Directly Across Her Path

God created Carole with great passion for people and an unusual passion for evangelism, but as a child she was paralyzed by polio from the neck down.[64] Because she had worked so hard to learn to walk again, it was especially devastating fourteen years ago, as she got weaker and weaker, that by doctors' orders she had to begin using a wheelchair. She told God that it hurt so much to have these limitations, and she begged him to please bring people across her path.

Because of her progressive limitations brought on by post-polio syndrome, she has made a decision to live each day to the fullest, taking advantage of every moment, though it takes great effort for her to do so. In the summer she signed up for an outreach mission from her church in Texas to go to Vancouver, Canada. On one of the mornings of this outreach, Carole was in a particular neighborhood passing out invitations for the church meeting that night from her motorized wheelchair. About a third of the way down the sidewalk, she noticed a man with a limp who literally walked across the path in front of her. As she drew up beside him, her story intersecting his story, and told him about the church meetings, they engaged in a conversation at which point he told her that he too had had polio. At that moment he asked her if she ever got mad at God. She said, "I have struggled most of my life, but now I am at peace. God wants me to live out my life and serve him from the place of this wheelchair." This Asian man from a Buddhist/Catholic background was very receptive to what she explained and within a very short time of interaction, just like the Ethiopian eunuch who responded to Phillip's instruction in Acts 8:26–40, he prayed to receive Christ as his Savior.

Only God could orchestrate this intersection, matching up a man within a story of great need with a woman within a story of great desire in a street in Vancouver at just the right moment of time as he walked across her path. This kind of encounter brings God, the Master story conceiver, great glory.

The very thing we fear as a limitation in our story may be what God

64. Carole Williams, as told to Gail Seidel, February 18, 2005, used by permission.

will use in us to bring him the greatest glory. God is in control of our circumstances, even when they seem outrageously out of control. He is never captive. His story is never thwarted by physical limitation, geographical boundary, or an oppressive political regime.

Charting the hand of God in my life by processing through my own life story and intentionally writing it out gives great encouragement in spiritual growth. God in his incredible mercy gives grace for the journey, comfort for the pain, and the Spirit's motivation for the future to embrace my story, which is really his story in me. Offering my story to the community contributes to the spiritual formation of the community and to my spiritual formation. Knowing and being known is a rich by-product of the vulnerability it takes to tell my story and promotes an awareness that contributes to corporate formation. God created me to bring him glory. He orchestrates my story intersecting your story for his story as story keepers to bring him the greatest glory.

And the story continues.

Protocol for Community: The "One Anothers" in the New Testament

John 13:14	Ought to WASH one another's feet
Romans 12:10	Be DEVOTED to one another
Romans 12:10	Give PREFERENCE to one another in honor
Romans 12:16	Be of the SAME MIND toward one another
Romans 15:7	ACCEPT one another
1 Corinthians 12:25	CARE for one another
Galatians 6:2	BEAR one another's BURDENS
Ephesians 4:2	FORBEAR one another
Ephesians 4:32	FORGIVE one another
Ephesians 4:32	BE KIND to one another
Ephesians 5:21	BE SUBJECT to one another
1 Thessalonians 5:11	ENCOURAGE one another
1 Thessalonians 5:11	BUILD UP one another

Hebrews 10:24	STIMULATE one another to love
James 5:16	CONFESS your sins to one another
James 5:16	PRAY for one another
1 Peter 4:9	BE HOSPITABLE to one another
1 Peter 4:10	SERVE one another
1 John 4:11	LOVE one another

Romans 14:13	Do NOT JUDGE one another
1 Corinthians 7:5	Do NOT DEPRIVE one another
Galatians 5:15	Do NOT BITE AND DEVOUR one another
Galatians 5:15	Do NOT CONSUME one another
Galatians 5:26	Do NOT PROVOKE one another
Galatians 5:26	Do NOT ENVY one another
Colossians 3:9	Do NOT LIE to each other
James 4:11	Do NOT SLANDER one another
James 5:9	Do NOT GRUMBLE against each other

Chapter 11

Preaching and Spiritual Formation

Harry Shields

> Sanctify them by the truth; your word is truth.
>
> —John 17:17

For almost sixteen years I served as a professor of homiletics and pastoral training at the Moody Bible Institute in Chicago, Illinois. Then in January 2001 I returned to pastoral ministry in a local church setting. It was not an easy decision. I loved the challenges of academic life. I enjoyed interacting with students about a variety of theological subjects. And I certainly enjoyed teaching homiletics and engaging in the weekly process of both preparing and presenting biblical sermons. It was the latter experience that played a major role in leading me back into pastoral ministry.

It wasn't long after my return to the pastorate that I attended a national conference on church leadership and community outreach. One of the keynote speakers paused in his address to give his commentary on the current state of the church. He said in no uncertain terms that preaching was an outdated, obsolete means of communicating spiritual truth to a postmodern world. As far as he was concerned, the film industry would be the next great center of spiritual outreach.

A former student of mine was sitting in the same row where I was sitting. He approached me after the speaker had finished and wanted my assessment of what had just been said. I must admit that I was not surprised by the comment. I had heard it before. When I first entered pastoral ministry, leaders in the so-called "church renewal movement" were suggesting that the sermon needed to be replaced with dialogue, visual effects, and small group discussions. Even a recent survey of individuals who attend worship services at least once a week stated that music contributed to their spiritual growth more than preaching, Scripture reading, or the ordinances.[1]

Why is that the case? Why is it that preaching is viewed as a relic left over from some of the glory days of the church? John Stott in his excellent book *Between Two Worlds* has captured, at least in part, how many people feel about preaching.

> The prophets of doom in [the] Church are confidently predicting that the day of preaching is over. It is a dying art, they say, an outmoded form of communication, an echo from an abandoned past. Not only have modern media superseded it, but it is incompatible with the modern mood.[2]

So how do we respond to such antagonists? Stott goes on to answer these skeptics. He writes later in the same text:

> In a world which seems either unwilling or unable to listen, how can we be persuaded to go on preaching, and learn to do so effectively? The essential secret is not mastering certain techniques but being mastered by certain convictions. In other words, theology is more important than methodology. By stating the matter thus bluntly, I am not despising homiletics as a topic for study in seminaries, but rather affirming that homiletics belongs properly to the department of practical theology and cannot be taught without a solid theological foundation.[3]

Yes, preaching is ultimately about theology. And there are at least three theological underpinnings that will help us see that preaching has been and always will be critical to the life of any local church. First, evangelical Christians believe that God exists and desires that human beings know him (1 John 5:20). God has not chosen to hide himself or his ways from us. He has made himself known and wants us to know him personally. Second, we also believe that God has revealed himself in a written revelation. The biblical record is more than reports about religious people. Evangelicals believe the words of Scripture are God's words and are to be obeyed (2 Tim. 3:16–17). And third, we affirm that the God who has made himself known is one who has also raised up people within the church to preach the Word of God to both believers and unbelievers (2 Tim. 4:1–5). Therefore, preaching is not a cultural or time-bound phenomenon. It is part of God's will for those who gather to worship him—both to know him and to make him known.

---

1. *Leadership* 27, no. 3 (Summer 2006): 71.
2. John Stott, *Between Two Worlds* (Grand Rapids: Eerdmans, 1982), 50.
3. Ibid., 92.

But what does preaching have to do with spiritual formation? It has everything to do with it, especially if we understand the place of preaching in the context of a local church, and if we understand what is meant by "spiritual formation." First, let me establish what I understand *spiritual formation* to mean. In writing to the Galatians, the apostle Paul had to respond to a congregation that wanted to turn back to what we might call "life by the law" or "spirituality without the Spirit" (Gal. 3:1–5). So Paul had to confront these first-century believers for their incorrect theology and spiritual practices. Yet he did not give up on them. He taught them afresh what it meant to be a Christian. He wrote,

> But now that you know God—or rather are known by God—how is it that you are turning back to those weak and miserable principles? Do you wish to be enslaved by them all over again? You are observing special days and months and seasons and years! I fear for you, that somehow I have wasted my efforts on you. . . . My dear children, for whom I am again in the pains of childbirth *until Christ is formed in you.* (Gal. 4:9–11, 19, emphasis mine)

Or as Robert Lightner states,

> *Spiritual formation* describes the continuing work of the Holy Spirit in the life of a believer which conforms the child of God more and more to the image of Christ (2 Cor. 3:18). This work of the Spirit is possible only as we cooperate with God by walking "in the light as He is in the light" (1 John 1:7); by setting our hearts "on things above" (Col. 3:1); by ridding ourselves of the deeds of the flesh (Col. 3:8); and by putting on a heart of "compassion, kindness, humility, gentleness, and patience" (Col. 3:12).[4]

In summary, spiritual formation can be described as any ministry extended to a believer in the power of the Holy Spirit so that a person can live, act, and think as Christ himself lives, acts, and thinks. That means that small groups have the potential of bringing about spiritual formation, as does Christian counseling, or music . . . and even PREACHING!

As stated above, preaching must be seen in the total context of church life. It is not the only ministry in the church but one ministry among many ministries. And I might quickly add, it is an *important* ministry. It is a ministry that God has used down through the centuries as an instrument of the Holy Spirit to enable people to live, act, and think as Jesus himself would. In the remaining pages of this chapter, I have explained three principles that

---

4. Robert P. Lightner, "Salvation and Christian Formation," in *The Christian Educator's Handbook on Spiritual Formation*, ed. Kenneth O. Gangel and James C. Wilhoit (Wheaton, IL: Victor Books, 1994), 39.

guide my study of spiritual formation and preaching. First, I want to develop the biblical foundation for preaching as a means of spiritual transformation. Second, I examine homiletical theory and its relationship to spiritual change. And finally, I propose a process by which preachers and students of preaching can prepare spiritually transforming sermons.

The Biblical Precedent

Dr. Billy Graham is famous for peppering his sermons with the phrase, "The Bible says!" Graham and other evangelical preachers appeal to the Bible as their primary source of authority. It is true that postmodern thinkers may not be moved by an appeal to Scripture. But even a casual reading of the Bible shows that preaching was highly valued in the early church. Haddon Robinson makes this observation:

> Preaching in the minds of the New Testament writers is God in action. Peter, for example reminded his readers that they had "been born anew, not of perishable seed but of imperishable, through the living and abiding word of God" (1 Peter 1:23). How did this word come to do its work in their lives? "That word," Peter explains, was "the good news which was *preached* to you." Through preaching they were redeemed.[5]

Throughout the pages of Scripture, especially the New Testament, preaching was the primary means that God used to transform people from those who were under God's wrath to a people made new by his grace.

The ministry of the Lord Jesus was characterized by preaching and teaching. Just prior to the famous Sermon on the Mount, Matthew's gospel tells us that Jesus "was going all over Galilee, teaching in their synagogues, preaching the good news of the kingdom, and healing every disease and sickness among the people" (Matt. 4:23 HCSB). The Savior's preaching was so significant that crowds of people would travel great distances to hear his message. The apostle Peter on another occasion described the Lord's message, a message communicated primarily through preaching, as containing "words of eternal life" (John 6:68). What Jesus preached was life transforming for many of those who heard.

Luke's gospel also indirectly portrays how Jesus envisioned the preaching of the kingdom. It wasn't always the kind of proclamation that brought about instantaneous change. Jesus likened it to the scattering of seed. Sometimes the seed was quickly taken away or stifled in its early growth. But Jesus does seem to indicate when the Word of God is proclaimed and falls on a heart prepared to hear it, growth will occur (Luke 8:4–8, 11–15). However, he is not suggesting that "hearing alone" will bring about spiritual growth. If that

---

5. Haddon W. Robinson, *Making a Difference in Preaching*, ed. Scott M. Gibson (Grand Rapids: Baker, 1999) 63.

were the case, all a preacher would have to do would be to simply read a passage of Scripture and sit down. But what was unique with the preaching ministry of our Lord was the fact that his proclamation was united with a sense of relevance in the mind of the hearer. That is, a person listening to Jesus (or any preacher) would say, "I understand what is being said, and I see where it fits into my life."

Following the resurrection and ascension of Christ and the establishment of the church, preaching played a very significant role. The apostles must have carried out some administrative responsibilities, but it was not their primary role. They certainly had a part in casting the church's vision (Acts 2:40; 3:11–26; 6:2; 2 Tim. 4:1–3). But the early leaders were of one mind when they told the early believers that "it would not be right for [them] to give up preaching about God to wait on tables" (Acts 6:2 HCSB). These men understood that preaching was both essential to their work and transformational at the same time.

As Paul took the gospel to the Roman world of his day, he unquestionably assumed that preaching was crucial to spiritual transformation. In writing to the Romans, he asks, "But how can they call on Him in whom they have not believed? And how can they believe without hearing about Him? And how can they hear without a preacher?" (Rom. 10:14 HCSB). And then two chapters later, Paul challenges these same Roman believers to apply the doctrine of justification by faith. How would they do that? In Romans 12:2 he indicates that spiritual transformation is a matter of "renewing the mind." Old fleshly habits of living are to be exchanged for new patterns of thinking in accordance with God's grace. And what better way for believers to learn of these new grace-based patterns of living than through preaching. So the New Testament believers assembled to hear God's Word proclaimed through preaching.

Similarly, the apostle Paul subtly revealed his approach to ministry when he wrote to the Colossians, "We proclaim Him, warning and teaching everyone with all wisdom, so that we may present everyone mature in Christ" (Col. 1:28 HCSB). It is true that one could proclaim God-inspired truth in a one-on-one dialogue, or even through the reading of a biblical passage. But the consistent pattern in the book of Acts and in the apostolic writings is that preaching played a significant role in the renewing of the Christian mind and the spiritual transformation of believers.

Throughout the New Testament, we see that the church employed preaching as a necessary ministry strategy. It appears to be the primary strategy to bring about the kind of spiritual change that God anticipated.

The Assumptions of Preaching Theory

I had the privilege of receiving my homiletics training under Dr. Haddon Robinson, one of the best-known teachers of preachers and a master preacher himself. Robinson has been instrumental in shaping the way preachers look at the Bible and ultimately how they view preaching. His definition of expository preaching indicates that the sermon is more than a public address. He writes:

> Expository preaching is the communication of a biblical concept, derived from and transmitted through a historical, grammatical, and literary study of a passage in its context, which the Holy Spirit first applies to the personality and experience of the preacher, then through him to his hearers.[6]

The key phrase is "*first applies to the personality and experience of the preacher.*" Robinson assumes that through studying the biblical text the Holy Spirit will transform the preacher. And then in turn, the preacher's message and personal change will be used by God to bring change to others. This has been the assumption of preachers throughout the centuries.

Another popular homiletics book in addition to Robinson's *Biblical Preaching* is Bryan Chapell's text, *Christ-Centered Preaching.* Like Robinson, Chapell assumes that preaching can bring about spiritual change. He writes,

> The fact that the power for spiritual change resides in God's Word argues the case for *expository* preaching. Expository preaching attempts to present and apply the truth of a specific biblical passage. Other types of preaching that proclaim biblical truth are certainly valid and valuable, but for the beginning preacher and for a regular congregational diet no preaching type is more important.[7]

Chapell is even more direct about the preaching of God's Word in spiritual transformation. He says,

> Since God designed the Bible to complete us, its contents necessarily indicate that in some sense we are incomplete. Our lack of wholeness is a consequence of the fallen condition in which we live. Aspects of this fallenness that are reflected in our own sinfulness and in our world's brokenness prompt Scriptures' instruction and construction.[8]

Both the New Testament authors and the most popular homiletics texts of the current day assume that preaching goes far beyond dispensing infor-

---

6. Haddon W. Robinson, *Biblical Preaching: The Development and Delivery of Expository Messages* (Grand Rapids: Baker, 1980), 20.

7. Bryan Chapell, *Christ-Centered Preaching*, rev. ed. (Grand Rapids: Baker, 2005), 22.

8. Ibid., 41.

mation. It is one of God's primary means of bringing about spiritual transformation. As one pastor says, "Preaching is the work of spiritually civilizing the minds of Christian disciples."[9] There are many ministries and practices that can be used by the Holy Spirit to make a person more and more like Jesus Christ. But preaching has been and will always be one of those primary agents of spiritual change.

A Process for Preparing Life-Transforming Sermons

All of this leads us to ask how sermons can be created so as to partner with the work of the Holy Spirit. And it is important to remember that it is the Spirit's work that brings about change (2 Cor. 3:18). Those of us who proclaim God's Word are his stewards, his servants, and the mouthpieces through whom God disseminates spiritual truth (1 Cor. 4:1). Philips Brooks is often cited for his definition of preaching as "truth poured through personality."[10] There is no need to diminish the role of the preacher, but it is absolutely essential to realize that the preacher's effectiveness is dependent on what the Holy Spirit chooses to do through the sermon. Therefore, in preparing the sermon, the preacher will want to give attention to three important areas: (1) the pastor's own spiritual formation; (2) the spiritual formation potential of the text to be expounded; and (3) the importance of sermon structures to spiritual formation.

The Spiritual Formation of the Pastor

In my own training as a pastor, I do not recall any textbook on preaching or any homiletics professor ever giving specific instruction on the care and nurture of the preacher's soul. It might have been strongly implied, but it was never presented as part of the formal process of sermon preparation. And yet how can we ever assume that listeners will be transformed without the preacher first being transformed as well? Robertson McQuilkin captures the need for Holy Spirit inspired preaching when he writes,

> It's quite possible to fascinate a congregation so that numbers steadily increase, to explain the Bible text so professionally one's reputation reaches back to the halls of *alma mater*, to inform the mind so carefully our people are recognized as Bible experts, and still miss out on spiritual formation. Without the energizing power of the Spirit, fresh each time one enters the pulpit, our people will not demonstrate any miracle quality of life.[11]

---

9. Lee Eclov, "The Danger of Practical Preaching," *PreachingToday.com* at http://www.preachingtoday.com/16666/ (accessed November 28, 2000).

10. Robinson, *Biblical Preaching*, 24.

11. Robertson McQuilkin, "Spiritual Formation Through Preaching (part 2)," *PreachingToday.com* at http://www.preachingtoday.com/skills/thespirituallifeofthepreacher/200010.8.html (accessed March 11, 2005).

But how does one go about experiencing this "energizing power of the Spirit"? There are steps you can take to complement your own spiritual formation. I want to recommend some practical habits that should characterize the sermon preparation process.

First, the preacher who is serious about spiritual formation will want to make prayer a daily habit. Much has already been written about prayer as a way of life for all Christians—a spiritual discipline of the utmost importance. But we would do well to pray for our preaching, the kind of prayer in which we implore the Lord of Life to enlighten us as to the meaning of his Word and to empower us to communicate it with power from on high. One preacher describes how prayer radically transformed his ministry:

> My confidence was taking a beating as some of the leaders let me know repeatedly that my pulpit work was not up to their standards. Previous pastors carried the reputation of pulpit masters, something I never claimed for myself. To make matters worse, we had numerous vacancies on staff and my sermon preparation was suffering due to a heavy load of pastoral ministry. But you do what you have to do. Most days, my goal was to keep my head above water. Every day without drowning became a good day. That's when I got serious about praying for my preaching. Each night I walked a four-mile route through my neighborhood and talked to the Father. My petitions dealt with the usual stuff—family needs, people I was concerned about, and the church. Gradually, one prayer began to recur in my nightly pleadings. "Lord," I prayed, "make me a preacher." Asking this felt so right I never paused to analyze it. I prayed it again and again, over and over, for weeks.

This same writer goes on to tell what happened when he made prayer part of the process of his own sermon preparation:

> I knew if my preaching improved, if the congregation felt better about the sermons, everything else would benefit. I knew that the sermon is a pastor's most important contribution to the spiritual lives of his members. To do well there would ease the pressure in other areas. So, I prayed.[12]

Do not misunderstand. Prayer is not a quick fix to "sermonic fatigue" or the lack of genuine study. Prayer is the pastor's humble admission that preaching is too important, challenging, and difficult to rely on human skill. Consistent, daily prayer is our way of joining forces with God instead of

---

12. Joe McKeever, "I Prayed for My Preaching," *PreachingToday.com* at http://www.preachingtoday.com/16755 (accessed June 24, 2006).

asking him to bless our efforts and our desires. In addition, prayer must be offered up for those who listen. Jesus warned that as the truth of the gospel goes forth, there will be forces that seek to rob the hearers of the spiritual benefit and power they so desperately need (Mark 4:1–20). So it goes almost without saying that prayer is an absolute essential to the preacher's own spiritual formation. And it is essential that we pray for our hearers as well because preaching always takes place on a spiritual battlefield.

I have personally found there is another essential resource that contributes to the spiritual formation of the preacher. It is Bible meditation. I am not referring to analyzing the Scripture that is to be expounded on any given Sunday. Rather I am talking about the spiritual habit of reading through the Scriptures on a systematic basis. I have friends in ministry who read one chapter of Proverbs every day. I know of others who use a reading guide that enables them to read through the entire Bible every year.

I also like to alternate my practice of Bible meditation. Usually in January of every year, I review and update my life mission statement and goals. But part of the process of review is to select four or five books of the Bible that I want to read and meditate upon. My goal is to spend at least two months in these books to get an understanding of what the biblical authors are saying. My purpose is not to do long-term sermon preparation but simply to understand the revelation of God in each of these books. I usually keep a journal of major truths I have discovered and try to review them during the time period I have allotted to study a given book. Again, the purpose is not to discover sermon topics, even though that might happen. The purpose is to nurture my own soul. I have found the practice of reading and meditation for my own spiritual enrichment pays rich dividends in other areas of ministry besides preaching, such as pastoral counseling and spiritual direction.

Another benefit to Bible meditation is that it gives birth to another spiritual habit, namely intentional reflection on God's sovereignty. Since all Scripture is a revelation of God's majesty and glory, Bible meditation will disclose the greatness of God down through the ages. And every pastor needs frequent reminders that God is sovereign over all things. He gives and he takes away. He allows us to go through times of apparent weakness and spiritual dryness. But when we reflect on the sovereignty of God in all things, we are reminded that it is God's prerogative to do with our ministries and our preaching whatever he chooses to do. We are his servants—he is not ours.

And then in addition to prayer, Bible meditation, and reflection on God's sovereignty, I have found another practice that has positively contributed to my own spiritual formation. I simply refer to it as a "thought journal." Let's face it. Pastoral ministry has its hazards. Our most carefully designed plans do not always materialize—contributing to our discouragement. People may misunderstand us or even work against us. And so it is important that we "take every thought captive" and surrender it to Christ and the truth of his Word. I do this in a couple of different ways. For instance,

I have for years had a section in my "thought journal" where I record recent events in my life, especially those events that have been troubling. I briefly record what happened and how that event made me feel. I also record what I did in response to the specific event that transpired. Then I take some time to reflect from God's Word on how the heavenly Father would want me to accurately think about the situation. On many occasions this simple practice has helped me to "shake off the blues" and enter into the more formal aspects of sermon preparation with enthusiasm.

One additional part of my "thought journal" is the recording of "thoughts of gratitude." Again, the experiences of ministry might sometimes be hazardous to our spiritual health. But that does not have to be the case. When we intentionally take an inventory of our lives, we will discover all around us that God has been active. When we seek to discover his spiritual, relational, and material blessings, we will have reason to give thanks to him in the ups and downs of pastoral ministry (1 Thess. 5:18). So I commend these daily habits to every preacher. When they are practiced—not as a way to gain God's blessing but to truly encounter him—the heavenly Father will nurture the preacher's soul, even as we seek to be used by him to transform others.

The Preaching Text and Spiritual Formation

The history of the church and the history of preaching lead us to believe there is little or no transformation without the Word of God. Jesus prayed for his followers that they would be sanctified "by the truth" because "[God's] word is truth" (John 17:17). Therefore, we must carefully handle the sacred Scriptures so that what is being proclaimed is truly what God is saying. The one who preaches for transformation must study the Bible in such a way that there is a high degree of confidence that what the preacher says is also what God is saying.

Living in the Text

But how do we come to that degree of confidence? It is important that we have a process, one that begins with a careful analysis of the text all the way through to the actual delivery of the sermon. There is one overarching goal in this process—the discovery and identification of what I like to refer to as the "transforming truth." This transforming truth is *a single sentence summary that tells the listener what God is saying in any given biblical text that is being expounded*. Robinson and others refer to this as the "big idea" or "central proposition."[13] In order to find that truth, the preacher needs to understand the spiritual dynamics that existed in the original biblical setting as well as the spiritual dynamics in the contemporary setting. Without understanding the original biblical audience and all it was facing, it will be difficult to speak into the hearts and lives of people in our own day.

---

13. Robinson, *Biblical Preaching*, 20.

I like Stott's imagery of "bridge building" when it comes to preparing sermons that are ultimately "transformational." That means that we need to live in two worlds. Stott explains his metaphor for preaching in the following way:

> It is because preaching is not exposition only but communication, not just the exegesis of a text but the conveying of a God-given message to living people who need to hear it, that I am going to develop a different metaphor to illustrate the essential nature of preaching. It is non-biblical in the sense that it is not explicitly used in Scripture, but I hope to show that what it lays upon us is fundamentally a biblical task. The metaphor is that of bridge-building.
>
> Now a bridge is a means of communication between two places which would otherwise be cut off from one another by a river or a ravine. It makes possible a flow of traffic which without it would be impossible. What, then, does the gorge or chasm represent? And what is the bridge which spans it? The chasm is the deep rift between the biblical world and the modern world.[14]

Our task is to help contemporary listeners to understand how God wants them to change to be more like Christ. And yet we have difficulty embracing that desired change because we spend all of our waking hours in the here and now. We are shaped more by our culture than by sincere critical thinking about what is and what should be. Men and women in local churches today develop their ideas about life not so much from biblical revelation as from culture. Social research shows that the social setting where we live influences our ideas, our feelings, and our values more than anything else.[15] That is why Christians need to be exposed to a worldview that is thoroughly biblical. And to say that it is "biblical" means we must draw the ideas for our sermons from the biblical text, so that we can address the ideas, feelings, and values of our listeners. As much as is possible, we need to *live* in the biblical world of any given passage of Scripture. And to use Stott's metaphor again, the preacher will have to cross over into the ancient world of biblical revelation to discover what God was first saying to an original audience before we can know what needs to be said to a modern audience. One has to "live" in the text, not just explain the text.

The place to start is to first develop a preaching plan, a sermon calendar of sorts that enables the preacher to know where his/her study will take place from week to week. Even though homiletics texts distinguish between sermonic forms such as topical, biographical, textual, and expository sermons, I believe that all sermons should be expository. That means

14. Stott, *Between Two Worlds*, 138–39.
15. Alice P. Mathews, *Preaching That Speaks to Women* (Grand Rapids: Baker, 2003), 21.

that even though a preacher might want to do a series of messages on such themes as "anxiety," "money," "ethics," or "fear," the source of information for any of these topics would be a single biblical text. If more than one text is used, those texts should be explained in terms of their original purpose and meaning. However, preaching that truly transforms lives will be the kind that systematically goes through a book of the Bible, passage by passage, to reveal what God is saying. And the best way to prepare to "live" in any of these texts is to develop a sermon calendar.

In my own preaching ministry, I develop a sermon calendar for a six-month time period. Experience over the years has taught me that unscheduled events and congregational needs can change a preacher's plans very quickly. So planning for each Sunday over a six-month time frame has reduced the number of changes that need to be made to the sermon calendar. At the same time, I would recommend that a preacher take some time away from the office in the form of a personal retreat to seek God's guidance as to what the congregation may need in terms of regular spiritual food. I also keep a page in a notebook of thoughts about sermon series that might be presented in the future. These thoughts come from casual conversations, pastoral counseling experiences, and articles that I read in magazines and newspapers. I have also placed a simple survey form in our church bulletin asking people to anonymously indicate what they would like to hear in future sermons. I then review this information as I prayerfully plan for the "ministry of the Word" over the next half year. I am also aware of preachers in other churches who assemble a congregational team to give feedback about future sermon series.

As to the sermon calendar itself, I have a single page for each month of the year (see below). I then include the date the sermon will be preached, the sermon series title, and additional subheadings for the weekly sermon title, the passage that will be expounded, and finally a comments column. The last category is a reminder as to what other features will be part of the worship experience, such as baptisms, Communion Sundays, or children's dedications. The comments section may influence the direction a sermon will take and its length. But the sermon calendar reduces speculation as to what the preacher will be studying from week to week. And reflection over an extended period of time also allows the preacher to evaluate the kinds of spiritual challenges the parishioners in a given setting may be facing.

[Month]			
Date	Sermon Series and Title	Passage	Comments

Once it has been determined what text or texts are going to be expounded, the preacher can then start the process of actually interacting with the text personally. As stated earlier, the preacher will want to engage in the regular discipline of prayer. And this is especially true when it comes to "living" in the text. So with the biblical text identified, the preacher will want to start the bridge-building process. I personally like to think of the process of exegesis and interpretation as "Triple A." That is, the preacher will want to identify the *audience*, the *aim*, and essential elements of textual *analysis*.

If the preaching text is to be more than a literary work to be analyzed, the preacher will need to spend time gathering information about the passage and meditating on the selected text. It is wise to bombard the text with several questions about the audience. For instance, who are the people who first received this text of Scripture? Who is the author, and why did this person sense a need to write at this point in history? What were the various challenges that the original audience happened to be facing at the time of writing? And it would be helpful for the preacher to engage in what Warren Wiersbe refers to as "imagineering," especially for the purpose of trying to identify with the original audience.[16] What specifically were their thoughts, feelings, and actions that precipitated the biblical author's intervention in their lives?

There are many helpful resources available to preachers that will enhance one's understanding of the original audience and its author. The introductory pages of critical commentaries, as well as background commentaries, can be of special assistance in knowing how an audience thought and lived. In addition, the preacher will want to read through the entire book of the Bible from which the preaching text is taken, so that one has a better understanding of the experiences and activities of the original audience.

Next, the preacher will want to spend time identifying the aim of the text. That is, what is the writer trying to accomplish by saying what is being said? Does the author want to change the biblical audience's belief system? Is there a need to confront unrighteous behavior so that it can be transformed into righteous actions? Is the author trying to empower the original readers to get a more accurate picture of God? Answering these questions will not only help the preacher live in the text, but it will be a bridge-building event in connecting with the contemporary audience as well. When we understand what a given author is trying to do in a passage of Scripture, the better the possibility of knowing what God wants to do to bring about spiritual transformation in our own lives and in the lives of our listeners.

The third element in the "Triple A" process relates to the typical practices of biblical exegesis, namely analyzing the text in its immediate context. Assuming that the preacher has access to the standard tools of exegesis—concordances, lexicons, commentaries, and other lexical resources—the preacher will want to read through the text several times. It is often helpful to read the passage in two or three different translations to sense the flow of the text. In my own study of a passage, I will "electronically paste" the passage onto a page on my computer where I can both read and analyze the text.

---

16. Warren Wiersbe, *Preaching and Teaching with Imagination* (Wheaton, IL: Victor Books, 1994), 24–25.

And then as I read the passage, I will try to identify the "major movements" or "blocks" that are within every text, even if the text is only one or two verses. Many times identifying these "blocks" is already done for us in modern translations that have paragraph divisions clearly identified. For example, while studying Matthew 7:13–23, I noticed that several translations had paragraph divisions starting at verses 13, 15, and 21. I used these verses as starting points for the major movements and thought divisions within the text. I then proceeded to do further analysis, trying to determine the relationships between each of the paragraphs. This type of analysis enables the preacher to read the text almost as if one is listening to the original speaker talk to the original audience. And it is this kind of "living in the text" that makes transformation possible—first for the preacher and then ultimately for the contemporary audience.

In narrative literature the preacher will want to identify this flow of thought in the same manner in which a story develops. Stories, whether in biblical or extrabiblical literature, have a *beginning*, *middle*, and *end*. Or to put it another way, a biblical narrative begins with some conflict or tension. The tension is followed by some increasing development of the conflict and ultimately leads to some climax or resolution of the tension. The preacher will want to be aware of this progression of thought, both to retell the biblical story with meaning, and to aid in ultimately identifying the passage's transforming truth.

Once the preacher identifies the flow of thought, it is time to engage in the more detailed work of textual analysis. At this point it will be helpful to make note of the literary genre through which the biblical message is being transported. Even though the author and the audience already may have been identified, it is often helpful to force ourselves to be aware of whether we are working with an epistle, a piece of biblical poetry, or narrative. Spiritual transformation is as much a matter of one's emotions as it is one's mind. We not only think deeply about life, but we also have strong "feelings" about what we believe and value. The preacher must be aware of how people feel—both the individuals that Scripture portrays and the people we address on any given Sunday. And various types of biblical literature evoke strong images and feelings. But the goal is not to focus on feelings alone, but the "feelings" and "images" communicated in the passage under study. Identifying these images will be one more step in bringing the preacher closer to understanding the transforming truth that God is ultimately trying to communicate.

One of the aspects of sermon preparation that is frequently overlooked is identifying literary images contained within any given text. This is especially true within biblical narrative. The images and metaphors of a passage help the preacher to answer the question, "What do I see, hear, smell, and feel in this text?" The answer to this question will help the preacher later on in shaping the sermon so that hearers will also truly experience the text. And when a listener experiences what is truly going on in the text and not just receiving information, one is better positioned for spiritual transformation. For instance, in 1 Samuel 24 the narrator tells us that David was in a cave, trying to protect himself from King Saul. In verse 4 we are told that Saul entered the same cave, unaware that David was there and in good position to kill Israel's king. But David did not kill Saul. Instead he "cut off" a piece of the king's robe. Later, David's conscience was stricken over what he had done. While standing some distance from Saul, David called out to the king and informed Saul that his life had been spared, when David clearly could have assassinated Saul. Saul's response was that David was more righteous than he. So he says to David, "Now swear to me by the LORD that you will not *cut off* my descendants or wipe out my name from my father's family" (v. 21, emphasis mine).

What is significant is that a picture, "cutting off" a piece of a garment, is used later to help communicate Saul's request to David (1 Sam. 24:21). The "picture" in the text can become a helpful means to communicate a vivid biblical concept to the contemporary audience during the actual delivery of the sermon, a concept that can enhance the listener's own spiritual transformation. For instance in 1 Samuel 24 God was communicating that only he has the right and the power to raise up a king or take him away. It is God's sovereign right, not that of a mere human being, to "cut off a man's claim to power." In answering Saul's question David was really acknowledging God's sovereign rule over his life and Saul's.

In addition, skill in studying the original languages will also enhance the preacher's understanding of the text. That is why the preacher will want to spend time doing lexical analysis. That is, it will be important to identify the meanings of key words contained within the passage under study. I would define a "key word" as any term in the passage the preacher or the members of the audience will not understand unless some explanation is given. So careful thought and time needs to be given to word meanings. Most students in Bible colleges and seminaries have received training in this type of textual analysis.

One other important aspect of textual analysis has to do with identifying "editorial comments." These are interruptions in the natural flow of a passage where a biblical writer gives information that is initially unexpected and seemingly unrelated to what is being said. But the comment is made to provide interpretive clues to the passage or to the larger context. For example, Judges 17:6 (cf. 18:1) contains an editorial comment. The writer states, "In those days Israel had no king; everyone did as he saw fit." The immediate context tells the story of an Israelite by the name of Micah who was in search of a priest for his own household, a practice forbidden in the Law. But the comment helps the reader to understand why there was serious moral and cultural decline, in the case of both Micah individually and the people of Israel corporately. Editorial comments may provide a point of connection between an ancient culture and the contemporary audience. And such connections can be bridge-building steps to change.

Identifying all of the above mentioned exegetical details might seem irrelevant to issues of spiritual transformation. But since preaching is aimed at addressing the listener's thinking and feelings, this exegetical data is foundational to assembling accurate biblical content. The issue is not simply defining the meaning of terms, but also seeing biblical pictures that the Holy Spirit will use to help a listener say, "OK, I *see* how this also fits into my life and calls for change."

Crossing the Bridge: Identifying "T-R-UTH"

If the preacher actually spends time meditating on the text—or as I prefer, "living in the text"—it becomes almost intuitive to identify what God's Spirit is communicating in any given passage. But once the preacher has gone through the steps of "Triple A," the preacher will be ready to identify the *transforming truth* of the passage under study. Homiletics texts consistently refer to the big idea, the proposition, or the central truth of the sermon. When I speak of the "transforming truth," I am affirming the relevance and significance of communicating one primary truth through the medium of a Sunday morning message. But there is one additional concept, especially as it relates to preaching and spiritual formation. That is, the sermon needs to have a transforming truth that is directed to both the mind and the will. Pastors need to help change the way people naturally think about life. This means helping to change their belief systems and then challenging them to act righteously based on what God has said in his Word.

Why must sermon ideas be aimed at both the mind and the will? It is because of our biblical understanding of human beings and the Spirit-empowered work of salvation. The New Testament portrays believers as people who have been delivered from the domain of darkness into the kingdom of God's Son (Col. 1:13–14). However, that does not mean that Christians always live righteously. At any moment they can make a choice to live in the power of the flesh or in the power of the indwelling Holy Spirit (Rom. 8:12–13). Everyone who attends a church service on any given Sunday will bring a personal belief system, which in turn impacts how the person makes moment-to-moment choices. These belief systems have developed over years of interpreting life experiences—personal rejection, humiliation at the hands of siblings, childhood sickness, job loss, and marital conflict. People attend church having lived many years of their lives in the "domain of darkness." Therefore, sermon propositions must not only be developed out of the God-ordained purposes of a biblical text but also out of a careful understanding of human beings. Old ways of unrighteous thinking and behavior must be confronted with truths that transform both the way one thinks and the way one acts.

After the biblical text has been carefully analyzed, the preacher will want to develop a summary statement that reflects God's purposes for both the original audience and the current audience being addressed today. This transforming truth is a single-sentence summary that declares what the sermon is communicating. In formulating this statement, the preacher will want to think in terms of the acronym T-R-UTH. These three elements refer to the Tension, the Revelation, and the actual summary statement that I call the Universal Truth (to) Heed. To put it another way, the preacher is trying to identify a truth that will transform lives by addressing both the mind and the will.

I am building on the assumption that all passages of Scripture were addressed to people who were facing some need for understanding or some need to change existing behavior. This is the "Tension" element in summarizing the passage. The tension element can be expressed in the form of a question. Robinson refers to a similar element as the "subject," or the answer to the question, "What am I talking about?"[17] Chapell talks about discovering the "purpose" of any given passage by first identifying what he refers to as the "Fallen Condition Focus," or the FCF. He discusses the need for the preacher to understand what the text is saying, what concerns the text is addressing, and what listeners share in common with the original audience.[18] Both Robinson and Chapell are indirectly referring to a tension within the passage being preached that has universal relevance. This specific tension must be discovered so that a T-R-UTH can be identified that relates to both the mind and the will of the listener, so that transformation can take place.

I find it helpful for my own understanding of the text and for later sermon development to state the tension in the form of a question. For example, 1 Samuel 25 describes the account of David being rejected by Nabal and subsequently being overwhelmed with bitterness and a desire for revenge. The overall purpose of the book of 1 Samuel is to reveal the development of Israel's monarchy and the transition from Saul's reign to that of David's. But if one was to represent Yahweh well as his earthly representative, that human king had to be a man who had a heart for God. First Samuel 25 tells about God's spiritual transformation of David. But in the immediate context there is also a theological purpose that has universal implications. First Samuel 25 seems to be answering the question, "What should we do when we have been treated unjustly?" This is the tension within the passage. It is the universal question that is consistent with the human author's original purpose as well as the need of listeners who must be challenged to move away from fleshly thinking to God's way of thinking. When people try to live the Christian life in their own strength instead of the Spirit's, or according to ideas developed without the influence of biblical revelation, fleshly thinking will control their behavior (cf. Eph. 4:17–24). Transformation will occur only when falsehoods are identified and biblical truth is made known. The preacher's job is to move the listener from these patterns of wrong thinking to knowing and living as God would have us live.

---

17. Robinson, *Biblical Preaching*, 45.
18. Chapell, *Christ-Centered Preaching*, 43.

Then there is a need to identify a specific "Revelation," a revelation about God's character or God's will that the biblical author is attempting to portray. The entire Bible is God's self-disclosure, an unveiling of his will and ways for his people. It is important in the whole process of spiritual formation that people understand that change is a divine/human endeavor. We do not change in our own strength and ingenuity but by availing ourselves of the power of God given to us in the Holy Spirit. Therefore, the revelation will be stated in terms of "who God is," or in terms of the "way God works." The revelation in the 1 Samuel 25 text can be stated as, "God alone is the ultimate Judge."

The combination of these first two elements will lead to a statement that summarizes what the text is revealing. It is a universal truth that could be applied to any given generation of God's people, a "Universal Truth (to) Heed." This statement ultimately becomes a transforming truth because it is fashioned in such a way that it aims at changing unrighteous thinking to godly thinking and unrighteous actions to godly actions. Again, the ultimate summary statement, the "universal truth to heed," for 1 Samuel 25 might be stated as, "Since God alone is the ultimate Judge, surrender your injustices to his justice." This summary statement can be reworked in a variety of ways so that it is concise and memorable. But whatever the ultimate wording, this summary statement will be the transforming truth that the audience will hear as God's will and way for them.

While working through the text, a preacher might be wise to develop a simple grid near the end of one's collection of notes. This grid includes the elements described above. In addition to identifying the transforming truth, the preacher will have a clear expression of the key elements of the sermon that can be referred to throughout the rest of the sermon development process. Keeping the "tension" and the "transforming truth" nearby will enable one to frequently rewrite and shape the sermon's idea to guarantee that its expression is aimed at changing both one's thinking and one's behavior. I regularly use a grid like the one shown below.

Tension	*Exegetical*	What was the specific tension facing the original audience?
	Theological	What is the related tension that faces all people?
	Homiletical	What is the related tension that is facing my audience?
Revelation	*Exegetical*	What was the original author revealing about God to the original audience?
	Theological	What is the text revealing to all generations about God?
	Homiletical	What is the text revealing to my audience about the way God is making himself known?
Universal Truth to Heed	How can the text's tension and the revelation of God be stated in universal terms to bring transformation to my audience?	

Shaping the Sermon

If it is true that preaching for spiritual transformation necessitates changing one's beliefs and behaviors, then a truly transforming sermon must be constructed to address the way people normally think. That is, when listening to sermons, people ask questions. We do the same thing in our daily conversations. We might hear what people are saying, but we process what they are telling us through a variety of questions—"Is this true? What is it that she is really telling me? How in the world would I ever be able to do such a thing?" Sermons should anticipate the questions people will ask, even if those questions are silently pondered while sitting in a church pew.

Therefore, the preacher will need to anticipate the kinds of questions people might ask with respect to the sermon's transforming truth or its subordinate statements. These same questions will become the "main points" or "movements" of the sermon. "Main points" have the tendency to convey the idea that people should be writing down a list of things to do or to avoid. But when the preacher identifies the questions that people are asking, the answers to those same questions—drawn from the biblical text—will sound more like a personal conversation or dialogue. And just like a personal conversation that "moves" from question to answer, and on to the next question, so the sermon can be structured around the most significant questions that listeners might raise. In turn, listeners will sense that their questions are valid and that the preacher respects where they are in life. If this kind of rapport can be established, it will also enhance the possibility of spiritual transformation through preaching.

There is no set structure that the sermon has to follow. It is not a matter of having three or four points that are cleverly connected through some alliterative pattern. Rather from the outset, the listener should be aware that the preacher is seeking to help resolve some human dilemma from the perspective of God's Word. At the same time, the preacher will need to anticipate where the resistance will come from the listeners. For instance, in a sermon on 1 Samuel 25, will the audience question whether or not God is actually at work to care for his people who have been mistreated? They may be inclined to disagree with the preacher, even if it is in the privacy of their own thinking. In fact, people will frequently think of examples where it seems like God has been oblivious to the suffering of his people. The preacher must anticipate both the objections and the common examples that bring resistance to the sermon.

Since the sermon at this point may appear to be little more than a collection of notes, the preacher will have to eventually develop some semblance of order. If the sermon has no sense of direction, no connectedness from one thought to another, people will simply tune out. So the preacher will have to think what the movements of the sermon will be and how one can clearly transition from one section of the sermon to another. The preacher who addresses both the mind and the will of the listener must arrange sermon material with a careful balance between explaining the meaning of the text and answering the questions of the audience.

In my own sermon preparation, I determine where the transforming truth will appear. That is, will the sermon be an inductive or deductive development? Homiletics textbooks frequently describe "deductive sermons" as sermon structures where the proposition or central truth appears in the sermon's introduction. "Inductive sermons" are those messages where the proposition or central truth appears later in the sermon, often at the very end. Because spiritual formation has to do with challenging the mind and the will of the listener, inductive sermons may have an advantage over deductive arrangements. If a sermon is crafted well and tension can be created at the very beginning, listeners will be inclined to listen to what the preacher is saying. But the key is carefully crafted sermons with introductory tension that begs for resolution.

After I determine the placement of the sermon's major theme, the transforming truth, I try to think in terms of four major movements. I refer to these movements as Our Story, God's Story, Our Resistance, and the Payback. As stated above, the transforming truth could appear in any one of these major movements. But the overall movement is designed to identify what needs to be changed in the listener's thinking that will ultimately lead to action. This focus on beliefs and behaviors is at the heart of spiritual change.

The first movement, "our story," refers to the "tension" that has been discovered in the biblical text that is common to all generations of God's people. In the case of the 1 Samuel 25 narrative, David was on the run, trying to protect himself from King Saul. To add to his personal struggles, Nabal, a man he had helped over an extended period of time, mistreated him. This led to David's desire for revenge. In the first movement of the story, the preacher will want to show how all of us have been mistreated in some way. The skilled communicator will want to give sufficient examples of mistreatment and injustice that are common to the contemporary audience. The preacher will also want to show how we also desire revenge, whether anyone else knows our thoughts or not.

This is "our story," the common story that every person faces. It is a "fleshly" way of thinking that needs spiritual transformation. But before that can happen, the preacher will want to identify in the listener's experiences what is parallel with the tension in the biblical text. This identification creates a compelling reason for listening to God's Word. In describing "our story," the one that is common to the contemporary audience, the preacher will want to raise one primary question. This question can be restated in a variety of ways, but it is the tool that challenges the listening audience to think about what needs to be transformed in one's spiritual life. The question can be as simple as, "We all know in our more sane moments that getting revenge is wrong. But what is the alternative? What would God want us to do that is both beneficial to us and honoring to him?" This primary question summarizes "our story" and prepares the audience to hear the Word of God.

Once the "our story" movement is concisely identified, there will be a need to move to the specifics of the biblical text. It is in this second major movement, "God's story," that all of our previous study of the passage will begin to generate dividends. However, that does not mean that we will be able to use absolutely every piece of information we have collected. We need to use those details of this second movement that will carefully lead to an answer to the question raised in the first movement. In narrative literature it is beneficial to retell the story of the text. Sometimes this can be done through a first-person narrative. At other times it will be done the way a reporter provides a "third-person" overview of a famous person's life. People are captivated by stories. And the stories of the Bible contain all the elements of the best stories in human history. So in a narrative text the preacher will want to think about retelling the story in such a way that listeners can see the events happening in their own minds.

But not every biblical text is a narrative. How do we retell "God's story" in a New Testament letter or a psalm? Every text is the revelation of God. And every text is lodged in some human drama. The Beatitudes seem like straightforward exhortations that Jesus gave to his disciples. But these "character traits" with their accompanying "blessings" are surrounded by the culture of Jesus' day. People were anticipating a Messiah. Jesus had been verifying through his miracles that he was the promised Messiah (Matt. 4:15–25). Therefore, it is not enough to explain word meanings in a text like Matthew 5:3–12. The setting and the potential reaction of the people listening to Jesus also needs to be described in meaningful ways. Contemporary listeners will need to see that "our story" parallels the story of the original audience, that is "God's story," which has been preserved in Scripture for all to see. It is "God's story" even if it has been woven through the lives of an ancient people.

As the preacher goes through the biblical text re-creating as many scenes as possible, there will be a natural progression that leads to the statement of the transforming truth. Somewhere near the end of this second movement, there should be a statement and restatement of the central proposition of the sermon. It should challenge the way listeners normally think about life. The transforming truth will answer the question raised in the first movement. In so doing it will also relieve the tension that was originally identified near the beginning of the sermon.

There is a third movement to a life-transforming biblical message. It is what I refer to as "our resistance." People will raise objections to what is being proclaimed. Questions will evolve out of our failed experiences in life or from a person's hit-and-miss attempts at trying to live holy lives in an unholy world. Robinson refers to these inquiries from the audience as developmental questions.[19] They can be stated in a variety of ways, but most listeners will say something like, "What do you mean by that statement?" This is a question that arises out of the listener's lack of information.

---

19. Robinson, *Biblical Preaching*, 79.

Or a listener might say, "I don't buy what you're saying. You're going to have to hear my objections and answer them." This "question" comes from skepticism over the preacher's proposed solutions. Postmodern listeners especially will not be satisfied with the data the preacher gives them from the biblical text. They want to be convinced, and spiritual transformation requires that we help to resolve their skepticism.

Or a person might say, "I've heard that before. But how do I do it?" This is a question of application. Another form of the question for application says, "I hear what you are saying. But where is this truth going to show up in my life?" People need to *see* in their own minds what life would be like if they were implementing God's Word into their own experiences. A simple exhortation to "go and do likewise" will not suffice. If listeners are being exhorted to be "salt and light" in the world, they need simple narrative descriptions of what that would look like when the truth is lived out in everyday experiences.

In order to answer a listener's objections, it can be helpful to construct a simple "application grid" as part of the sermon preparation process (see below). At the top of the grid insert the single-sentence summary, the transforming truth. Then in a left-hand column write down all the potential listeners who might be hearing your sermon. In a column next to each of the "people categories" identified, write down what their objections might be to the sermon. In addition, record what would be the most convincing responses to those objections. There is no limit to the different kinds of people who might be listening to a sermon. And there is no limit to the specific shapes that their objections will take. Identifying listeners, their objections, and the answers to those objections will be important if the preacher is to be used by the Holy Spirit to change both minds and wills.

TRANSFORMING TRUTH:	
High School Students	
Singles	
Divorcees	
Laborers	
Retirees	

The final movement in the sermon is what I call the "payback." Most textbooks on preaching refer to the conclusion as a place to review the sermon idea, summarize the points, and issue a challenge. However, people are not inclined to remember sermon points. They are more prone to remember a simple, memorable truth that summarizes the basic teaching of the text. But by the time the sermon is ready to conclude, most people will ask something like, "What's in this for me? If I embrace what you are suggesting, what will happen in my life?" The preacher will want to take some time to answer this final question. However, preachers will always be working to move people beyond "me-thinking." That is why I often try to describe for people what obedience to God will do for their families, their careers, and their Christian witness to others. And I also try to give them a vision of what personal obedience will do for Christ and his church. After all, life is not ultimately about what benefits the listener but what will exalt Christ in all things. Listeners need to see that there is a "payback" to obeying what God says in his Word.

After the "Amen"

Good preaching was never intended to be a single event. Many people see it as something that takes place between 11 A.M. and noontime on Sunday. But the mark of a good sermon is when it leads to discussion. People talk about it over Sunday dinner. It is the subject of conversation as parishioners leave the worship center. Life-changing preaching gets people to talk about God and his Word.

In my own ministry I often find that something I said in a sermon will set in motion another role that I have—the role of a pastoral counselor or spiritual director. Specific statements in the biblical text or applications that I have made within the sermon frequently foster more questions. Therefore, many preachers (like myself) will set aside a specific period of time every week to meet with people one-on-one. People will want to come and talk about their spiritual struggles and challenges. In this way the preacher will now become the "listener." And the listening will be designed to give attention to the condition of a person's heart. So don't assume that the sermon will end with a prayer and benediction. All too frequently a sermon designed for spiritual transformation becomes the vehicle for ongoing soul care and discipleship.

In addition, preachers can participate in the process of life change by intentionally constructing contexts where the sermon can become a matter of review. Some churches allow for a question-and-answer time following the sermon's actual presentation.[20] Other churches have midweek Bible studies where the sermon from the previous Sunday morning is discussed, and application is made a specific part of the discussion. Some churches have sermon feedback classes as one option for Sunday morning adult education classes. Other churches have web-based tools that allow individuals to listen to a recorded version of the sermon and answer a series of application-oriented questions.

There is one caution that must be raised with the use of new technology and its use in spiritual formation. There is always the temptation that a person can watch videos and listen to audio sermons in isolation. We can be thankful that modern technology gives us access to a wide variety of gifted preachers and teachers. But spiritual transformation in the New

---

20. Robinson, *Making a Difference in Preaching*, 131–33.

Testament does not take place in isolation. When the apostle Paul exhorted his readers to be transformed by the renewing of their minds (Rom. 12:2), he also quickly exhorted readers to function as a body with many individual parts (Rom. 12:3–8). That is why we must not create an atmosphere where sermons are listened to in isolation or without opportunity for discussion. At the same time, a local church can benefit from listening to the sermons of nationally recognized preachers. But those same preachers will not have insight into the needs of a distant local congregation. Rather the pastor/preacher in the local church will best know the needs of the congregation and be ready to address those needs in the weekly sermon. Both preaching and spiritual transformation should be viewed as a "local" community activity.

In many churches throughout the world the small group has become a primary venue for spiritual formation. When people gather together in groups of ten to twelve people, there is a tremendous opportunity to share life together and maintain accountability. The wise pastor will take advantage of small group settings to train the leaders of these groups to lead discussions on the content and implications of the sermon. In this way preaching will never become an isolated ministry of the church. It will become one of the many instruments the Holy Spirit uses to make his people more and more like Jesus Christ.

Yes, there will be some individuals who will assume that sermons are outdated and inefficient in changing lives. But the history of the church tells a very different story. God is at work, and he is changing lives everywhere. And until our Lord Jesus comes for his church, let us be faithful in preaching the kind of sermons that transform people to be more and more like our Lord Jesus Christ.

Conclusion

Paul Pettit

Taken as a whole, the contributors have presented a compelling need for spiritual formation occurring within an authentic, biblically based community group among the members of the body of Christ. Except for those called to periods of monasticism, Christianity was never designed to be lived out in isolated individualism. The community enjoyed within the Trinity should serve as our model for living the Christ-life *with* others.

Spiritual formation involves members of the body maturing together toward Christlikeness, by the power of the Holy Spirit and according to biblical standards. Individual members of the body shape each other like iron sharpening iron. God shapes and molds believers into the image of his Son like a potter shaping clay on a spinning wheel. Character transformation can get messy!

Spiritual formation, growing in community toward Christlikeness, is the critical need of all Christ followers. We cannot say that some Christians need spiritual formation while others do not. Neither can we say that some elite Christians finally arrive at a plateau in their maturity where they no longer possess a need to be spiritually formed. Growth in Christian maturity is a lifelong process and goal. As the apostle Paul wrote to the Ephesians, "From him [Christ] the whole body, joined and held together by every supporting ligament, grows and builds itself up in love, as each part does its work" (Eph. 4:16).

This conclusion highlights four key concepts of Christian growth, each principle building upon the previous one. These foundational ideas, interwoven throughout the book, are here explicitly spelled out for the sake of clarity. This conclusion summarizes our approach to spiritual formation and includes the idea of knowing one's own *identity in Christ*, so that one can make oneself known in *Christian community*, so that one can pursue a lifetime of *growth in integrity*, so that one can become fully equipped to glorify Christ by *serving others*.

Principle 1: Discovering My Identity in Christ

I cannot grow in spiritual formation unless I know who I am and who I am becoming. Christians must hold an accurate self-portrait by intimately knowing who they currently are and who they are becoming *in Christ*. This principle has to do with being both accurate and secure in our self-identity. One of the profound questions continuing to plague each of us through childhood, into adolescence, and on into adulthood is, "Who am I?"

There are two main outlooks or orientations that comprise our own understanding of ourselves: our earthly identity and our heavenly identity. Our earthly identity is comprised of all those factors that make up our self-perception of who we are. Factors such as the universal human nature that all possess, the different roles we play (parent, student, employee, friend), and how those roles differ from who we really are at the core of our being (regardless of the particular role we may be living out at any given moment).

Other areas of our earthly identity include our own ideas of the concept of gender, what we believe it means to be male or female, our own understanding of our unique temperament, and our own ethnic heritage.

For the believer, our heavenly identity consists of all of the factors that comprise our being born again from above: our identity in Christ, the fact that we are saints who still live on earth with fellow humans and thus still sin, the fact that we possess a spiritual gift, and the idea that we are a part of a corporate body made up of fellow believers. Each of these important factors plays into the makeup of our self-perception or identity.

As we become more confident in who we are and begin to understand our strengths and weaknesses, we are better able to set boundaries and serve others with proper motives. When we are insecure in who we are, we live life in a continual effort to please others or gain approval from or control over others. So growing in spiritual formation means we are more at peace with who we are, who we were created to be, and what we are becoming.

In the movie *Gladiator*, the two main characters are pitted against each other in stark contrast throughout the film. One, Maximus, a former military general who was betrayed and sold as a slave, is quite secure in who he is and what he wants. The other, Commodus, an illegitimate king, shows obvious signs of not knowing himself and his gifts, much less an accurate self-perception of who he really is.

Through the film's fascinating story line, Maximus emerges as the hero who is willingly able to serve; while Commodus is shown for the self-doubting, conniving, manipulator that he really is. In an amazing reversal of fortune, the slave with no social status becomes the savior of Rome, while the king with all authority is mired in self-absorption. Why is all this talk of *identity* a critical factor in one's spiritual formation?

Identity, or accurately knowing oneself, is vital to the process of spiritual formation because formation involves an individual becoming more Christlike as a member of an authentic community. However, one cannot truly become a contributing member of an authentic community unless one possesses a developing and accurate self-perception. I cannot become secure in a group of individuals unless I am becoming secure as an individual. A chain is only as strong as its weakest link.

In other words, I cannot allow others to see me for who I am, if I do not know who I am. I cannot reveal who I am in community if I have not undertaken the difficult task of introspection. It is a loving gift to myself and others to accurately know who I am, so that I can authentically share that same information with others who are attempting to know me, encourage me, love me, correct me, and even rebuke me.

As an individual believer in the body of Christ, I am a part but not the whole. In fact, I am one small part of a great whole. The goal of spiritual formation is not my own individual growth *apart from* the body, but my maturity and development *within* the body and *for* the body.

Jesus was secure in his own identity. He knew he had been sent from the Father, was on a mission at the behest of his Father, and that he was returning to the Father. Even though Jesus was secure in his identity, the Pharisees continually questioned him concerning his origin—about his Father.

John records the Pharisees protesting, "We are not illegitimate children. . . . The only Father we have is God himself" (John 8:41b). But still Jesus responded, "You belong to your father, the devil, and you want to carry out your father's desire" (John 8:44). Although the Pharisees were secure in their identity, they were deluded and self-deceived. Thus, they did not possess an accurate self-perception. Their identity was cloudy.

On the other hand, Jesus was secure *and* accurate in his identity and was therefore able to give of himself, love his enemies, and even lay down his life for the sins of the whole world. Socrates held that the unexamined life is not worth living. Going through the motions and routines of everyday life while not taking the time to truly understand who we are and what we do best is a miserable way to live. Wearing a mask and pretending to be someone we are not is draining. A large part of the spiritual formation journey is continually discovering who we are and who God is.

John Calvin wrote about a type of double knowledge, of accurately knowing oneself and also accurately knowing God. And the fact is, the more we know about ourselves in relation to God, the more we can know God; and the more we know about God and his interactions with humans, the more we can know ourselves.

In the movie *The Lion King*, the developing hero is unclear about many aspects of his identity. Instead of occupying his rightful position on the throne as legitimate heir, he cowers in a distant land and carries out his days in self-indulgence until a wiser, older character literally knocks him in his head, reminds him of his regal inheritance, and shouts, "You are Mufassa's boy!"

Not until Simba fully understood and literally embraced his identity was he able to carry out his preordained role as king of the tribe. I cannot grow in spiritual formation toward Christlikeness unless I know *who* I am, and *whose* I am.

Principle 2: Understanding Myself in Community

I cannot grow in spiritual formation unless I understand myself in relation to others. As we begin to grow and mature in our self-understanding, we are better able to enter into authentic community with other learners. As stated earlier, the individual believer is one small part of a greater whole. So as individual believers, we need to know ourselves as individuals *and* as individuals in relation to the other members of the body. Put another way, while discovering *my* place in Christ, I also need to understand *our* union with Christ.

Unity in the body of Christ does not imply sameness. The body is made up of many unique parts fitted and joined together to make a magnificent whole. The goal is for growth to take place for the whole body. It is wonderful if individual parts grow, but they need to grow along with other members of the body, not in isolated individualism. The apostle Paul wrote about this type of growth and used the metaphor of a temple building when he wrote, "In him [Christ] the whole building is joined together and rises to become a holy temple in the Lord. And in him you too are being built together to become a dwelling in which God lives by his Spirit" (Eph. 2:21–22).

As believers, our goal is not to be one glorious part of the body but a part of one glorious body. Paul wrote to the Corinthians and said, "Now you are the body of Christ, and each one of you is a part of it" (1 Cor. 12:27). Jesus prayed that his disciples would be one, just as he, as a part of the Trinity (three persons), experiences oneness.

This idea can be represented by a close examination of a family unit. Each member of the family is important. It is hoped that each individual in the family is growing and maturing. But it is also hoped that the family is growing as a unit as well. We could not say that a family is growing as long as some individuals within the family were failing to grow and mature. Growth as an individual would be desired, but growth on the part of the entire family is even more desirable.

How selfish would it sound for a parent to report, "Our oldest daughter and our youngest son are simply doing awful, however I am growing like crazy, so I am very pleased with our family!" And yet many of us sound like this when we report on our growth toward Christlikeness. It is not uncommon for someone to report, "Our church fellowship is really struggling, but I am doing wonderfully!"

From the same passage of Scripture on the body of Christ mentioned earlier, the apostle Paul wrote, "If one part suffers, every part suffers with it; if one part is honored, every part rejoices with it" (1 Cor. 12:26). True spiritual formation, therefore, is not an isolated, individualized, privatized endeavor but a corporate one.

Principle 3: Pursuing Integrity in Christian Community

I cannot grow in spiritual formation unless I am growing in wholeness. As believers we need to grow in a holistic manner as whole persons.

Some have incorrectly assumed, probably because of the name, that spiritual formation relates only to the inner life. However, if we are growing in Christlikeness, it should follow that we are growing in all areas of life—our inner life and outer actions should align.

In biblical times, potters would spin soft, wet clay on a wheel and then bake their products in a hot kiln. Some pieces were of no use since they had cracks or chips. These pieces had areas of lack and were not useful for their intended purpose. These pieces did not have integrity; that is, they were not whole and they could not be *integrated* into use alongside the other pieces of pottery.

Recently, some megachurch pastors have fallen from their lofty pinnacles. In these much-publicized cases, the message being proclaimed on Sunday morning did not match the lifestyle that was being lived out at other times of the week. Integrity has been defined as what one does when no one is looking.

When the U.S. government prints currency, a watermark is placed on the bills to help deter counterfeiters. The watermark serves as a mark of authenticity and lets consumers know whether or not the bill they hold in their hands is the real deal.

A growing Christian should behave like a watermark, a standard bearer of what it means to be a Christ follower. Christians ought to be maturing with other believers, and they also should be growing in every area of life. It is when we are with others who know us well that we can begin to see and work on our own blind spots. We should not lead a bifurcated existence where we profess Christ in some areas of our life yet coddle secret sins or known bad habits in other, private areas.

The results of Christian spiritual formation are ever increasing levels of love and peace (shalom, wholeness) in our life and in our communities as we partner with God and his people in our exciting journey of faith.

As a young boy growing up in Kansas, I loved staying out late with family in the summertime and playing backyard games or catching fireflies in glass jars. The warm, humid air guaranteed we were tired and sweaty by the end of the night when we knew it was time to go in for a bath. But wanting to watch television or eat ice cream, we would sometimes splash a little cold water on our face or even put some of our dad's cologne behind our ears in an attempt to fool our parents. Do you think this tactic worked?

We had no integrity at that moment. The sweet words we professed with our mouths did not match the sour smell emanating from our moist armpits. We had no wholeness, no shalom, no integrity in either our message or our behavior. Growing in wholeness and allowing the Holy Spirit to point out areas of weakness in our integrity requires increasing levels of maturity and trust as we open our lives to trusted friends in our biblical community group.

I'll resist the urge to relay some popular lawyer jokes, but it has become commonplace in discussions of integrity or honesty to talk about attorneys or politicians. While there may have been a time when most business transactions were conducted with a firm handshake and a person's word was his or her bond, today reams of paper are required to hold all the contractual jargon and loophole clauses for even the simplest of deals.

We are not being correctly formed if we are growing in a few areas of our Christian life and stagnating in others. We have no integrity if we hold secret bank accounts or talk about others behind their backs. I'm impressed with the Old Testament character Daniel. The Scriptures record that "the administrators and the satraps tried to find grounds for charges against Daniel in his conduct of government affairs, *but they were unable to do so. They could find no corruption in him*, because he was trustworthy and neither corrupt nor negligent" (Dan. 6:4, emphasis mine).

What would the leering press and the investigative reporters find if they went digging through your trash, recorded your private phone conversations, and examined your financial records? Would you pass through unscathed and corruption free as Daniel did?

We limit our service and usefulness to God when we harbor double-mindedness or wear masks. In fact, we may be the last ones to see the obvious faults that others, who know us better than we know ourselves, have observed all along. This is why practicing truth telling in an authentic biblical community group is a necessary and vital part of spiritual formation. Working on our blind spots requires opening ourselves up to a handful of trusted Christian friends who have our best interests at heart.

In an argument with Jesus, the Pharisees tried to emphasize that they were clean on the outside because of their ceremonial washings. However, Jesus reiterated that the outer and the inner life must be in alignment (integrity) when he asked, "Don't you see that whatever enters the mouth goes into the stomach and then out of the body? But the things that come out of the mouth come from the heart, and these make a man 'unclean'" (Matt. 15:17–18).

Principle 4: Practicing Service Toward God and Others

I cannot grow in spiritual formation unless I understand how my unique contribution affects my role in the body of Christ. For the developing Christ follower who is growing through spiritual formation, ministry is not an option but an imperative. Service toward God and others is the natural next step, the normal outcome of a life devoted to Christ.

Ministry is not merely activity for God. As we grow in our understanding of who we are, and as we mature with others in the context of Christian community, and as we shore up the areas of lack and weakness in our life, the natural outflow is dedicated service according to our divine design.

As we grow in trust and allow others to speak truth into our life, we become more aligned with our passions, talents, giftedness, and usefulness. We begin to function more and more according to who God created us to be. We start to live a life on mission for Christ and his kingdom.

The beauty of the body of Christ is the diversity of the individual members and the diversity of gifts. Our aim is to discern what we do best in the body by pouring ourselves out as a drink offering in service to Christ and the church. For example, one person may feel she is really good at singing. So she presents that gift as an offering to the church. However, when those who know her well are unable to affirm the offering, an honest reevaluation of her perception of her gift should ensue.

Another person may feel he is no good at teaching. And yet when he teaches, many people are edified and invitations to teach begin to arrive unsolicited. This person also should reevaluate his perception of his gift and calling.

Of course, this type of reevaluation should not take place in isolated, private moments. Rather, trusted friends who have the individual's best interests at heart, those who know the person's story, passions, and dreams, should offer words of affirmation and honesty. This is a beautiful portrait of Christian formation.

The ultimate example of humble service is the portrait of Christ as described by Paul when he admonished,

> Each of you should look not only to your own interests, but also to the interests of others. Your attitude should be the same as that of Christ Jesus: Who, being in very nature God, did not consider equality with God something to be grasped, but made himself nothing, taking the very nature of a servant, being made in human likeness. And being found in appearance as a man, he humbled himself and became obedient to death—even death on a cross! (Phil. 2:4–8)

What we do best is God's gift to us, what we do with that talent is our gift to God. Our ministry is our special place of service in and within the body of Christ. It is special activity done for God and others that is fueled by the power of the Holy Spirit. The apostle Paul wrote about this type of service in his letter to the Romans when he advised, "Just as each of us has one body with many members, and these members do not all have the same function, so in Christ we who are many form one body, and each member belongs to all the others" (Rom. 12:4–5).

The key factors in using our gifts "as unto the Lord" are that our activity be carried out in humility and that our service be accomplished with faith. After that, we need to be patient and leave the results (the effects) up to the Lord.

This conclusion has set forth the four-part notion that Christian spiritual formation consists of knowing your *identity* in Christ, so that you can make yourself known to others in a Christian *community*, so that you can pursue a lifetime of *integrity* in the context of community, so that you are fully equipped to glorify Christ by serving others in *ministry*.

Scripture Index

Acts

Romans

1 Corinthians

2 Corinthians

Galatians

Ephesians

Philippians

Subject Index

D

J

K

L

Bible Permissions

All Scripture quotations, unless otherwise indicated, are from the *Holy Bible, New International Version*®. *NIV*®. Copyright © 1973, 1978, 1984 by International Bible Society. Used by permission of Zondervan. All rights reserved.

Scripture quotations marked ASV are taken from the American Standard Version.

Scriptures marked CEV are taken from the Contemporary English Version. Copyright © 1995 by American Bible Society. Used by permission.

Scripture quotations marked ESV are from The Holy Bible, English Standard Version, copyright © 2001 by Crossway Bibles, a division of Good News Publishers. Used by permission. All rights reserved.

Scripture quotations marked HCSB are taken from the Holman Christian Standard Bible®, HCSB®, Copyright © 1999, 2000, 2002, 2003 by Holman Bible Publishers. Used by permission.

Scripture quotations marked KJV are from the King James Version.

Scripture quotations marked NASB are from the NEW AMERICAN STANDARD BIBLE, updated edition. Copyright © 1960, 1962, 1963, 1968, 1971, 1972, 1973, 1975, 1977, 1995 by The Lockman Foundation. Used by permission. (www.Lockman.org)

Scripture quotations marked NET are from the NET Bible® copyright ©1996–2005 by Biblical Studies Press, L.L.C. http://www.bible.org/. Scripture quoted by permission. All rights reserved.